Rugby For Dummies®

Cheat Sheet

Key Rugby Terms

- **Line-out:** Looks somewhat like a jump-ball in basketball, with both teams lining up ... other, but one team then throws the ball down the middle of the tunnel. Line-ou... ball, or a player carrying it, has gone out of bounds.

- **Maul:** Occurs when a player carrying the ball is held by one or more oppo... ...f the ball-carrier's teammates bind on the ball-carrier. All the players invo'... ...d moving towards a goal line. Open play has ended.

- **Ruck:** One or more players from each team, who are on their feet and in conta... ...nd the ball on the ground. Once a ruck has been formed, players can't use their hands to ... ball, only their feet.

- **Scrum:** A contest for the ball involving eight players who bind together and push against the other team's assembled eight for possession of the ball. Scrums restart play after certain minor infractions.

Rugby Tournaments at a Glance

Tournament	Description	Participants
Rugby World Cup	Held every four years to crown the World Champion	20 qualifying nations
Six Nations Championship	Annual international championship of Northern Hemisphere	England, Scotland, Wales, Ireland, France, and Italy
Tri Nations Series	Annual international championship of Southern Hemisphere	Australia, New Zealand, and South Africa
Super Cup	Annual international test series	Canada, England, Russia, and the United States
Churchill Cup	Annual international series for men and women	Canada, England, New Zealand (Maori and Black Ferns), and the United States
Super 12	Annual Southern Hemisphere interprovincial championship	Australia: Brumbies, Reds, Waratahs; New Zealand: Blues, Chiefs, Crusaders, Highlanders, Hurricanes; South Africa: Bulls, Cats, Sharks, Stormers
Heineken Cup	Annual European interprovincial/club championship	England: Leeds Tykes, Gloucester, Leicester, Nothhampton, Sale, Wasps; Wales: Cardiff, Gwent, Neath/Swansea, Llanelli, Ospreys; Scotland: Celtic Warriors, Edinburgh, Scottish Borders; Ireland: Leinster, Munster, Ulster; Italy: Amatori Calvisano, Treviso; France: Agen, Bourgoin, Perpignan, Stade Francais, Toulouse

A Team on the Attack

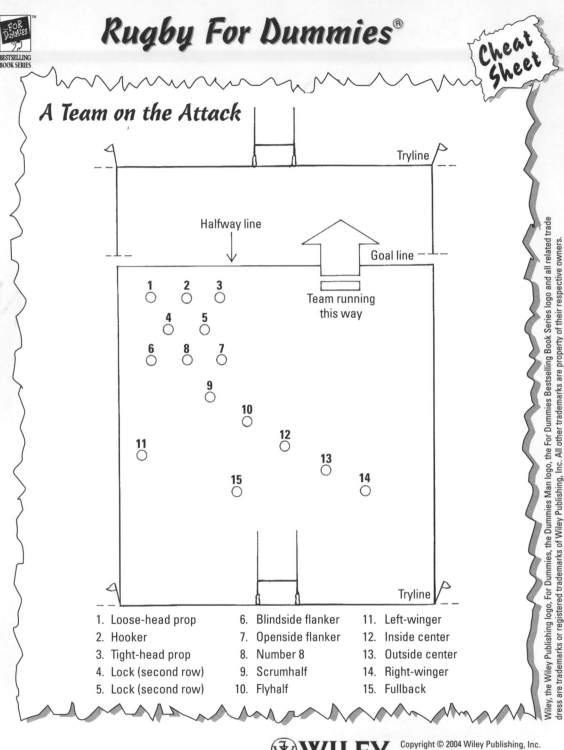

Tryline

Halfway line

Goal line

Team running this way

Tryline

1. Loose-head prop
2. Hooker
3. Tight-head prop
4. Lock (second row)
5. Lock (second row)

6. Blindside flanker
7. Openside flanker
8. Number 8
9. Scrumhalf
10. Flyhalf

11. Left-winger
12. Inside center
13. Outside center
14. Right-winger
15. Fullback

Wiley, the Wiley Publishing logo, For Dummies, the Dummies Man logo, the For Dummies Bestselling Book Series logo and all related trade dress are trademarks or registered trademarks of Wiley Publishing, Inc. All other trademarks are property of their respective owners.

WILEY

Copyright © 2004 Wiley Publishing, Inc. All rights reserved.

Cheat Sheet $2.95 value. Item 3405-6.

For more information about Wiley Publishing, call 1-800-762-2974.

For Dummies: Bestselling Book Series for Beginners

Rugby
FOR

DUMMIES®

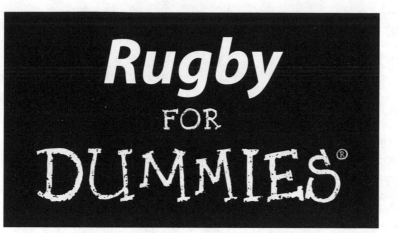

by Mathew Brown
Patrick Guthrie
Greg Growden

John Wiley & Sons Canada, Ltd

Rugby For Dummies®

Published by
John Wiley & Sons Canada, Ltd
6045 Freemont Boulevard
Mississauga, ON L5R 4J3
www.wiley.ca

Copyright © 2004 John Wiley & Sons Canada, Ltd. All rights reserved. No part of this book, including interior design, cover design, and icons, may be reproduced or transmitted in any form, by any means (electronic, photocopying, recording, or otherwise) without the prior written permission of the publisher.

National Library of Canada Cataloguing in Publication

Guthrie, Patrick, 1962–

Rugby for dummies / Patrick Guthrie, Mathew Brown.

Includes index.
ISBN 1-470-83405-6

1. Rugby football. I. Brown, Mathew (Mathew Timothy) II. Title.

GV945.G88 2004   796.333   C2003-906732-7

Printed in Canada

3 4 5 TRI 08 07 06

For general information on John Wiley & Sons Canada, Ltd., including all books published by Wiley Publishing, Inc., please call our warehouse, Tel 1-800-567-4797. For reseller information, including discounts and premium sales, please call our sales department, Tel 416-646-7992. For press review copies, author interviews, or other publicity information, please contact our marketing department, Tel: 416-646-4584, Fax 416-236-4448.

For authorization to photocopy items for corporate, personal, or educational use, please contact The Canadian Copyright Licensing Agency (Access Copyright). For an Access Copyright license, visit www.accesscopyright.ca or call toll free, 1-800-893-5777.

LIMIT OF LIABILITY/DISCLAIMER OF WARRANTY: WHILE THE PUBLISHER AND AUTHOR HAVE USED THEIR BEST EFFORTS IN PREPARING THIS BOOK, THEY MAKE NO REPRESENTATIONS OR WARRANTIES WITH RESPECT TO THE ACCURACY OR COMPLETENESS OF THE CONTENTS OF THIS BOOK AND SPECIFICALLY DISCLAIM ANY IMPLIED WARRANTIES OF MERCHANTABILITY OR FITNESS FOR A PARTICULAR PURPOSE. NO WARRANTY MAY BE CREATED OR EXTENDED BY SALES REPRESENTATIVES OR WRITTEN SALES MATERIALS. THE ADVICE AND STRATEGIES CONTAINED HEREIN MAY NOT BE SUITABLE FOR YOUR SITUATION. NEITHER THE PUBLISHER NOR AUTHOR SHALL BE LIABLE FOR ANY LOSS OF PROFIT OR ANY OTHER COMMERCIAL DAMAGES, INCLUDING BUT NOT LIMITED TO SPECIAL, INCIDENTAL, CONSEQUENTIAL, OR OTHER DAMAGES.

Trademarks: Wiley, the Wiley publishing logo. For Dummies, the Dummies Man logo, A Reference for the Rest of Us!, The Dummies Way, Dummies Daily, The Fun and Easy Way, Dummies.com and related trade dress are trademarks or registered trademarks of Wiley Publishing, Inc., in the United States, Canada and other countries, and may not be used without written permission. All other trademarks are the property of their respective owners. John Wiley & Sons Canada, Ltd is not associated with any product or vendor mentioned in this book.

About the Authors

Matt Brown began his rugby career at Occidental College. After a miraculous graduation he spent several seasons with the Oxy Olde Boys, then joined the Missoula All-Maggots. In 1995 he moved to Latvia, where he first played for Rigas Miesnieks, then was a founding member of the Riga Exiles. He appeared twice for Latvia, earning a cap in 1997 against Bulgaria in a World Cup Qualifying match. Since 1999 he has been a producer of Championship Rugby, writes a weekly column for Foxsportsworld.com and now hosts the FOX Sports World Rugby Report. He is planning a 2006 comeback for Oxy.

Patrick Guthrie is a product of the Oxy Olde Boys rugby juggernaut. In 1995, he pioneered the delivery of rugby on television creating Championship Rugby. He eats, sleeps and drinks rugby having produced 500 shows over the past 9 years. A two-time president of Oxy and SCRFU's General Counsel from 1994-1997, he's a graduate of the International Rugby Academy's Practical Coaching Course and is USA Level-1 certified. He's coached both the Occidental College Women & Olde Boys the past two years. He is currently a member of the USA Rugby Board of Directors and produces rugby for Fox Sports International.

Greg Growden is one of Australia's best-known sports writers. He began writing about rugby union in 1981, and since 1987 has been the chief rugby writer for the *Sydney Morning Herald*. He is also a regular on New Zealand television rugby shows.

Greg's other books include *A Wayward Genius: The Fleetwood Smith Story* and *Gold, Mud 'N Guts, The Incredible Tom Richards: Footballer, War Hero, Olympian*.

Dedication

This book is dedicated to rugby and all who have ever played, watched or enjoyed it. The sport has been the driving force in both our lives and we're hopeful that this attempt to enlighten the uninitiated will bring a greater audience to this fascinating and wonderful game.

— Matt Brown and Patrick Guthrie

Authors' Acknowledgments

Thanks to Vandy and Train for getting me started, and Godfree for instilling in me a deep and abiding love for the game. Thanks to all of the teammates I've ever played with, from Oxy to Missoula and Riga to Vail. Special thanks to Guthrie for convincing me to join him on the quest to bring rugby to the North American audience and to Dermot for giving me my first gig writing about rugby. Thanks to Reid for keeping me housed and my family for putting up with me forever.

— Matt Brown

My father comes first for his support, love, and recognition early on that I was on a crusade to grow the game, no matter the personal costs. Special thanks to Bo Kelly for his trust and financial backing to get the whole project started. Kudos to Bob Watkins, Ed Hagerty and Dennis Storer for being my three wise men. Thanks also to my boss Dermot for not firing me, yet. But most of all, thanks to the Oxy Olde Boys and Brownie in particular for introducing me to my life's great passion.

— Patrick Guthrie

Publisher's Acknowledgments

We're proud of this book; please send us your comments at canadapt@wiley.com. Some of the people who helped bring this book to market include the following:

Acquisitions and Editorial

Associate Editor: Michelle Marchetti

Developmental and Copy Editors: Colborne Communications

Cover photography: PhotoDisc/Getty Images

Illustrations: Paul Lennon, Adrian So

Production

Publishing Services Director: Karen Bryan

Project Manager: Elizabeth McCurdy

Project Coordinator: Robert Hickey

Layout and Graphics: Kim Monteforte, Heidy Lawrance Associates

Proofreader: Pamela Erlichman

Indexer: Belle Wong

Photo Credits:

Fig 8-2: Getty Images/Daniel Berehulak; Fig 9-2: Getty Images/John Gichigi; Fig 9-3: Getty Images/ Clive Brunskill; Fig 10-3: Sport the Library/Action Photos Rugby Union; Fig 10-4: Sport the Library: Tom Putt; Fig 10-6: Newspix/Mark Evans; Fig 10-8, 13-1, 15-1, 15-2, 16-4, 17-1, 17-2, 17-3, 19-2, 23-2, 23-3: Rugby Magazine USA; Fig 16-1, 16-2, 23-1: Doug Crosse; Fig 16-3: Rugby Action Photo; Figure 19-1, 21-3: International Rugby Academy; Fig 21-1, 21-2: Fox Sports World; Fig 22-1: Sport the Library

---

John Wiley & Sons Canada, Ltd

Bill Zerter, Chief Operating Officer

Robert Harris, Publisher, Professional and Trade Division

Publishing and Editorial for Consumer Dummies

Diane Graves Steele, Vice President and Publisher, Consumer Dummies

Joyce Pepple, Acquisitions Director, Consumer Dummies

Kristin A. Cocks, Product Development Director, Consumer Dummies

Michael Spring, Vice President and Publisher, Travel

Suzanne Jannetta, Editorial Director, Travel

Publishing for Technology Dummies

Andy Cummings, Acquisitions Director

Composition Services

Gerry Fahey, Executive Director of Production Services

Debbie Stailey, Director of Composition Services

Contents at a Glance

Table of Contents

Introduction

● ●

*W*elcome to *Rugby For Dummies*. This book is your introduction to a sport that has attracted a passionate following around the world for more than a century, but is just now exploding in popularity in the United States and Canada. As rugby devotees ourselves, we understand the natural appeal of the sport, and why you might have felt the need to find out more about it.

Rugby is the world's third most popular team sport and is played in more than a hundred countries. The non-stop action is breathtaking as the athletes confront each other over 80 minutes of gut-wrenching competition.

Although it was first introduced more than 130 years ago, up until very recently rugby was a mystery to most North Americans. In the past few years rugby has made the transition from being a totally amateur game to a fully professional sport. This revolutionary development has increased the fitness of the players, sped up the game, and created a vastly more entertaining, television-friendly product that is growing by leaps and bounds all across North America.

This book is intended to help parents, players, coaches, and their families get acquainted with the basic elements of this fantastic game. We hope this book will lift the veil of mystery that has shrouded the sport and enable you to appreciate both the excitement on the field and the camaraderie off it that makes rugby truly unique.

About This Book

Rugby For Dummies includes all the information you'll need to get started in the sport, whether you want to be a player, coach, or spectator. It's the first comprehensive guide to all things rugby and was written specifically for a North American audience. There are plenty of foreign books that talk about rugby, but to our knowledge (and we know it all!) this is the only one that explains the game in terms that Canadians and Americans can easily understand.

At all times, we've made ease of access and cross-referencing a priority, so you can use this book to quickly locate a specific topic, find the information you're looking for, and get on with your life.

Conventions Used in This Book

Rugby has its own language, so to help you understand what we're talking about, we've made a point of putting rugby jargon in *italics* and then defining those terms right away. If we missed one here or there, however, and you encounter a term you're not familiar with, check the glossary in Appendix B.

Why You Need This Book

If you tried to figure out rugby on your own, it would take you at least a decade of constantly watching, playing, asking questions, and absorbing the atmosphere for you to get a good feel for the game. We know, because that's how we did it. Until we wrote this book, there was no easy way to access and assimilate all the information needed to gain a solid understanding of the game — other than personal experience through trial and error.

Whatever your reasons for reading this book — whether you're barely acquainted with the game or possess a wealth of knowledge about it — *Rugby For Dummies* will answer your questions and increase your understanding of the sport.

How This Book Is Organized

This book is organized into seven parts. Each of the parts covers a major aspect of the game.

Part I: Rugby: Roots, Boots, and All

The first chapter details the history of the game and its worldwide organizational structure. Then we cover the basics of the field, explain the scoring system, and take a quick look at all the positions. To prevent you from showing up unprepared, we also list all the gear you'll need to play.

Part II: Getting Down and Dirty

The second course is the meat and potatoes portion of this book. We explain the various responsibilities and skills needed to play all 15 positions. Next, we introduce the Laws of the Game and the match officials, which leads to an explanation of the object of the game, what happens after a tackle, and the concepts of offside and foul play. Then we discuss the difference between tackles, rucks, and mauls. Next, we analyze scrums and line-outs. We then shift gears to address the individual skills of running, passing, kicking, and tackling, and finish off with a look at tactics and training for rugby.

Part III: Welcome to the Oval Planet

This part spans the globe to survey the annual calendar of provincial, inter-provincial, and international competitions. We move next to the Rugby World Cup and the International Rugby Board's (IRB) stable of events. Then we move back closer to home with a look at the USA National Team — the Eagles, followed by a look at the pride of Rugby Canada — the Canadian National Team. We conclude with a tour of the heart and soul of North American rugby — the club game.

Part IV: Coaching and Refereeing

Part IV covers the full spectrum of coaching — from the minis to the Super League — and explains how you can become a certified coach. The refereeing section reviews the responsibility of the ref, and what you need to do to become one, so as to address the current shortage of whistle-blowers.

Part V: Following the Game: The Informed Fan

The fifth part will bring joy to your household, as we lay out when and where you can watch rugby on TV. We survey the channels and tell you what's on tap so you can watch rugby across North America. Next, we tell you how you can find a local match to attend. In order to satisfy your thirst for more knowledge, we also detail all the rugby-related magazines, books, and websites.

Part VI: The Part of Tens

In the sixth part we offer three top ten lists. The first provides our ten best North American players. The second covers the ten best rugby moments of all time. The third list conveys ten peculiar facts about the oval game.

The Appendices

Finally, we've included three appendices for easy access to information you're likely to need. Appendix A includes the USA Rugby and Rugby Canada test records. Appendix B contains a handy glossary of rugby terms for your edification. If you need to get in touch with a particular group or organization mentioned in this book, Appendix C has the contact details for you to get hooked up.

Icons Used in This Book

To help you navigate your way through this book, we have created six icons that appear in the margins. The icons point you to a particular type of information, depending on your needs. The icons mean the following:

This icon indicates useful information for players looking to improve their skills. Even if you're not a player, they'll help you understand what players are trying to accomplish and elevate your knowledge and enjoyment.

This symbol is used when we offer advice to coaches. All of these suggestions have worked for us in our coaching experience, so we hope you'll find them useful and we encourage you to give us feedback.

Whenever we use a word or phrase that is unique to rugby speak, we employ this icon to identify the terminology and then define it.

Whenever safety is an issue, we use this symbol to alert you to the potential risk and then explain how to minimize or avoid harm.

If you see this icon, get buckled-in for an entertaining tale from his vast reservoir of rugby exploits, recounted from Brownie's unique rugby-centric perspective of the universe.

Whenever you find this icon, remember that Guthrie's been at the forefront of bringing rugby to the North American audience for ten years and has, by necessity, become a self-educated expert in everything related to the game.

Where to Go from Here

So now you're ready to start your incredible journey into the world's most amazing game. Where you go from here depends on your experience and the type of information that you're looking for. If you've got no clue at all, start at the beginning and enjoy the ride. If you have a question about a particular phase of play, head directly to that chapter and get the answers you need.

Regardless of where you begin, we're confident that by the time you reach the end of your trip through these pages, you'll see the light and will share our love for the game they play in heaven. Welcome to the rugby family!

Part I

Rugby: Roots, Boots, and All

The 5th Wave   By Rich Tennant

©RICHTENNANT

INNOVATIVE RUGBY FRONT ROW

Cullen Brown
Tighthead
Prop

Dirk Lee
Hooker

Fritz Bobblehead
Loosehead Prop

In this part...

To make you feel comfortable about everything rugby, this part provides an introduction to the game, explains how it began, what it's all about, and for newcomers, we lay out the basic parameters of the sport.

To start, we give you an outline of the beginnings of rugby and describe how it has become one of the most widely played and most popular sports around the world. We explain what is required to win, the scoring system, the field on which the game is played, and what goes on during a match. And finally, we tell you what gear you'll need to have when you show up for that first training session.

Chapter 1

Rugby's Allure, Beginnings, and the State of the Game

• •

In This Chapter

▶ Why rugby is an amazing sport

▶ How it all began

▶ The organizational structure of the game

• •

*W*hy do millions of fans around the globe watch 15 players chase an oval ball on a field of grass as if the world would end if they missed one pass, kick, or tackle? Because they are hooked on rugby, a game of passion that is full of action, excitement, beauty, unpredictable moments, and dramatic resolutions on the field and unique camaraderie off it. When played by the best exponents of the game, rugby union satisfies the soul like nothing else.

Ten Reasons Why Rugby Is Awesome

Rugby can be played by anyone. The game does not discriminate — rich or poor, male or female, young or old, every person can enjoy this fantastic game.

There's a position for everyone. Whether you are 7 feet tall or 5 feet tall, 100 pounds or 300 pounds, fleet as a cheetah or slow as an ox, there is an appropriate position for every body type.

Rugby players share a global bond. Played in more than one hundred countries, devotees of the game nevertheless belong to a select group. No rugby player is ever without a friend as long as another rugby player is nearby.

Everyone participates fully. Although there are 15 different positions, each player has to possess a skill set that includes running with the ball, passing, tackling, rucking, mauling, and kicking.

Rugby has a unique ethos on the field. Rugby is a hard, aggressive game that attracts fierce competitors. Regardless of the intensity, however, gentlemanly conduct is expected of all participants and you won't find the sort of trash-talking that pollutes most other professional sports in North America.

Rugby has a unique ethos off the field. The same players who do their best to legally smash each other for 80 minutes during a match will always shake hands and share a beverage and a chat afterwards. Whether at a club game or the highest international level, socializing with the opposition is mandatory.

Rugby tests athleticism and courage. Fast running, towering kicking, and fearless tackling are all elements of the game that challenge players to reach their athletic potential in the face of danger.

Rugby is easy to follow. Although it looks chaotic at first, rugby is easy to understand and appreciate once you become familiar with a few simple principles of play.

Rugby people are cool. Rugby brings together a gregarious, intelligent, diverse group of characters that are fun to be around.

Rugby has a proud history. While it is new to many North Americans, rugby has a long and storied tradition of competitive excellence, fair play, and sporting spirit that transcends the game itself.

The Birth of the New Handling Game

The game gets its name from Rugby, a town in England's Midlands, where it was first played at Rugby School. The legend goes that in 1823, a schoolboy by the name of William Webb Ellis first picked up the ball in the middle of a soccer game and ran with it, thereby breaking the old rules and setting the stage for an entirely new game (see the following section for the creation of this myth).

What is true is that the game was popularized and the rules codified at Rugby School. Its alumni spread it throughout Britain to other schools and universities like Oxford and Cambridge, and eventually to the far reaches of the British Empire.

The mythical pick-up of William Webb Ellis

William Webb Ellis was indeed a student at Rugby School in 1823, but that's about as much historical fact as can be determined about him in regards to his invention of the game of rugby. In reality, the myth was created years after his death in 1872 for a specific purpose — so the upper classes in England could justify their control of the game. Around the time the story was concocted, rugby was in the throes of a great battle between amateurism and professionalism that would eventually split the sport into two different codes.

Ellis's posthumous anointment as father of the game was a significant event in that battle and his name lives on today as the embodiment of the sports crowning achievement, the William Webb Ellis Cup, which is awarded to the winner of the quadrennial World Cup.

A century of amateurism

From its beginnings at English public schools, rugby was definitely an elitist pursuit that actively discouraged and prohibited the payment of players. In 1895, after the Rugby Football Union (RFU) refused to allow clubs to compensate players for missing work to play the game, 22 clubs broke away from the union to form the Northern Football Union. This forerunner of the professional rugby league eventually adopted its own set of rules and began paying players — something rugby union wouldn't do for another century.

Up until the 1990s, rugby union was a strictly amateur sport. While there were obviously numerous cases of cushy jobs, special treatment, and under-the-table payments, rugby administrators in both hemispheres diligently ferreted out cases of direct pay for play and banned those who were caught. Making the jump to rugby league meant no further involvement in union at any level.

That this prohibition against remuneration outlasted even the Olympic movement's similar rule is a testament to the amount of control the game's conservative governors exerted over a worldwide sport. By 1995, the pressures of money and television had become too great and under threat of losing the best players to league or upstart union competitions, the powers that be capitulated and the sport entered a new era of professionalism.

How the Game Is Organized

As an entirely amateur sport for most of its history, rugby was controlled by volunteer administrators in individual countries. Each rugby-playing country had its own organizational structure and was responsible for internal decisions regarding finances, eligibility, competitions, and development. Interaction between different nations was managed on a union–to–union basis. In the last quarter of the 20th century, however, the growth of the game led to the strengthening of an existing but limited governing body, the International Rugby Board (IRB).

Rugby's rulers — the IRB

The IRB was founded in 1886, but it didn't attain its all-powerful status until nearly a century later. Headquartered in Dublin, the IRB is the world-governing and law-making body for the game of rugby union. The day-to-day business of the board is conducted by a professional staff of over 40 people. IRB membership currently totals 96 unions and 5 regional associations.

The Executive Council, made up of representatives from the eight foundation unions, meets twice a year. The eight foundation unions — Scotland, Ireland, Wales, England, Australia, New Zealand, South Africa, and France — each have two seats. Argentina, Canada, Italy, and Japan each have one seat on the council as does FIRA-AER (the International Amateur Rugby Federation — European Rugby Association). The full membership meets every two years at the association's general meeting; regional meetings are held at regular intervals.

The IRB is now responsible for setting the international test schedule; developing the game worldwide; running the World Cup through a subsidiary organization, Rugby World Cup Limited; and generally acting as overlord to the sport.

There are a number of tournaments under IRB control, including the Women's Rugby World Cup, Rugby World Cup Sevens, IRB World Sevens Series, Under 21 World Cup, Under 19 World Championship, and the Super Cup. The principal money-making IRB property, however, is the Rugby World Cup, which is held every four years.

National unions

The first national union was formed in England in 1871 and called, appropriately enough, the Rugby Football Union (RFU). The union came about in response to the need for order and uniformity in the rapidly expanding game. Before the standardization of rules created by the RFU, matches varied significantly in rules and length, depending upon where they were played.

A national union is usually a large, professional organization that has a multitude of responsibilities. The union's composition and role depends on the size of the rugby-playing population and the popularity of the game in a particular country.

In a country like New Zealand, for example, the New Zealand Rugby Union (NZRU) negotiates with sponsors, staffs and runs the various national teams, hires coaches, and contracts professional players for their services. The staff at the NZRU are full-time employees engaged in developing and promoting New Zealand rugby in all its forms, from youth to international competitions.

In a small country like Latvia with only seven rugby clubs, it's a much different story. The national officials are usually either volunteers or they're paid a small stipend for their work. The responsibilities are often the same as in a large union, but the scale is much smaller.

The United States Rugby Football Union (USA Rugby) and Rugby Canada are somewhere in between New Zealand and Latvia. They both have paid professionals running the organizations, but they also rely heavily on volunteers from both countries to assure the smooth functioning of the game in all its aspects.

Provincial unions

In countries like South Africa, where rugby is entrenched in the nation's sporting landscape, provincial unions are powerful champions of their regional interests. In addition to training referees and coaches, running youth programs and academies, and selecting and funding teams for competition in national events, provincial unions have a say in how the game is run at the national level. North American equivalents are the regional or provincial unions like the Pacific Coast Rugby Football Union and the British Columbia Rugby Union.

Local unions

Local unions are concerned with administering the game within a certain geographical area. In the U.S. these are called local area unions and in Canada they're referred to as sub-unions. These unions are staffed by volunteers and are responsible for scheduling matches, providing referees, organizing playoffs, and resolving disputes between clubs.

Rugby clubs

The most basic rugby grouping is the club. In most parts of the world, rugby clubs are run by the members and players — they do everything from preparing the field to cleaning up after the reception. Depending on its size, a club may field teams from youth level up to senior and even masters levels.

In more established rugby countries it's common for the clubs to own their clubhouse and several fields to play and practice on. In others, the club is often just an association of like-minded individuals who get together to train and play the game they love.

GUTHRIE SAYS

Being on the Board

After years of being a vocal and very public critic of the way USA Rugby was run, in December 2003 I was elected to the USA Rugby Board of Directors. Prior to taking my seat, my impression of the Board of Directors was that they were a bunch of nincompoops who were easily herded in whatever direction the Executive Committee pointed them. Moreover, I felt that the top leadership had a self-serving agenda that had very little to do with developing the game. Control for it's own sake was their be-all and end-all. Numerous visionaries who took action to help the game grow had been frustrated, blackballed, sued, and otherwise ostracized by the iron-fisted control that a select few had over the national union. The Board, it seemed to me, was a total waste of time.

When I arrived in Denver for my first BOD meeting, I was determined to keep an open mind and see how things went. I kept a low profile and listened to the exchange of ideas and, to my surprise, was duly impressed by a Board membership that was very capable and knowledgeable. The collective experience around the table was impressive and the measured comments, and sometimes heated discussion demonstrated that I was totally off the mark in my impressions of the Board. The room was filled with passionate people from all walks of life who had volunteered to come from around the country to thoughtfully debate the future of the game. Doctors, way too many lawyers, engineers, professors, business people, government officials, former internationals, referees, and even a TV producer were committed to working together to address the needs of the country's players, referees, parents, fans and all others involved in the game. The new direction of USA Rugby, signaled by first hiring and then not firing CEO Doug Arnot, is an exciting one, as rugby is poised for massive growth over the next decade. So the next time you hear someone berate the job our leaders are doing, ask them if they've ever been to a Board meeting.

Chapter 2

The Basics

In This Chapter

▶ Finding your way around the rugby pitch

▶ Keeping score

▶ Timekeeping on the field

▶ Meeting the team

*L*ike most things in life, you need to understand the basics before you can really appreciate rugby. Whether you're a complete newcomer, have had some exposure to the sport, or are a full-fledged expert, the material we cover in this chapter will help you get that much more familiar with the ins and outs of the game.

In this chapter, we describe the playing field, outline how points are scored, explain timekeeping, and describe the positions of the players.

Figuring Out the Field

Rugby is played on a grass field, although sand, clay, and dirt surfaces are permitted, provided they are not dangerous. A permanently hard surface, such as asphalt or cement, is prohibited. The place where rugby is played is variously referred to as the field of play, the playing field, the rugby field, and the pitch, but they all refer to the same place, which is shown in Figure 2-1 on page 18.

Dimensions of the playing area

Rugby is contested on the playing area. The playing area is composed of the field of play and two in-goal areas. This is where the players do battle.

Basic rugby terminology

Before launching into the specifics of the pitch, a couple of key rugby terms require definition. A *scrum* is used to restart play after certain minor infractions. The scrum is a contest for the ball involving eight players who bind together and push against the other team's assembled eight for possession of the ball. A *line-out* is used to restart play after the ball, or a player carrying it, has gone out of bounds. The line-out looks somewhat like a jump ball in basketball, with both teams lining up opposite each other, but one team then throws the ball down the middle of the tunnel.

✔ **The field of play:** The area where the bulk of the action takes place is referred to as the *field of play*. It measures no more than 100 meters long by no more than 70 meters wide (109.4 yards long by 76.5 yards wide). The field of play does not include the touchlines or the in-goal areas at either end of the ground (see Figure 2-1).

✔ **The in-goal areas:** At each end of the playing area are the *in-goal areas*, which must be between 10 and 22 meters long and 70 meters wide (10.9 yards to 24.1 yards long and 76.5 yards wide). The in-goal areas include the goal lines, but not the touch-in-goal or dead ball lines.

✔ **The playing area:** This includes both the *field of play* and the two *in-goal* areas. The touchlines, touch-in-goal lines, and dead-ball lines are not part of the playing area.

What do all those lines mean?

Like most newcomers, when we first started playing rugby the field markings were an indecipherable mystery of seemingly random chalk marks. The rugby pitch has numerous lines marked on it, which can seem confusing, but once you know what they all mean and comprehend their strategic importance, your overall understanding of the game will be significantly enhanced. Keep reading and you'll learn in five minutes what took us five years to figure out! Here's a rundown of the lines and what each one means:

✔ **Halfway line:** The *halfway line* is a solid line that marks the center of the field, and is where the game starts. Play is also restarted at the halfway line after successful tries, drop goals, or penalty goals. One of the objectives in rugby is to spend as much time as possible in the opponent's half of the field (see Figure 2-1).

✔ **10-meter line:** There are two broken *10-meter lines* that are placed 10 meters on either side of the halfway line. When a team kicks off, the ball must reach this line for the kick to be legal.

✔ **22-meter line:** There are two solid *22-meter lines*, which are located 22 meters out from each goal line. Drop-outs, a specific kind of restart (discussed in more detail in Chapter 7), are taken from behind the 22-meter line. The 22-meter line is also crucial in positional play (see Chapter 9 to learn how the 22-meter line affects the kicking game).

✔ **Goal line:** The *goal line*, also called the *tryline*, is a solid line that delineates the beginning of the in-goal areas. There are two goal lines, one at either end of the field of play, which players must reach to successfully score a try.

✔ **Dead-ball line:** The line beyond the in-goal area at each end of the pitch is called the *dead ball line*. Once the ball touches, or goes over this line, the ball is considered "dead," or out of play.

✔ **Touchline:** The two solid lines that run from goal line to goal line are called the *touchlines*. These are just like the sidelines in football. They are called touchlines because when the ball contacts the line or the ground beyond them, it is considered to be *in touch*, which means out of bounds (see Chapter 9 for more on the touchlines).

✔ **Touch-in-goal line:** The *touch-in-goal line* is the continuation of the touchline between the goal line and the dead ball line. For newcomers to the game, grasping the meaning of the principal lines described above allows you to follow the flow of play. However, there are some other broken lines and dash lines unaccounted for in Figure 2-1.

✔ **5-meter line:** The *5-meter line* is a broken line that runs from one tryline to the other, parallel to the touchlines. It marks the front of the line-out and the minimum distance a line-out throw must travel (see Chapter 9 for more line-out particulars).

✔ **Dash lines:** Dash lines are 1 meter in length and provide reference points for both referees and players. There are three different types of dash lines:

  • **15-meter dash line:** There are seven dash lines that are located 15 meters in and parallel to both touchlines. The dash lines intersect the goal lines, the 22-meter lines, the 10-meter lines, and the halfway line. They define the back of the line-out, and also where scrums and penalties are taken after line-out infringements (see Chapter 8 for more on scrums and Chapter 9 for more on line-outs).

  • **5-meter dash line:** There are six 5-meter dash lines positioned 5 meters in front of and parallel to each tryline. They are placed in from each touchline at 5 and 15 meters, and one in front of each goalpost. The dashes mark the minimum distance from the defending team's tryline where a scrum or line-out can be set, or where a penalty can be taken.

  • **Halfway dash line:** This is a half-meter-long dash that intersects the halfway line at midfield. This is the spot where kickoffs and restarts are supposed to originate — even though most kickers will cheat a meter or two sideways in either direction.

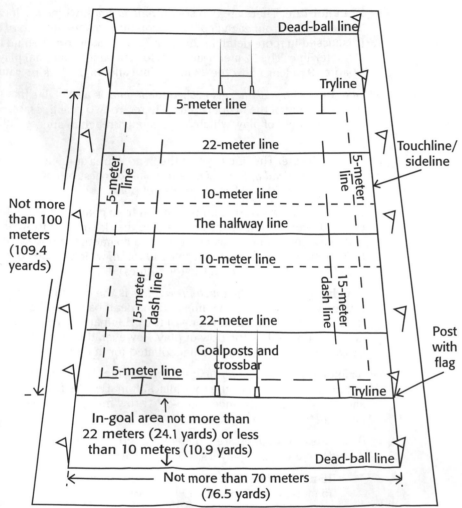

Figure 2-1:
The arena in which rugby is played.

Explaining the goalposts and flags

Old-time football fans will immediately recognize the H-shaped structures at either end of the pitch. We are referring to the goalposts that are situated at each end of the field of play, directly on the tryline. They must be 5.6 meters (6.12 yards) apart with a *crossbar* (the horizontal beam between the goalposts) that measures 3 meters (3.28 yards) above the ground. The minimum height of the goalposts is 3.4 meters (3.71 yards) above the crossbar. As a safety precaution, the goalposts are usually covered with padding to prevent injury if players crash into them. The goalpost pads also provide great advertising opportunities for sponsors!

There are 14 flags on the rugby pitch. Four of the flags mark the intersections of the dead-ball and touch-in-goal lines. These flags rarely come into play, as they mark the extreme corners of the field.

Another four flags mark the three-way intersection of the goal lines, touchlines, and touch-in-goal lines. These flags are not part of the in-goal areas, so if you make contact with any of them during play, you are out of bounds. Although it might seem self-evident, the game of rugby is meant to be played within the boundaries, with limited exceptions (see Chapter 9 for the times when you're allowed to play from out-of-bounds areas).

The remaining six flags are also outside the playing area, positioned 2 meters beyond the touchline, at the 22-meter and halfway lines.

Understanding the Scoring System

Football developed from rugby, so if you understand touchdowns, extra points, and field goals, getting a handle on rugby's scoring system is a breeze. How points are accumulated in rugby has evolved over the last hundred years, with the addition of awarding points for tries and conversions. Long ago, scoring a try didn't result in points — it just earned the right to attempt a kick at goal. The modern system encourages teams to score tries over simply kicking penalties.

There are five ways to tally points in rugby. The ease or difficulty of achieving each of them plays a crucial role in strategic decision-making by players and coaches. Once you understand what the five ways are, your enjoyment of the game really takes off, as you come to appreciate what's at stake on the field.

Scoring a try

Scoring a try is the quickest way to amass the most points in rugby. A try is the pièce de résistance of rugby, similar to scoring a touchdown in football. In fact, rugby is where the term "touchdown" came from, because the ball must actually be touched down for a try to be awarded. A try is scored when the ball is grounded by an offensive player in the in-goal area or on the tryline itself.

To signal a try, the referee raises an arm and blows the whistle at the spot where the ball came into contact with the turf (see Chapter 5 for a complete list of all the referee signals). The exact place is important because it determines where the conversion kick can be taken from (see "Converting a try" later in this chapter).

A try is worth five points, which is the highest number of points a rugby team can score at one time.

Awarding a penalty try

The awarding of a penalty try is one of the most contentious and misunderstood aspects of rugby, usually because of when and why it occurs. A *penalty try* must be awarded if the referee believes the defending team committed a penalty that prevented the attacking team from scoring a try that would probably otherwise have been scored. This gives the referee plenty of latitude to negate cynical or desperate acts of cheating by awarding points to override what happened on the field. This unique license to rectify the impact of unsportsmanlike conduct is in keeping with the gentlemanly ethos of the game.

When a penalty try is awarded, the referee runs beneath the crossbar in the center of the goalposts, raises an arm, and blows the whistle.

Just like a normal try, the attacking team receives five points, but gets to attempt the conversion as if the try had been scored under the posts.

Converting a try

Once a try or penalty try is awarded, the attacking team has the chance to add a further two points to the scoreboard by kicking a *conversion*. The referee marks the place where the try was scored and then the *goal kicker* can tee up the ball anywhere along a line parallel to the touchline, out from where the ball was grounded. In other words, if the try was scored 5 meters (5.46 yards) from the sideline, then the conversion must be taken 5 meters (5.46 yards) from the sideline. (Figure 2-1 shows the sideline.)

Usually the goal kicker takes the ball back as far as he needs to get a better angle in order to improve his chances of making the kick.

Another reason for taking the kick far back is that on a conversion, the opposition may charge the kicker and block his attempt. The defending team must stand on or behind the goal line until the kicker begins to approach the ball — then they are allowed to rush the kicker.

The goal kicker places the ball on either a specially constructed kicking tee or on a mound of hand-sculpted sand. A *kicking tee* is a small plastic device that's placed on the ground and holds the rugby ball upright. Making a sand castle is the old-fashioned way but, unfortunately for silica aficionados, it's rarely seen anymore.

Goal kickers have their own unique routines for kicking goals, including how many steps they take, where they aim, and how they position the rest of their body (see Figure 2-2). This used to be a long and drawn-out process that interrupted the flow of the game and wasted time. To speed up play, the

International Rugby Board (IRB) recently imposed a one-minute time limit for conversions and penalties, which begins when the kicker receives the tee from the sidelines. Gone are the days when a game consisted of a never-ending series of interminable stoppages for penalties and conversions, punctuated by short bursts of actual rugby.

Figure 2-2:
Preparing
to take a
penalty kick.

If the conversion kick flies through the uprights, the touch judges raise their flags and the referee blows the whistle. (See Chapter 5 for more on touch judges, the match officials who use signal flags to assist the referee.)

Conversion kicks are worth two points. Thus, a "converted" try is worth seven points in total: five for the try plus two for the conversion. If the goal kicker misses, the team gets only the five points for the try.

Kicking penalty goals

If the referee determines that a team has broken one of the laws of the game, a penalty can be awarded to the other side. The non-offending team can choose among several options of how best to utilize the resulting possession. One of those choices is to kick a penalty goal.

The referee signals a penalty by blowing the whistle and raising an arm in the direction of the team to whom the penalty has been awarded (there's a diagram of the penalty signals in Chapter 5). Next, that team's captain has to make a decision. If the captain chooses to kick at goal, the kicker places the ball on the spot where the penalty occurred, or anywhere on a direct line behind it, just like a conversion. Unlike a conversion, the defending team is not allowed to rush the kicker at any time while a penalty kick is being attempted.

A successful penalty goal is worth three points.

Drop-kicking goals

A *dropped goal* (also called a "drop goal" or "drop kick") is different than a conversion or penalty kick because it takes place while the ball is in play. A drop goal involves a player dropping the ball and trying to kick for the poles just after it hits the ground, as shown in Figure 2-3. (We discuss the finer points of the drop kick in Chapter 10.)

Figure 2-3: Scoring a drop goal with a drop kick requires a lot of skill.

The importance of a specialist goal kicker

In the modern era, having an outstanding goal kicker on your team is of paramount importance. Goal kickers are immensely valuable because their skills are so often called upon during the match when one player or another has committed any one of the indiscretions that result in a penalty. If you have a reliable goal kicker, your team can be outscored in the try department but still win the match because you've kicked enough penalties.

In the 2003 World Cup the boot of England fly-half Jonny Wilkinson was instrumental in his country's triumph. In the knockout stage of the competition England was outscored in tries by 5 to 2 but was able to come away with the trophy because Wilkinson accounted for 62 of England's 72 points, kicking 16 penalties, 4 drop goals, and 1 conversion.

Slotting a drop goal is a clever maneuver that most teams don't utilize. Drop kicks are rare because they require perfect timing and lots of practice to properly execute.

If the ball passes between the goalposts and above the crossbar, the team earns three points.

Timekeeping on the Field

Play is divided into two halves. Each half is 40 minutes with a 10-minute halftime in between. The referee has the power to extend play to make up for time lost because of injuries or delays. This is called *injury time* and is entirely up to the referee's discretion. Unlike most other clock-governed sports, the referee is the official timekeeper. When the referee determines that all time has expired he blows the whistle to signal the end of the match, which is called *fulltime*.

When the clock runs and when it stops

The 40 minutes in each half is running time, not elapsed time. In rugby, the clock counts up instead of down, beginning at the kickoff. Running time stops for injured players to be quickly treated or removed from the pitch, occasionally for water or for players' clothing to be replaced, and for times when the referee wants to speak with the respective captains, individual players, the touch judges, or the television match official (TMO).

When someone's injured

This is another decision made by the referee. If a player can be quickly treated, most refs will allow a slight delay in the game. Special dispensation and a little extra recovery time is afforded front row players if a scrum or line-out is required to restart play (see Chapters 8 and 9 for more on scrums and line-outs). The referee also has the option of letting the match continue while a player receives treatment, if the player isn't in the way. For serious injuries, time stops until medical personnel can remove the player from the pitch.

When the TMO is looking at play

The TMO is the equivalent of instant replay in football. In selected leagues and international competitions, if the match is produced for television, the referee has the option of checking with a fellow official, who can review various angles the referee didn't see (see Chapter 5 for the TMO's scope and responsibilities). When the referee and the TMO are communicating, running time is off.

When the hooter sounds

The hooter, or horn, or siren is a relatively new addition to most professional rugby stadiums. By keeping track of when the referee's time is running and when it isn't, the stadium timekeeper sounds the hooter when 40 minutes of running time has expired in each half. The hooter does not mean the end of the match, and play can continue after it sounds. It is more like a signal to players and fans that time is almost up. In many cases, the next time the ball goes "dead," the referee will blow the whistle to signal fulltime (the end of the match).

Introducing the Players

Rugby is one of the few sports that caters to all sorts of body shapes and sizes. A photograph of a rugby team often looks as if one specimen of every human body type has been assembled at the same spot, at the same time, to provide an illustration for an anthropological study.

A quick scan of any team out at training is proof that everyone can play the game. Within every team, the tall, the small, the fat, the skinny, and everyone in between can find a position that suits them.

Taking up position

Each *squad* or *side* — the group of players who make up a rugby team — is composed of 22 players. This includes the 15 who start the match plus the 7 reserves. The starting 15 take the pitch at the beginning of the match and the 7 reserves sit on the sideline in case of injury or tactical changes.

While most of the positions involve specialized skills, that doesn't mean players are stuck in the same position for the rest of their rugby lives. Players have scope to move about, especially if their body shapes change with age. In this section, we give you a brief overview of the positions on a rugby team. We discuss the positions in more detail in Chapter 4.

The 15 players who start the game are divided into 8 forwards (also referred to as the *pack*), and 7 backs (commonly called the *backline*). The forwards are primarily responsible for winning the ball and the backs are charged with doing something positive when they get it. An old oval adage says the forwards decide who wins a match and the backs decide by how much.

Regardless of position, however, every rugby player must possess a basic set of skills. Each player must be able to tackle opposition ball-carriers, catch the ball, run with it, and pass it.

Positions by the numbers

The 15 starters on a rugby side all wear specific numbers on their jerseys to designate their position. Even among English speakers, some of the names of the individual positions vary depending on where you are in the world (we cover these name variations in detail in Chapter 4), but the following terms are the most generally recognized:

- **Loose-head prop (jersey number 1):** A big, strong player who is responsible for scrumming in the front row and lifting the jumpers in the line-out.

- **Hooker (jersey number 2):** This front rower actually hooks the ball with his foot at scrumtime, hence the name; plus he or she does the throwing at line-outs.

- **Tight-head prop (jersey number 3):** The rock upon which the scrum is built, he has to be the strongest and most technically proficient player in the pack.

- **Locks (jerseys number 4 and number 5):** Locks form the second row in the scrum and are normally used as line-out jumpers and restart takers because of their superior height and reliable hands. Some teams number their locks according to left or right, others by seniority, or simply preference of the players for a specific number.

- **Blindside flanker (jersey number 6):** This player must be powerful and make an impact in contact on offense and defense. He must have excellent ball-handling skills.

- **Openside flanker (jersey number 7):** This is usually the most dynamic and best defensive player on the team, responsible for making critical tackles, creating turnovers, and ranging all over the pitch.

- **Number 8 (jersey number 8):** The number 8 (or eightman) plays a crucial role on the team. This player directs and controls the scrum from the rear and is often a pivotal link between the forwards and the backs.

- **Scrumhalf (jersey number 9):** Also known as the halfback, this player must be compact and quick, with excellent passing skills and the ability to operate in tight quarters.

- **Flyhalf (jersey number 10):** This is the player who runs the show on offense either by running, passing, or kicking the ball.

- **Wings (jerseys number 11 and number 14):** Two of the fastest players on the pitch, the wings must be able to kick and play good positional defense. Which side the two wings play on is usually decided by kicking ability and side-stepping preference.

- **Inside center (jersey number 12):** This is a physical player with quickness and power running the ball, and no fear when tackling.

- **Outside center (jersey number 13):** The outside center is a creative runner and ball-handler with very good speed and solid defensive skills.

- **Fullback (jersey number 15):** This is the backline general. This player must possess excellent tactical knowledge, have a strong leg for kicking, be an attack-oriented runner, and be the last line of defense.

Reserves

Players who don't start the match but come on as replacements or substitutes are called *reserves*. The reserves sit near the field of play ready to go on at any time. Coaches can replace players who are injured, make tactical changes to combat a threat posed by the opposition, or simply remove a player who is tiring or having a poor game. Each reserve has the same basic designated role as the players they replace. Wearing the jersey numbers 16 to 22, they are as follows:

- **Reserve hooker (jersey number 16):** The hooker replacement has to be able to come off the bench and hit the line-out jumpers with minimal warm-up.

- **Reserve prop (jersey number 17):** This player needs to be able to cover for both the tight-head and loose-head props.

- ✔ **Reserve forward (jersey number 18):** This player can be used to cover either lock position.

- ✔ **Reserve forward (jersey number 19):** This player can provide backup for all three back-row forward positions (the flankers or number 8).

- ✔ **Reserve scrumhalf (jersey number 20):** This reserve is a specialized scrumhalf replacement.

- ✔ **Reserve back (jersey number 21):** This player can play either inside center or outside center position in midfield.

- ✔ **Reserve back (jersey number 22):** The second reserve back is used to provide backup for the wings or the fullback.

Of the seven backup players who sit on the *reserve bench* (the name given to the place the replacement players sit), three are specialist positions: the hooker, the prop, and the scrumhalf. For a scrum, an injured prop must be replaced by another suitably trained prop, not by just any player filling in, because of the particular technique, strength, and experience required to safely compete in the front row.

Officials are deeply concerned about the risk of serious injury to front-rowers if a scrum is incorrectly set, or injury to someone who doesn't have the ability to withstand the pressure coming through from the opposition. Safety on all levels has improved in recent years, with a greater emphasis on injury prevention (player safety is discussed further in Chapter 18).

Clever use of the reserve bench can often mean the difference between winning and losing a match, particularly if it's going right down to the wire. With the faster and fitter game of rugby being played these days, the reserve bench has become a vital part of every coach's arsenal.

Bringing on players from the reserve bench for tactical reasons is a recent rugby phenomenon. It has changed the way coaches select their 22-person squad and their strategy throughout. Fresh players are brought on as impact players, usually in the second half, to try to take advantage of a tiring opposition. This does not mean that a team gets an unfair advantage, as the opposition also has the chance to use fresh legs whenever required.

Being a reserve is a tough assignment in rugby, especially if the conditions are foul. Sitting on the sidelines while your teammates do battle is never easy and is even more difficult when you have to be ready to join the fray at any moment.

Each player on the reserve bench is there for a specific reason. Whenever you're in the reserves you have to stay focused on how the game is unfolding. It's important to watch the players you're likely to replace and see what's working and what's not against the opposition. The key is to be mentally switched-on and ready to get stuck-in right away should the need arise.

Chapter 3

Grab Your Rugby Gear

• •

• •

Rugby is often referred to as football without pads. Of course that's not true, but it does highlight one of the main advantages of rugby — that you don't need to break the bank buying all those expensive football pads, helmets, and uniforms to outfit your team or yourself for action. All you need is a jersey, some shorts, a mouth guard, a pair of cleats, and a ball, and you're on your way to playing the game.

In this chapter, we describe the necessary items to pack into your bag, as well as some extra stuff that you may consider worthwhile — in rugby circles, your gear is collectively referred to as your kit, which you lug around in your kit bag. Next, we discuss the important issue of personal safety while playing rugby and the precautions you can take to protect yourself on the pitch.

Getting It Together: The Essentials of the Kit Bag

A strong, yet lightweight, sports bag is essential to carry your rugby kit around in. The bag should be big enough to hold a rugby jersey, socks, shorts, boots, football, and towel — plus a change of clothing. Bag sizes vary but you should look for one that is larger than a normal gym bag as you'll soon have it stuffed to capacity. Try and find a bag that has a separate pocket for your valuables and has a waterproof compartment, either on the outside or the inside, where you can stuff your muddy socks, shorts, and boots.

Before you rush out and purchase a kit bag, you should inquire whether your team has bags for sale. Many clubs periodically order personalized team bags, sometimes to commemorate tours or championship seasons. This is the ultimate in sophisticated rugby luggage.

Having a ball

A rugby ball is oval, not round. It can be made of leather or a strong synthetic material and consists of four panels. Some balls are designed to make them easier to grip when playing in muddy or wet conditions. The ball used in youth rugby is slightly smaller than the one for adults. Whatever your age, though, it's important that you train with the same size ball that you play with in a game.

A rugby ball is the first item any aspiring rugby player buys. Even though rugby clubs usually have an abundance of balls, it's still a smart idea for you to have one to practice with on your own. Coaches recommend that you have a ball in your hands as often as possible so you can practice your kicking, passing, catching, and handling skills.

Finding a rugby ball in a sporting goods store in North America is more serendipity than certainty. Your best bet is to order a ball online from one of the many online rugby stores.

The dimensions of a rugby ball are as follows:

- **Length:** 280–300 millimeters (11–12 inches)
- **Circumference (end to end):** 760–790 millimeters (30–31 inches)
- **Circumference (width):** 580–620 millimeters (23–24 inches)
- **Weight:** 400–440 grams (14.5–15.5 ounces)
- **Air pressure:** 0.67–0.70 kilograms per square centimeter, or 9½–10 pounds per square inch

Maintaining the proper air pressure is important. Make sure that your ball has enough give in it for you to push your fingers in slightly at one end. A softer ball is easier to catch, handle, and pass, and is therefore better suited for training purposes.

There are two categories of rugby balls. A *match ball* is usually a rock-hard, top-of-the-line rugby ball. Match balls are well balanced to pass, kick, and punt consistently. You'll pay $50 US or more for a match-quality ball.

A *training ball* is virtually the same as a match ball but is less expensive and should be used for practicing. Don't bother buying a match ball to kick around the neighborhood. While a training ball isn't as good as a match ball, it's perfectly fine for your needs and is much more affordable. The average training ball costs about $30.

Kicking in with a kicking tee

Over the last few years, the introduction of kicking tees has made life a lot easier for goal kickers. This small plastic apparatus is placed on the ground and holds the ball upright, as shown in Figure 3-1. A kicking tee holds a rugby ball in the same way as a golf tee holds a golf ball when a golfer prepares to hit a drive. In rugby, it's used when a team attempts to kick a conversion or a penalty goal (the scoring system is explained in Chapter 2).

Figure 3-1: Placing the ball at the correct angle on the kicking tee.

Kicking tees are quicker and less messy than the old method of kicking off a hand-sculpted mound of sand or dirt: You used to have to wait for a ball boy to run onto the pitch with a sand bucket, wait for the goal kicker to build a sandcastle, wait for the goal kicker to be satisfied with his work, wait for the kicker to place the ball on top of his castle, check the wind and gauge the distance one last time, and then finally kick it.

It is not compulsory to use a kicking tee, as some players still prefer sand. Try both and see what's most comfortable for you.

Different goal kickers like to place the ball on the kicking tee at different angles, depending on their kicking style — the kicking tee caters to all the different variations.

It's not imperative for every player on the team to own a kicking tee, especially if you have no interest in goal kicking. However, if you want to kick for goal, it is a must-have on your shopping list. You won't use your own tee in a game because clubs have plenty of them, but you will need a kicking tee to practice with. Your club may even let you have one of their spares, particularly if you start kicking match-winning penalties or conversions.

Kicking tees are a one-time purchase, usually costing between $10 and $20, and can be found online and in selected sports shops.

Miscellaneous kit items

If you're lucky, your club will sell team bags, hats, T-shirts, jackets, and warm-up outfits. There's nothing like showing up for a match with the whole squad decked out in matching outfits. Even if you get thumped by 100 points, you'll look good, improve team morale and make a much-needed contribution to the club's treasury.

To heighten your experience, there are a few more handy items to toss into your kit bag for use on match day. To supplement the team's medical kit, bring some plastic bandages and antibiotic ointment to treat the minor cuts and scrapes that are inevitable if you've played hard enough. Bring a roll of white cloth athletic tape to keep your ears fully attached to your head and for other running repairs. Invest in a pair of good sunglasses, a wide-brimmed hat, and sandals to wear after the match, while you root your second-side teammates to victory from the sideline.

Getting the Gear

The International Rugby Board (IRB) in Dublin, Ireland, sets the standards for rugby union regulations. The IRB allows for pads made of soft, thin material to be incorporated into an undergarment or jersey, provided the pads cover the shoulder and collarbone only. No part of the pads can be thicker than 1 centimeter when uncompressed, or have a density of more than 45 kilograms per cubic meter.

Rugby jerseys

Rugby jerseys can be short- or long-sleeved, and have traditionally featured a full collar. They are made of thick cotton, or synthetic fibers, which tend to breathe more than other materials. Because rugby involves tackling and binding onto one another it's important to wear a jersey that won't be easily destroyed by the constant aggression.

Game-day rugby jerseys are usually supplied by the club, but you'll need your own to wear at practice. You can purchase a proper rugby jersey for about $40, which should get you through your first season of play. Your jersey needs to be sturdy enough to withstand the punishment, so don't make the mistake of buying a department store knock-off.

Rugby shorts

Similar to the jersey, rugby shorts must be able to withstand punishment. Most rugby shorts have pockets, but you can find some varieties without them. Generally, you want a pair of shorts that are thick enough to last (and provide some protection to sensitive areas) and don't give your opponents too much to hold on to.

New players usually have to obtain their own shorts. The color and style are determined by the club you play for. There may even be two different colors, for games at home and away. Different brands fit differently and over the years we have found that Canterbury (New Zealand) and Barbarian (Canada) shorts are the most durable and comfortable shorts available.

Make sure the shorts you buy are comfortable and not too tight or too loose. If anything, the shorts should be bigger rather than smaller. We also recommend that you buy shorts with a drawstring in the waistband to ensure that they remain snugly in place around your waist. It is hard enough tackling an opponent without your efforts being impeded by a pair of shorts heading south. Moreover, if you're a line-out jumper (see Chapter 9 to see if you'll soon be launched to new heights), you'll be lifted by your shorts — so they better be fastened well or you'll get a serious wedgie.

Rugby shorts are usually priced between $20 and $35. They can be purchased online, in Canterbury clothing shops, or at specialty sporting goods stores.

Looking after your feet

Of all your rugby equipment, footwear is probably the most important. A perfectly good rugby game can be ruined by the discomfort caused by a pair of ill-fitting boots. If your feet aren't happy, brace yourself for an uncomfortable afternoon on the pitch.

BROWNIE SAYS

The boots that wouldn't die

My first real rugby boots were Patrick Parcs that I bought at the OMBAC tournament in 1988. They lasted for eight seasons, thanks to several rolls of duct tape. After about two years, the boots separated from the soles, so before each match I would carefully tape them together on my feet and then cut them off after the final whistle. I loved those boots because they were phenomenally comfortable and perfectly molded to my feet. I took a lot of grief from both team-mates and opponents over my silver footwear, but I didn't care, because they were the ideal fit.

Sadly, they met their end in Missoula, Montana, in 1995 after a particularly wet Maggotfest (see Chapter 16 for a full description of the exploits at the Maggotfest) when I left them on a friend's porch to dry. His girlfriend, now wife, threw them away, not understanding how anyone could be so attached to such ragged and dilapidated footwear. It was a crushing blow and it took me seven more years to forgive her and to find another pair of boots that fit as well. Today, I play in a pair of Canterbury Mokos that I also love and will be wearing for many years to come.

Booting up

Rugby boots (or cleats) are similar to soccer shoes or football cleats, but the studs need to be circular and otherwise meet IRB specifications. You can wear football cleats for rugby, but you'll need to remove the toe stud for them to be legal.

Forwards' boots are generally mid- to high-cut with different stud patterns designed for the rigors of scrumming and close-in work. Backs' boots are more often low-cut, built for speed and easy direction change. It doesn't really matter if you're a forward or a back — it's more important that you buy the boots that are most comfortable on your feet.

The first rule of *boot law* is to make certain that your boots fit snugly around your feet, side to side and heel to toe, to prevent blisters caused by friction. Boots should be comfortable and have the required traction on the pitch.

The best place to buy boots is online, or if you're one of the geographically fortunate few, at a rugby shop in your area. Also keep in mind that at most large rugby tournaments you'll find vendors offering their wares. This is a good opportunity to try on a variety of makes and models to find the boots that are just right for your feet. Once you've found the right fit, you'll have more confidence ordering online.

PLAYER TIP

When you buy a new pair of boots, walk around in them for a while to get comfortable before practice, and never use a brand-new pair for a match. At your first training session with new boots, apply a little petroleum jelly along the back of the heel and inside, above your toes, to prevent blisters.

Although rugby boots range widely in price, you'll find good reliable brands that start at $50. While a lot of rugby gear is available at fairly low prices, please don't economize in the boot department — cheap can be very painful and take all the fun out of the game.

When heading off to the game, always remember to check your kit bag to ensure that your boots are included. If you forget your socks, jersey, or even your shorts, there's usually someone on the team who can lend you his or hers, but if you leave your boots behind and wear a teammate's that don't fit, you'll be cursing your forgetfulness with every step. When it comes to rugby players and boots, once you find a pair that fits right, there's no limit to what you'll do to keep them in action.

Socking it to them

Rugby socks are similar to soccer socks and are worn to the knee. Soccer socks from any sporting goods store will get you started until you can purchase your game socks from your club; just make sure that they stretch up slightly above your knee, enabling you to roll the top back over to just below the knee.

Make certain that each sock has an elasticized band near the top so that it stays up during the match. To have your socks dangling around your ankles is not a recommended fashion statement. If your socks have a propensity to sink to half-mast, get a couple of short lengths of shoelace and tie a piece around each sock just below the knee and then fold the top of the sock over. Don't tie it too tightly or you'll impede the flow of blood to your legs, which could give you cramps or cause your lower legs to turn blue, wither, and eventually fall off. Old-style rugby socks used to be secured in this way before the advent of elastic (your co-authors still keep theirs up the old-fashioned way).

Finding gear in North America

There are three ways to get gear in North America. If you happen to live close to one of the few rugby supply houses, consider yourself lucky. For the vast majority of rugby players, your best options are to either buy online (or by mail order) or attend one of the many annual tournaments where rugby retailers set up mobile stores to display their wares. Other than mouth guards, don't expect to find proper rugby gear at your local sporting goods store and, whatever you do, don't try to adapt football, hockey, or other sports' pads for use in rugby (one of the best places to start outfitting yourself online is at www.worldrugbyshop.com).

Depending on the club you play with, you may be supplied with rugby socks to ensure you are wearing the right club colors. If not, the club can tell you where to buy the right pair. Socks are not expensive and the type for players at club level are available at sports shops starting at about $4 a pair.

Protecting Your Assets

After you experience the joy of playing rugby, you're likely to regard the myriad bumps and bruises as badges of courage, and come to enjoy the horrified reactions of family, friends, and co-workers who cringe at the sight of your occasional black eyes and minor facial stitches. Despite temporary trivial cosmetic alterations to your visage, rugby is actually very safe, considering the fact that it is a full-contact sport.

In Chapter 18, we address safety and the truth about injuries in rugby. Here we detail the variety of protective clothing available to lessen your chances of getting hurt.

Choosing protective equipment

In recent years, the increased emphasis on safety has led the IRB to approve the use of more and more articles of protective gear. Responding to the challenge and commercial opportunity, manufacturers have improved existing devices to protect teeth and have developed new products to lessen the impact of collisions. Below is a list of the most widely used safety items.

Before you buy headgear or shoulder pads, make sure they comply with the IRB specifications. The IRB has strict standards for rugby gear, and manufacturers must have their products approved by an IRB testing house. Once the item is approved, the garment label is marked with the IRB logo and the words "Approved Clothing," and given an approval number. Don't get too intimidated by all this IRB stuff. When buying protective gear, the packaging should indicate whether or not they are approved for use.

✔ **Mouth guards:** Almost all professional players wear mouth guards to protect their teeth from wayward fists, boots, or bodies. Mouth guards are an essential piece of protective gear and anyone who takes the pitch at any level should always wear one. Most sporting goods stores stock them for football and they can be molded to fit your teeth at home by following the directions on the package. Compared to the cost of dental reconstruction, they are a worthwhile investment at less than $5.

✔ **Headgear:** Regardless of whether you're a forward or a back, if you feel more comfortable or confident wearing padded headgear, you shouldn't hesitate to use it. Headgear must be made of soft and thin material and the IRB has set standards for what is legal. You should look for the IRB logo to be sure that your headgear is approved for use. Good, comfortable, reputable brands can be purchased for between $35 and $75.

✔ **Shoulder pads and vests:** Shoulder pads and padded vests, as seen in Figure 3-2, provide rugby players with shoulder, collar bone, and chest protection. Those made with Lycra allow more air circulation and dry more quickly. They also come in various sizes, so you can choose the amount of padding that you're comfortable with. Some are short, covering mainly the upper chest and shoulders. Others are long and will protect the entire torso as well as biceps. Female rugby players should look for vests that are designed for women. These vests are longer, and have more padding for chest protection. The IRB states that these chest pads can be made of soft, thin material, as long as no part of the pad is thicker than 1 centimeter when uncompressed. Keep in mind that shoulder protection alone won't prevent injury — you need to use good technique at all times during contact sports. Vests are generally priced at $50, but can be more expensive if they have special features.

✔ **Sports bras:** Most female rugby players also wear sports bras to reduce breast pain and limit movement. There is no specific bra designed for rugby players yet, but it's important to find one that provides good support and protection. Sports bras help to protect women as long as they fit properly. If you've never purchased a sports bra before, it's a good idea to get measured by an expert so you can get the right one. A good sports bra will cost around $30.

Figure 3-2: Shouldering the load with protective shoulder pads.

✔ **Compression shorts:** These are worn under your rugby shorts to provide extra protection and support. They also help prevent and repair hamstring and groin injuries. The shorts are usually made of thick Lycra or cotton, allowing for maximum air flow. Prices vary, but a good pair shouldn't cost more than $25.

✔ **Jock straps:** As an alternative to compression shorts, jock straps provide support for men who prefer the more traditional method of protection. These can be found at any sporting goods store and cost about $10.

Avoiding serious injury

While mouth guards, headgear, and shoulder pads offer some protection if you are hit in a certain spot, they do not guarantee a totally pain-free experience.

The best way to avoid serious injury is to play hard and at full throttle every minute you're on the pitch: "The half-hearted are the first to get hurt" is an old adage. Your club will teach you how to take other precautions, such as tackling safely and falling properly.

Rugby administrators are on the side of the player, instituting numerous laws to protect those on the pitch from serious injury. The referee is also required to stop any play that he or she determines to be dangerous and where a player might get hurt.

Do not hesitate to use any form of protection allowed by the IRB. Don't listen to any nonsense about forwards who wear shoulder vests and headgear being cowards — try telling that to the Canadian team captain Al Charron, or United States skipper Dave Hodges, who both wear protective gear. Like so many other professional players, they choose to wear it — if you've ever stood next to either one of them, you'd know that whatever they want to wear is A-OK with us.

Knowing what's barred on the pitch

You need to take note of things that are not allowed on the rugby pitch. For safety reasons, players cannot wear or take onto the pitch:

✔ Anything contaminated with blood

✔ Anything sharp or abrasive

✔ Anything containing buckles, clips, rings, hinges, zippers, screws, or bolts

- ✔ Jewelry, such as rings or earrings
- ✔ Communication devices, such as two-way radios tucked into rugby boots
- ✔ Shorts with padding sewn into them

In addition, players are not allowed to have any toe cleats on the soles of their boots. Nor are players allowed to wear gloves onto the pitch, other than the fingerless variety. If you wear a knee brace that is reinforced with metal parts, you'll need to pick up a soft brace to play rugby.

Referees are required to examine both teams before the game to ensure players are not equipped with anything that might be dangerous. Part of this inspection is the boot check — when the referee looks at both teams' boots for worn-down studs or other prohibited items.

BROWNIE SAYS

Jewelry removal

After some offhand comments in support of women's rugby fuelled by being awarded a beer mug for occasionally helping out the women's team plus the consumption of ample liquid refreshment at my club's end-of-the-season banquet a few years back, I found myself coaching the Occidental College Women's team the next fall, which I had supposedly agreed to do at said party. The experience was fantastic overall, but one aspect was definitely different from my own collegiate days on the pitch — the abundance of jewelry in all forms. In my day,

the occasional earring or class ring would hastily be removed just before kickoff and tossed to the sideline. With the Oxy women at the beginning of the 21st century, it meant unscrewing multiple earrings, nose studs, tongue studs, belly rings, and pieces of jewelry from unmentionable areas. This was a process that usually took a good 15 minutes or so, even longer with the more heavily accessorized players. Regardless of its decorative value or strategic placement, all jewelry had to come off because metal is a serious safety hazard on the pitch.

Part II
Getting Down and Dirty

In this part...

Now that you have a basic knowledge of rugby, it's time to get serious and find out exactly what's required to play the game.

In this part, we start off by explaining the various playing positions and outline the skills you need to be a star. We then move onto the all important laws of the game, where you'll learn what not to do to stay on the right side of the referee. We also detail the object of the game and then demystify the scrum, rugby's signature formation that is used to restart play. Then we cover the lineout, and finish this part with a chat about training smart to win.

Chapter 4

Location, Location, Location: Positions on the Pitch

*W*hen 30 strapping rugby players all take the field at once, there's a rush of beef to rival the greatest cattle stampede. To the rugby-watching novice, it can look like total confusion. But do not despair. Rugby has a major advantage over a lot of other sports — the number on each player's back actually determines the exact position they play.

In this chapter, we help you sort out which number goes with which player and what the person is trying to do in the game.

A Place for Everyone

Rugby is an equal opportunity game. Whether you're 5 feet tall or 7 feet tall, 100 pounds, 300 pounds, or anywhere in between, there's a place for you on a rugby team. If you want to play rugby, it will be easier to decide which position best suits you if you understand the typical characteristics and role on the team of each player.

A *side* is made up of 15 players — 8 forwards and 7 backs. The forwards (known collectively as the *pack*) have the primary role of winning the ball, while the backs are responsible for doing something productive with it. Generally, the bigger you are the more likely you are to become a forward; the faster you are the more likely you are to become a back.

Regardless of position, every rugby player needs a basic set of skills. Everyone on the team plays both offense and defense throughout the match. This means that the smallest player and the tallest, the lightest and the heaviest, must be able to perform various duties such as tackling, carrying the ball, catching, and passing it when necessary.

Playing the Numbers Game

Unlike American football, where the players' numbers are individually selected within a certain range for each position, and baseball, where numbers are random, rugby union uses specific jersey numbers to identify each position on the field. In this regard, rugby is spectator-friendly. On the field, the players who start the game are numbered from 1 to 15, and the reserves are numbered from 16 to 22 (check out Chapter 2 for more about reserves).

Jersey numbers indicate the position each player occupies on the team. Numbers also let spectators, players, and coaches know who to cheer for when something wonderful happens. At the same time, everyone, including the referees and touch judges, can identify who is to blame if something goes wrong. Once you are clear about the designated role and responsibilities of the player in each position, you'll be able to pick the stars from the slugs.

Figure 4-1 shows the forwards and backs in typical attacking formation. It might be helpful to refer to this figure often while you are reading about each of the positions.

A quick word on rucking and mauling

Before we discuss the responsibilities of the respective positions, a quick primer is in order to explain rucks and mauls. A ruck usually forms after a tackle is made when two or more players are in contact over the ball on the ground. The goal is to compete for possession by driving over the ball and using your feet to move it back to your side. A maul, in contrast, requires a minimum of three players and occurs when a player carrying the ball is held by one or more opponents and one or more of his teammates bind onto the ball-carrier who has the ball in hand off the ground. In a maul, everyone must be on their feet.

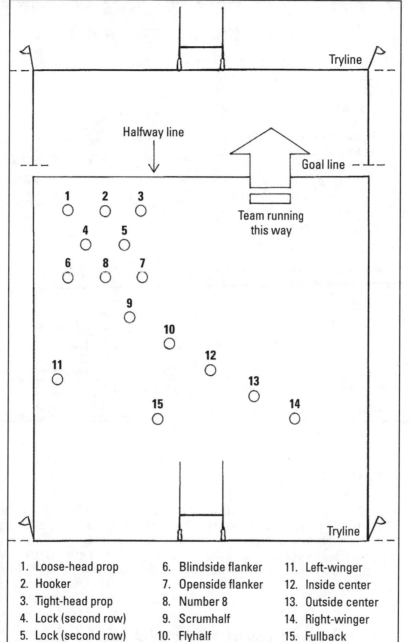

Figure 4-1:
The forwards and backs getting ready to attack.

1. Loose-head prop	6. Blindside flanker	11. Left-winger
2. Hooker	7. Openside flanker	12. Inside center
3. Tight-head prop	8. Number 8	13. Outside center
4. Lock (second row)	9. Scrumhalf	14. Right-winger
5. Lock (second row)	10. Flyhalf	15. Fullback

What's in a name: Positions around the world

Rugby originated in England in the mid-1800s and has spread throughout the world over the last 180 years. As such, the game has developed on similar, but somewhat divergent paths, depending where in the world you are. One of the by-products of these unique threads of evolution is reflected in the proliferation of different position names. While most of the positions on the rugby pitch have standardized names all over the English-speaking world, a few regional variations that can be confusing crop up in certain countries.

Here's a list of these differences:

These terms are interchangeable with the standard nomenclature and are not specific to any country or region.

- Scrumhalf — halfback, inside half
- Flyhalf — pivot, first receiver, outside half
- Lock — second-rower
- Flanker — wing forward, breakaway, break

- Flankers and Number 8 — loose forwards, or loosies

The following names are a product of regional variation.

New Zealand:

- Flyhalf — halfback, first five-eighth
- Inside Center — second five-eighth
- Outside Center — center, center three-quarter
- Wing — three-quarter

United Kingdom and Ireland:

- Flyhalf — standoff, outhalf

South Africa:

- Flankers — numbers are reversed
- Openside — wears jersey number 6
- Blindside — wears jersey number 7
- Eightman — eighthman

Fearless Forwards

Eight players make up the forwards (or pack) of a rugby union team — two props, the hooker, two locks, two flankers, and the number 8. This group's main goal is to win possession of the ball. These players are usually the heavyweights of the team, using their bulk and strength to try to overpower their opponents. Forwards can be broken up into three groups: front-rowers, second-rowers, and the back row.

Getting in tight with the tight five

The *tight five* is the group of players who wear the jerseys numbered 1 to 5. This group consists of the three front-row players (tight-head prop, hooker, and loose-head prop — or "front-rowers" collectively) and the two second-row players (two locks, or "second-rowers" collectively) who line up behind them. The tight five forms the core of the pack. The group's main function is to keep the scrum steady and productive, in the hope that when the ball is placed in the scrum it ends up in their team's possession. After an infringement occurs, the three front-rowers bind together and are joined by the two back-rowers to compete for possession of the ball in a *scrum*.

A scrum is the term used for the interlocking formation of the team where the forwards' arms are around each other's shoulders, their knees are bent, and their heads are down. As shown in Figure 4-2, all eight players bind together and face their opponents. Both units then come together on the referee's call, creating a tunnel in the middle. The ball is put in this tunnel by the scrumhalf and both teams' hookers attempt to channel it back to the rear of their own scrum with their feet. This is one of the signature elements of rugby and is used to restart play after an infraction. A scrum is over when the ball has been released from the web of players and is in play (see Chapter 8 for more details on the scrum).

Figure 4-2:
Forming a scrum, ready to compete for the ball.

Picture those wildlife documentaries where two huge rams slam together and head-butt each other for supremacy of the herd and you've got some idea of what goes on when a scrum is engaged. Brute force and strength are only half the battle. Proper, usually hard-learned, technique will invariably prevail over simple bulk in the tight five. Understanding play is a little bit easier if you take the tight five positions one by one. We'll start by explaining the function of the three front-rowers (tight-head prop, hooker, and loose-head prop), and follow by talking about the two second-rowers (the locks).

Facing off in the front row

The front row is easy to pick out: The loose-head prop wears the number 1 jersey; the hooker wears number 2; and the tight-head prop wears number 3. Don't panic — we explain these unusual names in the next few paragraphs. (Remember, the location of these players is outlined in Figure 4-1.)

The front-rowers form the platform upon which the whole team is built. These three players must be uncompromising, technically sound, and committed to doing whatever it takes to win the battle up front. If the front-rowers are weak or off their game, the team is at risk of collapsing.

Front-rowers take enormous pride in their scrummaging technique and revel in the fact that it is literally the only head-to-head confrontation in the game. Other rugby players may make jokes about props' less-than-svelte physiques, but there's also a huge amount of respect involved in the ribbing, because everyone loves playing behind a solid front row.

You won't find many flashy or cocky front-rowers, but they believe they are the three most important rugby players on the field and, in many respects, they're right.

Propping up: Tight-heads and loose-heads

The *props* are the players who wear numbers 1 and 3. They can be found on either side of the hooker in the front row. Since props take most of the physical impact in the scrum, they must possess superior upper and lower body strength.

The term "prop" comes from the fact that these two players "prop up" the hooker when the scrumhalf (more about this position later in the chapter) puts the ball into the scrum. Figure 4-3 shows the scrumhalf putting the ball in at the scrum and the hooker being supported by his loose-head and tight-head props.

The words "loose" and "tight" simply describe how the props are positioned in the actual formation of the scrum. Because of the alignment of the scrum, the loose-head prop has his head outside the scrum and can see what the others are doing. The tight-head prop, however, positions his head between the opposition's hooker and loose-head prop. In other words, the loose-head has no other head to his left, whereas the tight-head's noggin is sandwiched between two opposing players' heads (we talk more specifically about scrums in Chapter 8).

Figure 4-3:
The
scrumhalf
putting the
ball in at
the scrum.

Don't be discouraged if it takes some time to tell the difference between a tight-head and a loose-head prop. The best way to remember exactly who is who is that the loose-head is on the left-hand side of the scrum and the tight-head is on the right-hand side of the scrum. The way to remember this is that "tight" rhymes with "right."

Tight-head props and loose-head props have exactly the same aim, though their techniques are different. The tight-head is the anchor of the scrum, requiring enormous strength to keep the scrum straight and intact. The loose-head is more of a technician, using different tricks to give his team an advantage in getting the ball away from the scrum.

Props are crucial performers at the *line-out* (a line-out is how play is restarted when the ball has been taken out over the sideline or kicked into touch; we discuss line-outs in detail in Chapter 9), when they are required to lift their teammates at the right time and place. This takes excellent footwork, quickness, and strength. They are also prized defenders who take on other hard-charging forwards in tight quarters. In attack, one of a prop's main tasks is to drive defenders back a few yards whenever they touch the ball; the occasional long run is a bonus, not a requirement.

BROWNIE SAYS

Technique beats athleticism

Years ago there was a beautiful annual rugby tournament on the polo grounds at Pebble Beach in Monterey, California. About three or four years after I took up the game, my team, the Oxy Olde Boys, was scheduled to play a side from Sacramento that was made up mostly of Pacific Islander players. As we watched them warm up in their sweats prior to kickoff, all of us focused on one particular athlete who was about 6'2", 225 pounds, incredibly fast, and looked menacing in his athleticism and obvious strength. A long ponytail and a glowering countenance completed the effect. Somebody eventually muttered what everyone was thinking: "Who is going to have to play directly against that guy?" As the other team took off their jackets just before kickoff, I saw the number 3 on his back, indicating that he was a tight-head and would be opposite me, a loose-head, in the scrum. As luck would have it, that must have been his very first outing in the front row because I had my way with him, relentlessly bending him every which way, lifting him off the ground (that was before it was made illegal for safety reasons), driving him mercilessly backwards at each scrum, and generally making his life miserable to the point where he eventually took to trying to punch me as a means of self-preservation. The thumping he took in the scrums totally negated his effectiveness in the rest of play as well. At the time I was still a relatively inexperienced prop but I had the basics down and was therefore miles ahead of this newcomer and it showed on the pitch. Rugby is a game where physical attributes are important but technical proficiency is even more significant and nowhere is that more true than in the front row.

Highlighting the hooker

In between the two props is the *hooker*, who wears the number 2 jersey. This is the most versatile of the three front-row positions. The hooker is seen around the field more often because this position has a wider range of responsibility. The hooker needs to have superior hand-eye and foot-eye coordination, flexibility, agility, upper body strength, and quickness. Powerful legs are also an asset.

At the scrum, the hooker is supported by his two props, enabling him to hang suspended over the scrum opening. When the scrumhalf puts the ball into the tunnel between the feet of the opposing front rows, the hooker is required to "strike" at the ball with his foot, guiding it back behind the feet of the players in the second row and back row so that his team gets possession.

The hooker must also be right on his game at every line-out, because he has the tough task of throwing the ball in and making sure that it is on target to one of the line-out jumpers. Since line-outs are used to initiate play more than any other restart, it's imperative that a hooker is able to accurately hit his jumpers on a consistent basis.

Hookers can make or break their reputation based on their ability as a line-out thrower. The ranks of former internationals are littered with hookers who were great in every other aspect of the game, but couldn't regularly maintain possession at the line-out with their throws. If throwing isn't one of your strengths, then this probably isn't the position for you.

The hooker is often expected to function as an extra loose forward, so he must be a courageous tackler and able to provide a link between forwards and backs in support play.

The second row: Exerting in the engine room

The second row of the tight five is made up by the two *locks*, who wear numbers 4 and 5. This pair is referred to as the *engine room* because this is where the power is generated in a scrum. While the front row sets the platform, the locks drive it forward, or keep it from being driven backwards.

Locks are typically tall, athletic players with strong backs and powerful legs. These two (who often look like they got lost on the way to an NBA game) are the players who are lifted high in the air to catch the ball tossed in by the hooker in a line-out. Because of their height, they are also usually the two key ball-takers on kickoffs. Simply being tall isn't enough, locks also need to have good hands, balance, and coordination in the air. The ideal lock will have legs like springs and hands like glue.

Most locks either have athletic tape wrapped around their heads or they wear protective headgear. This is done to prevent their ears from chafing when they pack down in the scrum.

Locks are the workhorses of the pack. They bind to each other and the props in front of them to attain the cohesion required to ensure that the scrum stays stable and doesn't collapse. This position generally requires someone tall and sturdy enough to not snap in two when pressure is applied in the scrum.

A truly great second-rower is almost superhuman. While a second-rower may have a physique that at first sight doesn't look as if it belongs on a rugby field, he needs to be an outstanding ball-carrier, have tremendous agility, and be an enforcer on defense.

The back-row forwards: Breaking loose with the loosies

The back row consists of the players in jersey numbers 6, 7, and 8 (blindside flanker, openside flanker, and number 8). Collectively, these players are referred to as the "loose forwards" (or loosies), because they are the first players to break away from the formation when the scrum ends. An excellent back-row combination is vital for a successful team because the three players are involved in so much of the game, creating numerous opportunities and thwarting many of the opposition's tactics.

These three players must be strong, quick off the mark, agile, and fearless in order to effectively tackle, carry the ball, and compete for possession.

Foraging with the flankers

The primary role of the two *flankers* is to tackle everything that moves and to steal the ball whenever possible. Flankers are built like football linebackers, with excellent quickness, agility, strength, and courage. These players are willing to sacrifice their bodies in a mission to gain possession of the ball and prevent their opponents from doing so.

The terms "openside" and "blindside" refer to which side of the scrum the flankers line up on. A scrum is usually set up on either side of the field, with open field on one side and the sideline on the other. The openside flanker joins the scrum beside the open field. The blindside flanker joins the side of the scrum closest to the sideline. The flankers bind to the locks' bodies on the "flanks" of the scrum, switching from one side of the scrum to the other depending on field position.

Toughing it on the blindside

The *blindside flanker* (number 6) has to be industrious. Along with the number 8, he is usually the second or third to arrive at the breakdown. He must be an outstanding defender, particularly as many opposing teams attempt to attack down the blindside from a scrum. The blindside flanker has to always be mindful of this and be ready to cut off this option immediately with a devastating tackle. Usually, he is also required to be the third major line-out jumper. And like the number 8, the blindside flanker must also be one of the real hard men in the team, and take on the enforcer's role if need be.

Discipline is a critical component of this flanker's make-up, because if he can't regulate his emotions and behavior, his actions will often get him in trouble. A flanker's mantra should be controlled aggression in search of and maintenance of possession. Flankers also need superior handling skills to support other ball-carriers and must be ready to transfer the ball on in any situation.

Patrolling the openside

The *openside flanker* is usually the smaller and speedier of the two because he patrols a greater amount of field. His prime aim is to be the first to the ball wherever it is on the pitch. He has to be quick to arrive at the scene after a tackle has occurred so he can wrestle the ball away from the opposition on defence before others get there and the ruck forms (see Chapter 7 for more on the intricacies of the ruck). For offensive support, the openside must reach the breakdown first to make sure that possession is maintained if his teammate is stopped by a defender.

The good, and the not so good, things that openside flankers do are often obscured by the heaps of bodies on the ground where they do a substantial amount of their work. They fight and tussle for the ball whenever there's a chance to take it away, but must also know when to give up the struggle for possession to avoid a penalty. If they are good enough to pilfer the ball without upsetting the referee, they are worth their weight in gold. A good openside must have a perfect knowledge of rugby law and be able to adapt to individual referees' interpretations.

Piloting the pack at number 8

The pack leader is the *number 8*, who, surprise, surprise, wears the number 8 jersey. The ideal number 8 is shorter than the locks and taller than the flankers, with a bit more bulk to smash through opposing defensive lines. This position usually goes to the most skillful and savvy forward because so much of the match happens around him; he is often the first to receive the ball from scrums, line-outs, and in open play. He has responsibilities all over the field, so he has to make his presence felt from sideline to sideline.

From any scrum, the number 8, working in tandem with the scrumhalf and flyhalf (we explain the roles of these players later in this chapter), decides how the team initiates the attack or structures their defense. If the team is attacking, the number 8 must decide, as the ball arrives at his feet, whether to run with it, pass it to the scrumhalf, or protect the scrumhalf while he plays the ball.

A good number 8 always knows exactly what the opposition is up to and seizes any opportunity to take the ball forward himself if he believes he can expose a defensive weakness by making a quick run from the base of the scrum. He basically has to be anywhere and everywhere, always thinking and anticipating the flow of the game to stay near the ball, especially when there is a breakdown in play.

The best in the business — Richie McCaw

New Zealand's Richie McCaw exemplifies all the skills, athleticism, and rugby IQ needed to excel on the openside. He's big and strong at 6'2", 218 pounds and has tremendous quickness and agility, plus the stamina to maintain a high work rate for the entire 80 minutes. His greatest asset, however, is his command of the subtleties of the breakdown. Along with Australia's George Smith, he's the best in the world at contesting for possession after a tackle occurs. He draws a couple of penalties every game because he always plays right on the edge of the law. He more then makes up for his infractions by regularly producing multiple turnovers. As teams get better at maintaining continuity on offense through multiple phases, having a player on your team who can create turnovers in general play each game is a huge advantage.

The player to watch for anyone aspiring to wear the number 8 jersey is England's Lawrence Dallaglio. His vision and work rate are outstanding, which means that in many matches he leads the tackle count statistics and is among the players who have touched the ball most in the match. Dallaglio cannot afford to make mistakes and get lost on the field, because he is usually the player who inspires confidence in the rest of the team through outright feats of courage and skill.

Get to the Back of the Line

The seven remaining players, who wear jersey numbers 9 to 15, are often referred to collectively as the "back line" (not to be confused with the back row of the forwards).

Like in football, where the linesmen do all the dirty work in the trenches and the quarterback, running backs, and receivers get all the glory, in rugby, an old oval adage says that the forwards win the ball and the backs win the game. A team with great backs and mediocre forwards will find themselves starved of ball to work with. The opposite will produce plenty of possession, but few chances to attack and score. To play winning rugby, you need 15 players totally committed to their roles and each other.

Passing and pestering for profit: The scrumhalf

The *scrumhalf* wears number 9, and is the border collie of the team. This is the team's organizer, who commands the forwards, directing their movements at ruck and maul time. Scrumhalves are usually the smallest players on the field and must have exceptional balance, be lightning-quick, and have superior passing skills. The very best scrumhalves are considered to be part of the pack by admiring forwards.

The scrumhalf's main aim is to be the team distributor. Because he is supposed to be one step away from everything that's happening, he is the person who usually distributes the ball from the scrums, line-outs, rucks and mauls, and whenever there is any form of breakdown in play. (We discuss the scrumhalf's passing skills in Chapter 10.)

The scrumhalf must be agile, intensely courageous, and the best passer in the team. The scrumhalf upholds communication between the forwards and the backs, and constantly urges the scrum on to greater heights, directing the rolling maul, and calling for runners to take it up hard off of rucks.

The world's best scrumhalf — George Gregan

Australian scrumhalf George Gregan is the best number 9 in the world. His mastery of the multiple-phase attacking game and uncompromising defensive skills place him clearly above the rest. He has the vision and rugby savvy to anticipate defensive openings and knows where his teammates are at all times, which enables him to select the best option in every situation. Almost instinctively, Gregan always seems to be in just the right place at just the right time, so he can quickly recycle possession and launch the next phase of attack. His ability to recognize breakdowns in the opponent's defensive structure and attack them repeatedly, through multiple phases, until the line is broken, is the main reason behind the offensive success of the ACT Brumbies and the Wallabies. He constantly barks out directives to his forwards, calling for crash runners off the fringes of rucks and coordinating the advancing Wallaby maul from the rear. On defense, he's one of the surest and toughest tacklers in the world (at any position!). While he might not make the biggest hit, even if he gets dragged for a meter or two, his tenacity results in the ball-carrier going to ground. Since his elevation to the Wallaby captaincy, his ability to maintain self-discipline has suffered; he has sometimes got on the wrong side of referees by losing his composure and disputing their decisions too vociferously.

The scrumhalf usually works in tandem with the flyhalf, and the pair decides on the best attack and defensive options (for more about game tactics, see Chapter 9). When you see the scrumhalf and flyhalf making weird hand signals, or cupping their hands around the mouth so that they won't be heard by the opposition, it means they are calling plays for the next phase of attack, and something interesting is about to occur.

A scrumhalf has to be able to kick over the top to both relieve and impose pressure. On defense, a scrumhalf has to repeatedly tackle much bigger players, so his technique must be exemplary.

Feeling footloose and fancy-free: The flyhalf

The *flyhalf* wears number 10 and is the chief play-maker on the team, making big decisions that often determine whether a team wins or loses. He is usually the player with the best combination of tactical acumen, kicking ability, and distribution skills.

The flyhalf is sometimes called the pivot because so much turns on what the player does. The flyhalf dictates the flow and style of the team's game plan, determining whether the team adopts a running game, relies instead on midfield kicking, or uses forward power to grind out a victory. (Chapter 11 further discusses the flyhalf's role in devising winning tactics.) The rest of the backline has to be on the same wavelength as the flyhalf. He generally calls the various moves and plays, and chooses who will be chasing his variety of kicks downfield. In this sense he is very much like a quarterback in football, deciding where the ball is going and to whom. On most teams, the flyhalf is the first-choice goal kicker, but not always.

A flyhalf of any note must have a very cool demeanor and an ability to think clearly under pressure. He also needs to possess good all-round skills, because every one of those skills is usually put to the test. Flyhalf is a very demanding position, but it is also one of the most rewarding.

Mastering the midfield: Centers

While both are called *centers*, the players wearing numbers 12 (inside center) and 13 (outside center) fulfill slightly different roles. The aim remains the same: trying to elude their opponents so that they can set up tries. Typically, centers have excellent kicking, passing, and handling skills, and can deliver a mean tackle.

Attacking from the inside out

Number 12 is the *inside center*, the player who stands closest in attack to the flyhalf (number 10) and who often acts as a back-up flyhalf, being the second midfield organizer of the attack. In simple terms, the main goal of the inside center is to keep attacks in some sort of formation by providing the link between the flyhalf and the outer backs.

A good inside center must be dependable, able to straighten the attack when required, and fearless in all facets of play. Few players touch the ball more often than the inside center, so he needs to have exceptional ball-handling skills and a tough hide to know when exactly to pass, when to run, or when to try and mix it up a bit with a "chip kick" (we explain kicking skills in Chapter 10). Most importantly, he cannot drop the ball, especially as he is invariably playing in a confined area with opponents hovering all around him. He has to be the coolest of customers with great hands. Centers are more likely to be drawn into rucks than other backs, so they should have more highly developed skills in this area.

Like the flyhalf, the inside center often has to decide whether to straighten the attack by running directly upfield with the ball, or to push the attack wider by passing to either the outside center or the fullback. He often plays a "battering ram" role in running the ball hard into the opposition's defensive line, plowing into defenders, and challenging them to tackle him. Ideally, he's strong enough to maintain the appropriate body position in the tackle so that his teammates have a better chance to recycle the ball — the quicker the better! (We talk about running with the ball and tackling in Chapter 10.)

On the defensive side of the ball, the inside center's job is to stop his opposite number from breaking through the line. Missed head-up tackles by inside centers are anathema to any coach's defensive stratagem. This means taking on a speedy, aggressive runner, built like himself, over and over during the course of 80 minutes.

Attacking from the outside in

Number 13 is the *outside center*, who is generally the faster of the two centers and, along with the wings, is among the team's more important attacking players. The prime aim of the outside center is to set up teammates playing outside him, in particular the fullback and wings. This usually involves luring the opposition's defense into pursuing him and, through that, creating enough room to throw what must be a perfectly timed pass, putting a teammate through the opposition's defensive line. But he must also have the attacking instinct to know when to attack the line himself and have faith in his own speed to get him through. The outside center is the player who tries to ruin the opposition's defensive pattern by providing that unpredictable, attacking spark.

The outside center usually has more space to work with than the inside center. Many tries have been achieved after a number 13 has broken his way through the opposition defense, and then put his wing or fullback over the goal line with a precise kick into the corner of the field, well behind the opposition defense. (Shown in Figure 4-1, the goal line is the line on or over which the attacking team must ground the ball in order to score a try.)

Just as important, the outside center must also be one of the best defenders, especially as a fast-running fullback is usually charging at him with ball in hand. This is no position for the faint-hearted.

To be successful, the two centers must work together. Good chemistry between this pair is an important element of a rugby team's dynamics. Centers who work well together are able to read each other's intentions without giving them away — like bridge partners or old married couples.

Running wild out wide: The wings

Each team has two *wings*. Number 11 is usually the left wing and number 14 is the right wing. When facing the defenders, the left wing is on the left-hand side of the team and the right wing is on the right-hand side.

Wings have to be the fastest players on the team, possessing extraordinary acceleration and the ability to beat their opponents and then out-sprint them to the tryline. Wings need to be fast in attack and able to work well in a limited amount of space; they also need to be furious in defense, especially when the attack is focused on the outer reaches of the field.

The demands of playing on the left and right wing are basically the same. However, who plays on which wing is usually determined by which foot a player prefers to kick with, or if he has a better left- or right-footed *sidestep* (sidestepping is where you dart off in a different direction to that anticipated by the opposition; we discuss it further in Chapter 10).

Wings are regarded as the "glory boys" of the team, whose primary function is to finish off attacking moves and score heaps of tries. On any team, they should be the most prolific try scorers, because their teammates devote so much of their energies into putting them in a perfect position to get over the opposition's tryline.

Roaming the range: The fullback

The *fullback* wears the number 15 jersey and has more freedom to roam than any other player on the pitch. The fullback's prime responsibility is to be the last line of defense to prevent tries. Fullbacks are generally well-rounded rugby players. They must be able to catch the opposition's high kicks during attacks, or become the extra player in an attack.

The fullback has to have a leg on him equal to that of the flyhalf because he will invariably be forced to clear the ball from deep in his own territory. Accuracy in kicking is paramount because if his kick doesn't find touch, he has to chase it down and put his teammates on-side before they can participate again (we cover the complexities of the Offside Law in Chapter 6).

A good fullback is like a chess player who uses intuition to anticipate what's going to happen a few moves ahead, and then gets himself into the right place to deal with it. The best fullbacks also use their skills to predict their opponents' next move to take advantage and counter before the other side can react.

When the opposition has the ball, the fullback has to know where and when to join in the team's defensive line, to ensure that the right number of players are in the right spot to stop the opposition from scoring. This could mean joining the defensive line between the centers, or among the forwards, to fill any gaps that may occur. Or it could mean placing himself in a strategic position behind the defensive line so he is in the right spot to catch a clearing kick from the opposition, or even a chip kick, which is aimed at turning around and disorientating his side.

Forwards and the midfield attackers have relatively defined areas of ground to work in and cover. However, the fullback, as the team's "gatekeeper," has a lot of territory to patrol.

A fullback's normal position on the pitch is standing several meters behind his attacking line. This means he usually has half the pitch to cover, and even more when his own side is close to the opposition's tryline. So it is important that he knows how to cover that area. No other player on the pitch is on his own so often without the support of a teammate. It's a demanding position, which explains why a good fullback is so vital to a team's prospects of winning. It also explains why this is probably the most stressful position on the field — the fullback is the last tackler and if he misses, the entire team is let down and the other side gets five points!

Surprising the enemy

A fullback can really make his mark in an attack. Because he's relatively free to move about the field, the fullback should be used as the surprise attack weapon — he can pop up anywhere and everywhere on the pitch. A running fullback radically improves the attacking prowess of any backline, particularly if he is able to read play, knowing when it's time to hit the line at pace, or to join the line to create the extra man.

The aim of most rugby attacks is to create an overlap where the attacking team has more players than the defensive line in front of them. The fullback can create that overlap if he chooses to enter the back line either near the centers or wings at an opportune moment.

Defusing bombs

In addition to being a sure tackler and intuitive attacker, the fullback needs to be cool under pressure. To break up their attacking patterns, teams often kick high balls to test the fullback. A *high ball* (or an *up and under*), is a kick from the opposition which is aimed downfield, traveling high in the air, usually 20 to 30 meters above the heads of the players. It takes great intestinal fortitude for the number 15 to maintain total concentration when fielding the ball, all the while knowing that tacklers are bearing down on him. The ball usually swirls in the air and is often tricky to catch, making it the fullback's nightmare.

The fullback is usually the first opposing player a team tests. If he's not up to the task of fielding the high ball, you can be sure your opponents will target him and keep applying pressure. If your fullback mishandles the ball, the attacking side usually gains an advantage, if not a try.

Chapter 5

Laying Down the Laws

• •

• •

*I*t is significant that rugby is a game governed by laws rather than rules. This is because rules are imposed to regulate behavior, whereas laws are implemented to achieve a desired result. In the case of rugby, the laws are designed to produce a free-flowing game whereby two teams should score as many points as possible with the team that scores more being declared the winner.

Arguing about interpretations and discussing the laws of the game is a noble pastime which takes place in pubs, clubhouses, and rugby grounds all over the world. In this chapter we introduce you to the laws by telling you where they come from and how they've evolved, we explain how you too can get a copy of the coveted book, and we detail the responsibilities of the people who are charged with running the game on the pitch from start to finish.

The Laws of the Game

There are 22 laws that cover every aspect of how the game is played on the field. From how the pitch is laid out and marked, to what happens in the in-goal area, the laws of the game encompass all the information necessary to allow the game to be played. (There is also a set of regulations that involve how the sport itself is governed.) While regional variations may develop in terms of style and technique in playing the game, the laws at the senior level are exactly the same whether the match is the World Cup final or a third division match in a lesser developed country (laws for younger rugby players are age-appropriate for safety reasons; see Chapter 17). Rugby is a centrally administered sport, which means that the International Rugby Board (IRB) decides on the laws and controls when and if they are to be changed.

The International Rugby Board

The International Rugby Board (IRB) was founded in 1886. The IRB is the world-governing and law-making body for the game of rugby. The Executive Council meets twice a year. It consists of the eight founding nations — Scotland, Ireland, Wales, England, Australia, New Zealand, South Africa, and France. Each founding nation has two seats. Argentina, Canada, Italy, and Japan each have one seat on the Council as does FIRA-AER (the International Amateur Rugby Federation — European Rugby Association). The day-to-day business of the Board is conducted by a professional staff of over 40, the majority of whom are based in Dublin. Rugby is played by men and women and boys and girls in more than a hundred countries across 5 continents, and the IRB membership currently totals 96 unions and 5 regional associations.

The IRB writes the law

Until the 21st century, there were 28 laws, many of which overlapped in a mishmash of repetitive jargon. Fortunately, the IRB saw the detrimental effect this was having on the development of the game and simplified the jumble quite a bit by consolidating the essential knowledge into 22 laws with far less repetition and a lot more clarity. While still seemingly daunting to the rugby novice, the newer version of the laws has been instrumental in producing some of the finest examples of rugby matches ever played in just the last few years.

The IRB does not make light-hearted changes for the sake of seeing bigger numbers on the scoreboard, but instead has a detailed process for updating the law book. Pursuant to the organization's by-laws, a Laws Committee is empowered to consider changes proposed by the individual unions which make up the IRB, to recommend changes and amendments to those submissions, and to clarify real-life situations that occur during the course of each year. In this way, the IRB can respond to trends in the game happening around the world and also prevent harmful alterations that detract from the overall spirit of the laws. From time to time, the IRB will authorize the application of experimental laws in prescribed matches to test whether or not they would benefit the sport. The IRB also continually amends the language of the law book to clarify points of confusion, without making material changes.

The laws are dynamic and ever-changing

If you were to pick up a law book from the early days of the game it would be pretty unrecognizable in content compared to today's version. Rugby did not start with a complete set of laws handed down from on-high like basketball did. What happened was that the early attempts at codification reflected what was already occurring on the pitch. As the game spread throughout the world, modifications were instituted to ensure continuity.

Over the years many laws have been changed to promote specific strategic objectives, to rein in wayward practitioners of dubious techniques, and to correct imbalances in the way offense and defense interact. The best way to understand this process is to take a close look at a specific law relating to one part of the line-out that has undergone radical changes in the last few years.

The line-out is a means of restarting play after the ball has gone into touch, or out of bounds. One team throws the ball in as both team's jumpers are lifted to precarious heights in an attempt to gain possession and produce a quick ball for the back line to use. Line-outs have become an intricately choreographed phase that requires coordinated timing from everyone involved. But it wasn't always so.

Until 1999, lifting in the line-out was done surreptitiously under the guise of supporting the jumper, who had to rely on good old-fashioned vertical leaping ability and natural height to secure the throw-in. There was also a lot more contact between the two teams and fewer clean takes that allowed the ball to be spun out wide in a hurry. When the law changed and lifting was brought into the open, a whole new set of skills had to be learned and the sport of rugby gained by highlighting its enormous collective capacity for ingenuity and the athleticism of its players. As of this writing there are very few advocates of returning to the older, slower, less exciting incarnation of the line-out law.

Of course there are always unintended consequences to any change and lifting was no exception. If lifting was legal in line-outs, then why not on restart kicks? It is now common to see jumpers positioned at various points on the pitch with an individual lifter ready to propel them skyward in hopes of cleanly fielding the kick. This has also made the game more interesting and put more strategic emphasis on what was a neglected area of play.

Then some coach or player somewhere had the bright idea of lifting jumpers to snatch penalty and conversion kicks out of the air before they could clear the crossbar. It actually worked a few times over a couple of seasons, but this was too much for the traditionalists at the IRB, so the Laws Committee deemed that it contravened the spirit of the law governing penalties (a viewpoint we both agree with), and an amendment was added that made the practice illegal. This episode points out the fact that the laws are evolving with the game — but never at the expense of the all-important ethos of the sport.

Reading the law book

We played rugby for many years before ever actually holding a copy of the laws in our hands and daring to look inside. We spent years committing penalties for unknown reasons, believing mistaken interpretations, and generally limiting our effectiveness for our teams. Knowledge of the laws came from older, more experienced players who spouted knowingly about "hands in the ruck," "offside at the tackle," and other vague terms. In retrospect, what we heard varied from almost right to completely wrong.

Delving into the law book opened up a whole new world. Referees' calls that previously seemed unfathomable were suddenly made clear. Confidence soared at the breakdown where strength and technique were supplemented with an almost magical sense of knowledge. Our enjoyment of the game expanded exponentially as the mysterious shield of ignorance surrounding referees' decisions melted away.

Our advice for any aspiring rugby player, coach, referee, or fan is to get a copy of the laws and dig in. Versions can be downloaded from the Internet, but it's best to go to the IRB's official web site (www.irb.com) so you'll know the version is up to date. Getting your hands on a hard copy is a little more difficult, but not impossible (Appendix C gives a full list of options).

Building up your knowledge

You don't have to spend long days and nights poring over the laws — far from it. However, an hour or two going through the main points of the law is time well spent. You'll begin to have a better understanding of what the referee is doing on the pitch if you've done your homework. In fact, you are more likely to know what's going on than some of the players, many of whom, sad to say, don't have a clue what the referee is going on about.

A good way to familiarize yourself with the laws in action is to focus on the referee during a game. Watch his every move and try to figure out why he makes the decisions he does. Through close observation, you'll get to know the various signals and recognize the types of play that lead to important decisions (all 40 of the referee signals are discussed later in this chapter).

You can quickly enhance your knowledge of the game by approaching the referee at the reception following a local match — most of them love the game every bit as much as the players do and enjoy talking about it. Also, referees are probably the most cooperative and friendly group to deal with in the rugby world, and are always eager to help people improve their knowledge of the laws of the game.

Approach referees in a friendly manner that reassures them that you aren't going to start arguing the merits of a decision they just made. You'll soon find yourself immersed in the intrigue of what actually happened at the bottom of a ruck or why a certain transgressor was judged to be offside. You'll begin to understand the finer points of some laws that were once absolutely bewildering.

Another way to increase your level of understanding is to ask questions of your coach. Your rugby coach is often a good source of information about the laws. You may find that coaches are instant experts on referees, even though their views may be more derogatory than flattering. For all this, however, most coaches have a good basic knowledge of the law book — it's an essential requirement if they want their team to succeed (see Chapter 18 for more information on coaches).

Don't hide behind your law book

A few years back, after a hard-fought match between my club, the Oxy Olde Boys RFC, and San Luis Obispo RFC, both sides gathered at the reception to take in some grub, liquid refreshment, and good old-fashioned rugby camaraderie. As the evening wore on, the match referee felt compelled to vehemently defend one particularly questionable call (the first and only sending-off of my co-author) by repeated reference to his law book. It was as if pointing to the text of the law would transform his suspect decision on the field into the unassailable act of a refereeing deity. It was painfully obvious to all of us that he was hiding behind the authority of the law book itself. Eventually, liquid intake necessitated a pit stop and the whistle-blower went to the bathroom.

What happened next was pure theatre. The president of San Luis Obispo, Bo Kelly, seized the opportunity — the ref's book from the table. Bo pronounced that the ref didn't know a thing about the game and without his precious little law book to hide behind, he'd be hopelessly lost. Showing good skills, Bo then produced a lighter and proceeded to set the law book on fire, to the cheers of both teams. Soon after, the referee emerged from the restroom to see what the commotion was all about. When he saw Bo holding his burning law book, the non-verbal message was self-evident — Bo was not at all impressed by the referee's incessant references to his law book.

Now please don't take this as an endorsement of book-burning generally, or law books in particular, or of being disrespectful to referees in any way. The lesson here is that a law book is nothing more than paper and ink. You get no authority whatsoever by simply carrying one around. The value of a law book is directly related to your approach to understanding the game and how you use it. Properly used, it's a good general guide, but you need to use your head to adapt the principles of the game to fit the particular situation you find yourself in.

Your coach should tell you during training sessions if you are doing something that would cause a referee to come down on you like a ton of bricks. If you repeat the offense in a match, your coach's behavior towards you is going to be less congenial, to say the least. Finding yourself banished to the reserve bench is a good indication that your knowledge of the laws is flimsy, and that you need to spend some quiet time with the law book. Just as a lack of knowledge of the laws can hurt your team immensely, an understanding of them will reap enormous benefits.

Match Officials

Running the game is a tough job that often attracts more criticism than praise. The referee is the main player in this drama but he has help from other members of the refereeing fraternity who are there to make his job easier. Collectively, the referee, the touch judges, the substitution official, and the Television Match Official (TMO) are known as the match officials. Should you aspire to become a referee or a touch judge, check out Chapter 20 for all the details.

The referee: The one with the whistle

Whether you are a player or a spectator, the referee is the person to watch. The referee is the single most important person on the field during a game. The primary function of the referee is to manage the match and help create a spectacle for the fans to enjoy.

The referee is the official who has the ultimate power over what occurs in a rugby match. What he says, goes. He is the sole judge of fact and law during the match. The referee's position is probably the most demanding of all, requiring a broad depth of knowledge, a high level of fitness, and a very thick skin.

Players prefer referees who don't talk down to them. No one likes a dictator. The best referees understand what the players are doing and, whenever possible, try to let the game flow. Referees should be firmly in control without feeling the need to constantly assert their authority. This is a tough balance to strike for any referee. The ultimate accomplishment for a referee is when, at the end of the match, no one remembers who held the whistle.

Referees are passionate about the game and fervently believe they have the best job in the world. The top-level referee's job has been transformed by the advent of professionalism. Full-time referees are now needed to work the various competitions around the globe. Formerly, police officers, school teachers, and business people volunteered their time as referees. Now there is a small but expanding group of professional referees who work matches all over the world, covering competitions from the Six Nations to the Tri Nations to the Super 12. (For a description of these organizations, see Chapter 14). Travel is often long distance, because southern hemisphere referees sometimes officiate at northern hemisphere matches, and vice versa. The reward is that you get to spend time in some of the most entertaining cities in the world — while getting paid well for doing something that you thoroughly enjoy.

The vast majority of referees are, and will always be, amateurs. Regardless of their status, however, the same duties and responsibilities are entrusted to them. Before the match they conduct a coin toss to determine which team will kick off and which end the other side will defend. They also do a pre-match inspection to ensure that players are in compliance with the relevant laws on equipment and clothing.

It is worth stating again that during the match the referee is the sole judge of fact and law. His decisions are final, with no appeal to a higher authority available. The referee is additionally charged with keeping the official time and score, sending players off for serious offenses, and regulating the comings and goings of substitutes and replacements. In all these duties they are assisted by fellow refs in subordinate roles, depending upon the level of match being played. (The further one travels down from the highest echelons, the less likely it is that a referee will have two other referees as touch judges.) A referee is allowed to consult with the other match officials, but the final decision in all matters is the whistle-blower's alone.

Your rugby-playing experience will be far better if you try and keep the referee happy; antagonizing the person with the whistle is not a good idea. Rugby players should always treat referees with respect and address them as "Sir" or "Madam." One of the ways that rugby maintains its reputation for sportsman-like conduct is a zero tolerance policy toward players and coaches at any level who are not civil in dealing with the referee. The badgering and brow-beating of officials that occurs in other professional sports is totally unacceptable in rugby and is contrary to the spirit of the game.

To avoid being targeted by the referee, act as if you never intended to break the law, never question a ruling unless you're the team captain, and be courteous at all times.

Touch judges: The ones with the flags

The two touch judges, one on each side of the field, play a very important role in a rugby match. As the name indicates, their primary responsibility is determining where a line-out has to be formed and which team throws the ball in to the line-out after it has gone into touch (we cover line-outs in Chapter 9).

The touch judges have to determine exactly where the ball crossed the touchline, which team was the last to touch it, and which team will throw the ball back in. They signal this by standing at the spot where the line-out is to be taken, raising a flag over their head, and pointing in the direction of the team that will throw it in.

A further duty is judging whether or not penalty and conversion kicks have been successful. To do this, the touch judges move to a spot behind each upright that will afford them the best view of the kick. If the kick goes over the crossbar and between the posts, they raise their flags to indicate that fact.

Touch judges also act as the referee's second and third pair of eyes. They advise the referee whenever they witness incidents of foul play that the referee didn't see. At the provincial and international levels, a touch judge is in radio contact with the referee and can alert him via a microphone built into his touch flag. In matches at the lower levels, a touch judge alerts the referee by holding the flag horizontally and pointing infield at a right angle to the touchline.

Once you've watched a few games, you begin to realize that the touch judges are almost as important as the referee, and have to be as fit and alert as the one with the whistle.

The substitution official: The one with the numbers

In the not-so-distant old days of rugby, it was rare for the 15 starting players of a match not to be the same players who finished it. In international matches a doctor used to have to certify that an injured player was no longer able to continue before he could be replaced. With the liberalization of the substitution law, which encourages coaches to make numerous changes as a strategic matter of course, the need arose for an extra official to supervise this activity.

The substitution official, sometimes called a reserve touch judge, handles the parade of players entering and exiting the pitch for trips to the blood bin, the sin bin, and the subbing and replacing of individuals from the reserve bench. For changes made by the coaching staff, this official will hold up two numbers, one for the player leaving the game and the other for the one joining it, letting spectators and the referee know exactly who is contesting the match at all times.

The duties don't stop there though, as the substitution official has to be wary of teams trying to get around the various substitution laws through nefarious means. The reason this person has to be a qualified referee is that on rare occasions the match referee will suffer an injury and have to be replaced by one of the touch judges, necessitating his move up the ladder to touch judge.

The TMO: The one with the video screen

At most major rugby matches involving professionals, a referee is also required for a fourth important job, the television match official (TMO), or video referee. The TMO spends the game in a quiet room somewhere in the stadium perched in front of a television set. In case you're thinking this sounds like quite a cozy little job, the video referee has to be an actual referee because it requires someone with an intimate knowledge of the laws.

The video referee's role has expanded from when it was first introduced. Initially, only in-goal decisions could be considered and the referee had to ask specific questions of exactly what he wanted to be reviewed. The original purpose was basically to determine whether or not a try had been scored, as well as other in-goal issues, but that responsibility has evolved into helping the referee to identify players who have been involved in committing foul play.

Scoring a try: When referees are uncertain whether a player has properly grounded the ball on or over the tryline, they make a hand signal that resembles a mime outlining a large imaginary box, to indicate a television screen. This means they've asked for the video referee to watch a replay of the incident and determine whether or not someone actually scored a try. At the same time, the referee contacts the video referee via a radio microphone hook-up and explains what he wants the video referee to look for. Usually the video referee watches the play several times before informing the referee whether or not a try was scored. Occasionally, the replay won't definitively show the incident in question; in this case, the TMO will send it back to the referee without a recommendation. Either way, the final decision rests with the referee on the field.

Identifying foul play: Beginning in 2003, the TMO was given the added burden of figuring out who was involved in an incident of foul play if the offender can't be singled out by the referee or the touch judges. The referee contacts the TMO and asks for help in unmasking the offender. In this case, the video referee can only look at the incident specified by the referee.

Recognizing the Referee's Signals

If you are watching the match on television, you have the advantage of being able to listen to the referee's calls, as they now wear microphones. Having the referees miked allows you to hear what they say to the players in the heat of battle; it also lets you eavesdrop on their conversations with touch judges and the TMO.

Many signals a referee makes are somewhat understandable because they mimic the infraction being called. Referees give signals to indicate what penalties have been given, all scoring plays, and whether a team has been awarded a free kick or advantage in play. The referee also signals when the clock is stopped. While the time left in the game is often shown on the scoreboard, remember the referee is the final arbiter of time — what he says, goes.

Some signals are not so easily understood, though, and may take a little time to learn. But don't worry; the signaling system becomes very clear when you can identify each specific signal. The signals you will see the referee make during a rugby match are shown in Figure 5-1.

Figure 5-1:
The Referee's Signaling System.

Penalty kick

Free kick

Try and penalty try

Advantage

Scrum awarded

Forming a scrum

Throw-forward/ forward pass

Knock-on

Not immediately releasing ball in the tackle

Tackler not letting go of tackled player

Tackler or tackled player not rolling away

Entering tackle from wrong side

(continued)

(continued)

 Unplayable ball at ruck or tackle

 Diving to ground near tackle

 Intentionally falling on a player

 Intentionally bringing down a ruck or maul

 Entering a ruck or a maul in front of the back foot and from the side

 Unplayable ball in maul

 Prop drawing down opponent

 Prop pulling opponent

 Wheeling scrum more than 90 degrees

 Foot-up by front-row player

 Throw-in at scrum not straight

 Failure to bind fully

 Handling ball in ruck or scrum

 Throw-in at line-out not straight

 Closing gaps in line-out

Barging in line-out

 Leaning on player in line-out

 Pushing opponent in line-out

(continued)

(continued)

 Off-side at scrum, ruck or maul

 Off-side at line-out

 Obstruction in general play

 High tackle (foul play)

 Off-side option: penalty kick or scrum

 Off-side under 10-meter law or not 10 meters at penalty and free kicks

 Dissent (contesting referee's call)

 Award of drop-out at the 22-meter line

 Punching (foul play)

 Physiotherapist needed

 Stamping (foul play: inappropriate use of boot)

 Ball held up in in-goal

 Timekeeper to stop and start watch

 Doctor needed

 Bleeding wound

Chapter 6

Understanding the Fundamentals

. . . .

. . . .

*U*nderstanding the fundamentals of the game is the first step to becoming a full-fledged rugby enthusiast. Whether you're a player, spectator, parent, or coach, being familiar with the basic principles will make every rugby experience better and more fulfilling.

When you first watch rugby on TV or in person, it can appear confusing as 30 players run around the pitch in what appears to be semi-organized chaos. Their collective actions are mysteriously orchestrated by the whistle-blowing referee who shouts indecipherable commands and periodically stops and starts play at seemingly random spots on the pitch. That is how we first saw rugby as well, attracted to the overall physicality of the sport but lacking even the most basic grasp of what was happening.

Our knowledge of the game developed from asking questions of more erudite fans along the sidelines and using the trial and error method on the playing field. Many light bulbs of awareness have gone off in our heads over the years as murky concepts suddenly became clear while watching and playing in countless matches. In this chapter, we discuss the object of the game, detail the skills that every rugby player needs, and clarify some of the most confusing rugby regulations, so you'll be able to bypass the initial confusion stage and move right into understanding the action.

Running with the ball

Until I reached college, the only sport I played competitively was baseball. At Occidental College I decided to play football in my freshman year and after one look at my bulky frame the coach declared that I was an offensive lineman. I didn't mind the physical contact involved but never really grasped the intricacies of the lineman's art needed to be successful. I felt I would have been better as a defensive player but the coaches deemed otherwise and I stayed at guard. Then in the off-season I discovered rugby. Suddenly, I was both an offensive and a defensive player. I was allowed to make tackles on ball-carriers of all sizes in addition to having a designated role in scrummaging and at line-outs. Best of all, I was encouraged to run with the ball and force others to tackle me. This opened up a whole new world of sporting enjoyment. I was actually playing an entire game instead of just fulfilling a narrow set of arcane duties. Once the athletic fullness of rugby came into my life, I never put on a helmet again.

Object of the Game

The game of rugby has one simple objective — to score more points than the opposition. This is an aim common to most ball sports, but where rugby differs is that the Laws of the Game prescribe that it be done by carrying, passing, kicking, and grounding the ball, and, most importantly, by observing fair play and doing it all with a sporting spirit.

While there are specific duties in individual positions, all players are allowed to participate in offensive and defensive aspects of the game, and thus must have a universal set of skills enabling them to do so.

Accumulating points in rugby can only be done by possessing the ball, either in scoring tries or kicking goals. This has led coaches and strategists down divergent paths with the same endpoint. Some focus on building excellent defensive teams that can withstand pressure and ultimately create enough turnovers and mistakes to produce opportunities to score points. Another school of thought stresses attacking prowess, placing a premium on creativity and speed.

Both approaches attempt to build squads that can capitalize on the concepts of interaction between offense and defense inherent in the Laws of the Game. The best teams are ones that master both disciplines and easily transition from one mode to the other. Too much emphasis on either one leads to a concentration of players without sufficient overall skills, exposing exploitable weaknesses.

Running, Passing, and Kicking

Since the key to rugby is scoring points, there is an obvious need to move the ball towards the opposition's half of the field to either ground the ball in their in-goal for a try or to get into range to successfully make a kick at goal. All the while, the defense will be attempting to stop this progress downfield. The three ways that teams change their position on the field are by running, passing, and kicking the ball.

Running

Any of the 30 players on the pitch can run with the ball to his heart's content, provided he can maintain possession. Being a valued ball-runner entails never losing possession of the ball, either when tackled or by throwing errant passes. Unless you're superhuman, odds are pretty good that you're going to be tackled before you reach the tryline. To avoid being brought down, you can pass the ball backwards to a teammate who is behind you.

Passing

Requirement number one in passing the rugby ball is that all passes must go either backwards or exactly horizontal, often called a *flat pass*. This standard is in relation to a team's own tryline, not the position of the player. If a player throws the ball and it travels parallel to the tryline then it's a legal pass. If

PLAYER TIP

Creating space

By first running and then passing the ball at just the right time and place, you can draw the defenders around you, thereby *creating space* for your teammate to carry on with the charge. The ability to create space, or to entice the defenders in your immediate area to focus on you and therefore forget about your supporting teammates, is a critical skill that can make a good player into a great one. If you can draw the defenders slightly away from where the attack will come next and then time your pass perfectly, you will have created space, and unlocked the secret to winning rugby. The key here is that

you never want the player receiving the pass to be in a worse attacking position than you were. Passing the ball should be done to accomplish something. Simply passing because you're about to be tackled, without considering whether the receiver is in a position to advance the attack, will not help your team and might get your best buddy injured.

In rugby parlance, throwing a ball that forces your teammate into a defenseless position as he attempts to catch it, setting him up for a monstrous hit by the tackler, is called a *hospital pass*.

its arc takes it anywhere behind that parallel line then it is also perfectly acceptable. (Illegal forward passes are discussed on the opposite page. A variety of passing styles are explained in Chapter 10.)

Kicking

The third method of advancing the ball downfield is by kicking it. Every player is allowed to kick the ball but most coaches want this chore to be handled by backs unless circumstances dictate otherwise. There are a number of different types of kicks, but they fall into three general categories: short, medium, and long. (We go over these kicks in greater detail and give them specific names in Chapter 10.)

Short kicks, whether along the ground or in the air, are usually designed to be regathered by the kicker and then carried farther. These kicks make sense when the defensive line has come up fast and flat, cutting down the space and time available to run or pass the ball through them.

Medium kicks are mostly booted high in the air to test the catching abilities of the opposition under pressure as members of the kicker's team converge on them. If the chasers, or the fastest of the kicker's teammates, get there in time, they can contest the ball in the air.

Kicking also plays a crucial role in field position. Since it's harder to score points from your half of the field, you need a reliable kicker who can punt it long with good accuracy, to move play into your opponent's half of the pitch.

Long kicks are meant to gobble up large chunks of territory in one fell swoop. When a team is backed up behind their own 22-meter line these kicks are generally intended to go over the touchline so that play can be restarted with a line-out. At other times, long kicks are supposed to stay in the field of play and are followed up by marauding defenders to attack the ball-carrier before his teammates can retreat in time to help out.

What Can Go Wrong?

If rugby just involved players running, passing, and kicking the ball up and down the pitch unopposed, it would be about as exciting as lawn bowling. What makes the sport a thrilling spectacle is that for every player attempting to run, pass, or kick, there is a corresponding player doing his darndest to prevent that from happening. When athletes collide in any competitive endeavor there are bound to be errors, especially if the goal of one team is to force the other into making mistakes. In rugby, these mistakes have specific names and the two most common involve ball-handling.

Knock-on

The most recognizable form of a knock-on looks very much like a fumble in football. A knock-on happens when a ball-carrier loses control of the ball for whatever reason and it goes forward (meaning towards the opponent's dead ball line) and touches any other player or the ground before the player can regather the ball. If the ball goes flat or backwards, that's not an infraction. The same is true if a player bobbles the ball in the air but is able to haul it back in.

A knock-on is also called when the ball hits a player's arm or hand — whether they're trying to catch it or not — and bounces forward. The distance the ball travels forward is irrelevant; it could be a couple of centimeters or 9 meters, it's still a knock-on. Barely nudging the ball ahead with your hand while trying to pick it up is the same as having it ripped from your grasp in a tackle.

A ball that bounces off a player's head, chest, or shoulder is not a knock-on, provided that no hands or arms are involved. It's embarrassing to get hit in the face with the ball when it's passed to you — but it's a relief when the referee shouts, "off the head, play on."

The one exception to the Knock-on Law is when a player is trying to block, or charge down, a kick. The law is written to reward aggressive play, so if the ball hits an outstretched hand or arm of a player while he's attempting to block a kick, it's not an infringement, as long as the player doesn't try to catch it.

If play stops after a knock-on (see the Advantage Law section for when play stops and when it doesn't), the non-offending team gets to put the ball in at a scrum on the spot where it occurred. A knock-on is then, in effect, usually a turnover by the team that had the ball.

This is why coaches should always place an emphasis in training on practicing the basic handling skills. The better your team handles the ball, the less likely they are to knock it on during the game.

Forward pass

Throwing the ball forward — meaning towards the opponent's dead ball line — is strictly prohibited. If you pass the ball and it travels forward as it leaves your hands, you've made a forward pass. From the safety of the sidelines a forward pass seems eminently avoidable. In the heat of battle, passing the ball forward is easier than it looks. Location on the pitch becomes jumbled and pressure from tacklers can be intense, causing wayward passes that are intended to follow the tenets of the law but somehow run afoul of it.

Mistakes — intentional and otherwise

Rugby referees have to be some of the most perceptive beings on the planet because they are called upon to determine intent as well as assign blame for mistakes on the field. There are a number of errors that, when they occur in general play and there is no hint of purpose behind them, result in a scrum to the non-offending team. A knock-on is one such case. If, however, the referee thinks that a player intentionally knocked a ball on in an attempt to spoil the offensive move to keep it from going quickly out wide, that is dealt with by awarding a penalty to the other side, giving them possession and a better tactical position than a scrum.

Once again there is an exception. If the ball is thrown backwards and hits the ground and then bounces forward, that is not an infraction. The same exception applies if a pass is released backwards and the wind catches it and takes it forward. You are only responsible for what you do with the ball, not what the ground or the elements cause it to do.

A good way to judge whether a pass is forward or not is to imagine a line running through the ball that is parallel to the goal lines at either end of the field. A pass that goes along that line or behind it is legal; a pass in front of it is illegal. (The same standard helps determine whether a ball has been knocked on.)

The Tackle Law — Where Football Ends, Rugby Begins

When football emerged from the sport of rugby early in the 20th century, the biggest initial change was the concept of ending each play when the ball-carrier was tackled. In football, that's the signal for everyone to stop and head back to their respective huddles and spend the better part of the following minute getting ready for the next five seconds of action. In rugby, after the ball-carrier is tackled, the game continues and gets even more interesting. What happens next may seem muddled and disorganized but if you know what to look for, it is actually well orchestrated and usually follows several different laws that govern the tackle situation, or what is known as the *breakdown*.

The tackle situation and continuity

For years, rugby administrators at the International Rugby Board (IRB) have been fiddling around with the tackle laws in a bid to quicken up the game. The admirable intention has been to speed up the process of making the ball available for further play. Concerned that matches were being slowed down by unsightly pile-ups of bodies fighting for the ball, the law-makers have tried to simplify things. The result has been the assigning of responsibilities to both the tackler and the tackled player, which, if unfulfilled, draw the referee's whistle and the awarding of a penalty. Even though the changes have been somewhat effective, this is still the most contentious area of the game.

The Tackle Law is written like this: "A tackle occurs when a ball-carrier, in a standing position, is simultaneously held by one or more opponents, and is brought to the ground, and/or the ball touches the ground. That player is known as the tackled player. Any opponents of the tackled player who go to ground are known as tacklers." The definition of "brought to ground" includes a player who is on one knee, sitting on the ground, or on top of another player.

The tackled player

When players are tackled, they must immediately let go of the ball when their bodies hit the ground and their momentum stops so that play can continue. It is illegal to lie on the ground and keep tight hold of the ball. Tackled players must either pass the ball immediately or release it at once by placing it on the ground in any direction (ideally, the ball should be placed backwards but that isn't always possible).

Once the tackled player has released the ball, he must attempt to roll away from the area, which in practice means that he can't lie on top of the ball, and can have no further involvement in play until he regains his feet. If the tackled player tries to play the ball in any way while still on the ground, he is liable to be penalized.

As a ball-carrier, your primary goal is to not lose possession of the ball for your team, whether you are on your feet or on the ground. Therefore, the best thing to do when being tackled is to manipulate your body position so that you fall with the tackler on the opposite side from where your teammates are. That way, when you release the ball back, your team will have first crack at securing possession and the opponents will have to step over both the tackler and you to the grab the ball (we offer more tips for the tackled player in Chapter 7).

The tackler

When a player tackles an opponent and they both go to ground, the tackler must immediately release the tackled player. Then he must immediately get to his feet or move away from the tackled player and roll away from the ball. Exactly how far away the tackler must roll is not defined, but it is clear that he must not interfere with play until he's back on his feet. If he makes the mistake of grabbing the ball while he's still on the ground, he attracts the whistle and the opposition is awarded a penalty.

If by the time he gets to his feet a ruck is already formed, he cannot then play the ball because he is now subject to the Ruck Law, which we discuss fully in Chapter 7. After a tackle, all other players must be on their feet when they play the ball. Players are on their feet if no other parts of their body are supported by the ground or players on the ground.

Tackling no-no's

In addition to the restrictions we've just described, the following rules also apply:

- A player cannot stop a tackled player from passing the ball.
- A player cannot stop a tackled player from releasing the ball, or from getting up and moving away from it.
- A player is not allowed to pull the ball from a tackled player before the tackled player has released it.
- A player may not fall on or over the tackled player.

What happens if the ball doesn't come out? Sometimes so many bodies are heaped together on the ground that neither the tackler nor the tackled player can move away no matter how hard the players try. If the ball becomes unplayable at a tackle, the referee orders a scrum, with the put-in given to the team that was moving forward prior to the stoppage. If no team was moving forward, the scrum feed goes to the attacking team. Most tackles turn into rucks soon afterwards and we cover how and why that occurs in Chapter 7.

The Advantage Law — When Play Stops and When It Continues

When you watch a rugby match you'll notice that some of the things that we describe in this chapter happen, yet play doesn't stop. Even those who are more familiar with the game may ask, "Why not?" The answer is because of the Advantage Law, which allows play to continue even after an infraction has been committed. The goal of the law is to keep play flowing by minimizing stoppages. The referees who tend to earn the highest accolades in the public's eyes — meaning they are the least complained about — are the ones who properly utilize this critical piece of judicial wisdom.

The Advantage Law is easy to understand if thought about in the right way. Simply put, when one team commits an infraction, the other team is afforded the opportunity to gain an advantage from the mistake. Instead of immediately blowing the whistle for every little blunder, the referee lets play continue, waiting to see if the non-offending team can profit from the miscue.

Let's say, for instance, that a player from the United States is running with the ball and is tackled hard by a player from Canada. When she hits the ground the ball spills forward from her hands. That's a classic knock-on. But instead of stopping play with a whistle blast, the referee calls out "advantage Canada," (or more likely identifies the team by the color of jersey the players are wearing) and points an arm in their direction. Now the Canadian team knows that they can try to make the best of the situation on attack. If they are successful and can capitalize on the error, the referee will call out "advantage over" and the contest progresses without play being interrupted. If they are stopped or otherwise stymied in taking their opportunity, the referee will blow the whistle and bring the teams back to the spot of the infringement for a scrum, where the ball will be put in by the Canadian scrumhalf.

So what exactly does a team have to do to gain an advantage? There are two criteria that referees consider: territorial and tactical. To illustrate, we go back to our North American example.

To gain a territorial advantage, the Canadian team would have to advance the ball beyond where it was originally knocked on by the American player and end up gaining more territory than if the referee had ordered a scrum. They could accomplish this by running it downfield or kicking it and having it go out farther down the touchline. Territorial advantage gained must be clear and real — the possibility of gaining it is not enough to forestall a stoppage in play.

A tactical advantage can be gained by having the freedom to use the ball as they wish. In the same example, if the Canadian team decided to pass the ball out wide along the back line to give their winger some space to run, they might have gained a tactical advantage even if they didn't get past the point of the original infringement. Referees have to ask themselves, "Was the team able to make a conscious choice to employ a tactic that would have gained them an advantage?" Whether or not the option was successful is irrelevant.

Tactical advantage is harder for referees to judge than territorial because it involves more interpretation, whereas a territorial gain is easy to discern with the naked eye.

One of the oldest coaching sayings is directly related to advantage. Coaches from the international level down to the beginner level should always encourage their players to "play to the whistle." Newcomers to the game will often see an opponent make a mistake and immediately let up, assuming that the referee is going to blow the whistle. If you train your team members to continue playing at full speed, they'll have more chances to cash in on the opposition's errors. Besides, you never know if the referee will see every infraction.

The Advantage Law takes precedence over the rest of the laws because it is responsible for cutting down on the number of times the action is halted for inevitable infringements. Advantage can be played for all but five situations in a game of rugby; these instances are safety-oriented and four of them deal with scrums. A whistle must be blown at once with no consideration for advantage when:

- A player is lifted in the air on a scrum.
- The scrum collapses.
- The scrum is wheeled around more than 90 degrees.
- The ball comes straight out the other side of the tunnel from where the ball was put into the scrum by the scrumhalf.
- The ball, or a player carrying it, touches the referee.

Recently players with a good tactical head on their shoulders have figured out an interesting use of the Advantage Law that might help you score some extra points for your team. If you are within range of the goalposts and you hear the advantage call, try to make a drop goal. If it goes over the post, great, you've added three points to your team's score. If you miss, it's no big deal, because the referee will bring it back to the original spot of the infraction. When you're trying this, be sure that you take the drop right away while the advantage is still on, otherwise you might waste a shot at goal that you could have gotten from the penalty kick.

Observing the Offside Law

Without doubt, the most important rugby law involves what is offside and what is onside in general play. Like soccer, rugby is a sport that revolves around the Offside Law. The main difference is that in soccer, offside is really only a concern near the goals, whereas in rugby, offside is in operation from end to end and sideline to sideline.

Spectators and players alike are often totally bewildered by the Offside Law, but it really is quite simple, as we explain.

In general play

A player is *offside* in general play if he is in front of a teammate who is carrying the ball, or in front of a teammate who last played the ball. If you are behind a ball-carrying teammate, you are *onside*.

Players who are offside are temporarily out of the game and should either stay where they are or get back onside. Figure 6-1 shows a team moving towards the opposition's tryline, with two players in the offside position.

To get back onside (and thus be able to take part in the game again), a player must retreat behind the ball. A player can return to being onside in one of four ways:

- ✓ The offside player runs behind the teammate who last kicked, touched, or carried the ball.
- ✓ A teammate carrying the ball runs in front of the offside player.
- ✓ A teammate who has kicked the ball forward runs in front of the offside player.
- ✓ A teammate runs past the offside player towards the opponent's tryline.

A player can also be put onside by a member of the opposition in three ways:

- ✓ An opponent carrying the ball runs 5 meters.
- ✓ An opponent kicks or passes the ball.
- ✓ An opponent intentionally touches the ball, but does not catch it.

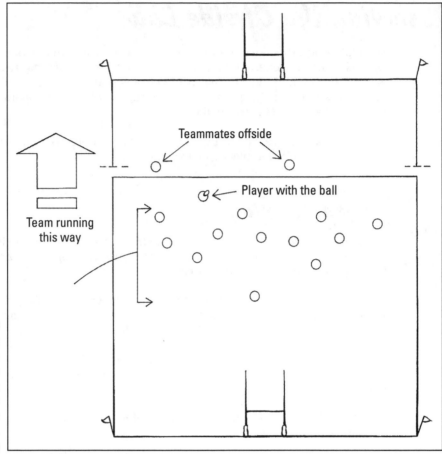

Figure 6-1:
Players
who are
offside are
temporarily
out of the
game.

When an offside player cannot avoid being touched by the ball or by a teammate carrying it, the player is *accidentally offside*. If the player's team gets no benefit from this (meaning that no potential tacklers were blocked by the action), play continues. If the player's team does benefit because the offending player shielded the ball-carrier from a defender, a scrum is formed with the opposing team putting in the ball. The same applies when a ball-carrier hands the ball to a teammate who is in front of him. If it's accidental, it is remedied with a scrum to the opposition.

A good way to remember this law is to imagine that you are the player with the ball. Everyone who is on your team and who is behind you is onside, and any teammate who is in front of you is offside. That should give you a better understanding of the most mysterious law of rugby.

Being penalized for going offside

At some stage of the game, all players find themselves offside. However, it's important to remember that players are not penalized for being in an offside position unless they:

- Interfere with play
- Move forward towards the ball
- Fail to comply with the 10-Meter Law (we talk about this little beauty in the next section)

If the referee catches you offside — and you are offending — he awards the opposition a penalty (we discuss all the options after a penalty has been awarded at the end of this section). When a player knocks the ball on, a teammate who happens to be in front of him can be penalized for playing the ball if he prevents an opponent from trying to play on.

Offside players must be careful that they are not caught *loitering*. This quaint rugby term refers to someone who is standing or retreating in an offside position and preventing the opposing team from playing the ball as they wish. South African referee Andre Watson has popularized the term *lazy runner* to denote this individual. If you find yourself in this situation, either fall back or get out of the way completely, or you'll attract the ire of the referee!

The Offside Law may sound rather tricky, but one simple solution applies if you are concerned about getting a penalty for being offside — get back behind your teammates before rejoining the fray.

Crossing the 10-meter line

Players are penalized if they fail to comply with the 10-Meter Law. This law applies when a player kicks the ball ahead and a teammate is standing in an offside position in front of the kicker. The offside player is prohibited from moving towards the opposition or going within 10 meters of where the opponent is waiting to play the ball.

The offside player is considered to be illegally taking part in the game if he is in front of an imaginary line that runs the width of the field, which is 10 meters in front of the opponent waiting to play the ball, or from where the ball lands. The offside player must immediately retire behind the imaginary 10-meter line. If he doesn't, the referee penalizes him for being offside and intentionally obstructing an opponent by awarding the opposition a penalty.

Figure 6-2 shows a player who is inside the 10-meter line and who must move back behind it or he will be penalized.

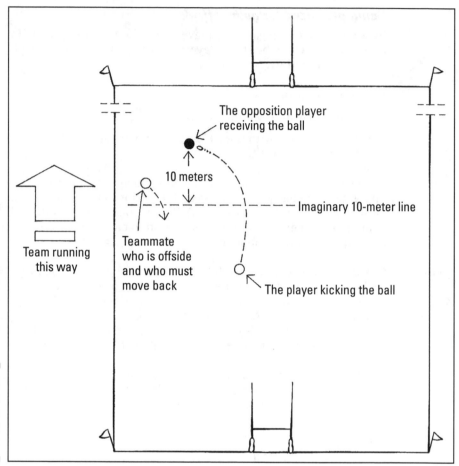

The opposition player
receiving the ball

10 meters

Imaginary 10-meter line

Team running
this way

Teammate
who is offside
and who must
move back

The player kicking the ball

Figure 6-2:
Move back
or break the
10-Meter
Law.

While retiring, the offside player cannot be put onside by the opposing team. However, before the player has moved the full 10 meters, the player can be made legal by any onside teammate who runs in front of him. The key here is that he must be retreating when passed. If he is standing there waiting, he cannot be put onside.

From set pieces

The offside laws are slightly different for the *set pieces* — which are scrums and line-outs. At a scrum, the offside line for every player except the scrumhalf runs through the hindmost foot of that player's team in the scrum. This is usually the number 8, so all of the back line players have to stay behind this player's back foot. The offside line for scrumhalves is a line running through the ball, allowing them to follow the ball as it makes its way towards the back of the scrum. This law is in place to ensure that the team that wins the ball has clear space to use it (we give more comprehensive details about the scrum in Chapter 8). The only players who ever really get called for being offside at the scrum are the scrumhalves, and even then very rarely.

At a line-out there are two separate offside lines, parallel to the goal lines, for each of the teams. One offside line is for the players taking part in the line-out (the ones standing there waiting for the ball to be thrown in). Until the ball has been thrown in and has touched a player or the ground, this offside line runs down the middle of the two sets of forwards on a line from where the ball was thrown. After that, the offside line is wherever the ball is. Basically, this is to keep players from crossing over the initial line until the ball can be played.

The other offside line applies to the players not taking part in the line-out, usually the backs waiting for the ball to be passed out to them. For the backs, the offside line is 10 meters behind where the ball is being thrown in from, or their goal line, if that is nearer. Until the line-out is over the back line players cannot advance beyond that line. If not closely watched by the referee, backs are naturally inclined to edge forward in anticipation of getting their hands on the ball or putting themselves in a better position defensively to stop the expected attack.

At tackles, rucks, and mauls

The offside laws for tackles, rucks, and mauls are similar to those highlighted above, with minor differences specific to the nature of each situation. After a tackle is made, if a tackler gets to his feet and plays the ball before a ruck has formed there is no offside line. Any other player attempting to pick up the ball must enter the area from a position on his side of the tackled player, no matter when he gets there. This forces other players to come back behind the tackle before playing the ball.

The sight of the ball on the ground must hit a certain circuit in some players' brains that turns them from thinking individuals to starving hyenas after a piece of meat, willing to risk anything to possess it. Not getting back behind the offside line before entering the tackle area will more often result in a negative outcome than in a successful poaching of the ball. The best thieves at the tackle situation are the ones who use their wits first and their quickness second.

A *ruck* is the term used when the ball is on the ground and at least two players from each team are in contact over it. Once a ruck has been formed there are two offside lines. Each offside line runs through the rear foot of the player furthest back in the ruck, parallel with the goal line. A player may join the ruck alongside the last player but not from the side or he is liable to be penalized. If you are not part of the ruck you can't be in front of this line. (We provide more information about this when we get to rucks in Chapter 7.)

Rucks are not neat tidy things so sometimes the temptation to help out in a hurry is greater than the discipline needed to join in at the proper place. Keep in mind that it doesn't help your team to win the ball only to have it given back by a penalty called against you.

It's virtually the same story for a *maul*, which happens when a player carrying the ball is held by one or more opponents: one or more of the ball-carrier's teammates then bind on the ball-carrier, and everyone involved is on their feet. Once again there are two offside lines parallel to the goal lines, one for each team. Players joining the maul have to do so from behind or alongside the hindmost foot of the player bringing up the rear of the maul. If you aren't joining the maul you have to stay behind this last player's foot. (Mauls are discussed in more detail in Chapter 7.) In most mauls there is usually an inviting place to slot into on the side, but you must resist the urge to do so.

Being offside at any of these phases of play is punishable by a penalty awarded to the non-offending team at the spot where the player was judged to be offside.

Playing Foul

The laws are written with an eye toward proportional punishment, reflecting a widely held belief that the penalty should fit the crime. The Foul Play Law has four parts with progressively stiffer sanctions meted out to wrongdoers. It includes obstruction, unfair play, repeated infringements, and misconduct.

Obstruction

The first level of foul play is obstruction. When a player and an opponent are running for the ball, the players cannot charge or push each other. Other players cannot run in front of the player carrying the ball or block the tackler. This transgression is dealt with by calling a simple penalty. This is generally considered to be a heat-of-the-moment-type offense.

Unfair play

The second level of foul play is unfair play. These are intentional actions in direct opposition to the laws and result in a penalty and sometimes a warning that continuation of said behavior will be severely dealt with. A player cannot waste time by making the ball unavailable to an opposition player, throw the ball into touch or over the dead ball line to slow the game down or prevent an attacking movement, or repeatedly commit the same penalty. If done subtly, the best players can get away with these callous infractions by hiding their intentions from the referee, but normally that only works once.

Repeated infringements

The third level of foul play is repeated infringements, which are judged to be even more cynical and disruptive than unfair play. Rucks and the tackle area seem to breed this type of behavior. After a player or a team has committed several of the same infringements, drawing a penalty each time, they are cautioned. If the behavior persists, the player must be shown a yellow card.

A yellow card forces the player into the sin bin for 10 minutes to think about his evil ways, forcing his teammates to soldier on with 14 men on the field. If he doesn't demonstrate that he's learned his lesson upon his return to action, the next step is a red card, signifying total banishment for the remainder of the match.

Misconduct

The fourth level of foul play is reserved for the most serious type of misconduct. A player cannot punch, strike, stamp, trample, kick, or trip an opponent. A player must not tackle an opponent above the shoulders, tackle an opponent who has jumped into the air to catch a high ball, or *late charge* someone who has kicked the ball. A late charge means to tackle or hit someone late, or well after the ball has left the area. Depending upon the severity of the misconduct, most often reflective of the referee's perception of malicious intent on the part of the offender, either a yellow or red card will be issued.

With the advent of television coverage at almost every major match, players guilty of misconduct are also subject to citing commissions that can issue suspensions and fines for an offense that the referee or his touch judges didn't see. Citing commissions usually consist of three officials who conduct a hearing with the offending player present to determine whether or not the player should be suspended for the offense. If the commission rules against him, the player may be suspended for further matches, depending upon the severity of the misconduct.

Taking Penalties

There are a multitude of actions on the rugby pitch that can cause the referee to award a penalty. The primary result of being awarded a penalty is that your team gets possession of the ball and a choice of options on how to use it. The decision on what to do on the field rests with your captain and the choice is governed by field position, how the match is progressing, time left, and the score.

The captain on a rugby team is responsible for making all the on-field decisions during the match, and must be a rugby savvy individual with a command of the strategic nuances of the game.

Kicking at goal

When your team is awarded a penalty kick, one of the options is to take a shot at scoring three points by attempting a penalty goal. To do this the captain or kicker informs the referee that they want to kick. Once chosen, no other options are allowed. Unless a law states otherwise, the mark for a penalty is at the place of infringement. On a penalty kick attempt, the opposing team must stand still with their hands by their sides from the time the kicker starts his approach until the ball is kicked. After receiving the tee from the sidelines, there's a one-minute time limit on taking the kick. Once the ball is kicked it is live again and in play.

The decision to take a shot at goal is determined by a number of situational factors. The game score, time remaining, kicker's range, and the relative difficulty of scoring tries all figure large in the calculus of whether or not to kick for goal.

Kicking for touch

Another option is to gain territory by kicking the ball downfield into touch. Normally a ball kicked into touch results in a line-out with the other team throwing the ball in, but on a penalty kick, possession is retained by the kicking team. The key is to make sure the kick actually goes out of bounds. Most teams decide to do this if they are out of the range of their goal kicker or if they need to score more than three points.

Choosing a scrum

A third choice for the non-offending team is to have a scrum formed at the place of the infringement with their put-in. This is a strategic decision that is usually made when there isn't enough time left to choose a line-out or when a team doubts their ability to get the ball to their jumpers. Also, an attacking scrum is a very difficult situation to defend against, even more so when the spot of the penalty is close to the defending side's goal line.

Taking it quick

A *quick tap* is when the non-offending team immediately kicks the ball *through the mark* and continues play as soon as a penalty has been given by the referee. Through the mark means that the kicker must kick the ball a visible distance at or directly behind the spot where the penalty has been awarded. If the kicker is holding the ball, it must clearly leave his hands. If the ball is on the ground, it must clearly leave the mark.

Taking a *quick tap* can be an extremely effective weapon because the opposition's defense has little time to react and realign. However, this choice should be used judiciously, because when you take it quick, you're giving up a shot at three points, or a chance to gain territory.

A team also has the option of kicking through the mark and attempting to run the ball straight at the opponents or to use a designed play, particularly when they are close to the tryzone. This type of quick tap is referred to as a *tap and go*.

Free kicks

A lesser degree of infraction, usually for technical violations rather than conduct, is called a free kick. The signal for a free kick also differs from a penalty, signified by a bent arm, raised in the direction of the team that will get the ball (see the "Recognizing the Referee's Signals" section in Chapter 5 for what this looks like). This gives the non-offending team possession but with far fewer benefits than a penalty. A scrum is one choice available on a free kick but kicking for goal is not. When kicking for touch from a free kick, possession is not retained at the ensuing line-out and ground is only gained if the kicker is behind his team's 22-meter line, making this an unattractive choice (the hows and whys of line-outs will be covered in Chapter 9).

Chapter 7

Playing the Game

● ●

In This Chapter

▶ Starting and restarting the match

▶ Defining tackler and tacklee

▶ Understanding the breakdown

▶ Recognizing the ruck

▶ Manipulating the maul

● ●

At the heart of rugby is the notion that in every situation there must be a fair contest for the ball. The Laws of the Game have changed over the years to promote this goal and as a result the game has become faster and more technically demanding of all the players on the pitch.

The modern game is meant to be continuous and fast-moving with as few stoppages as possible. If players just ran about from end to end this could be easily accomplished, but the confrontational nature of the sport demands that one team try to stop the other from advancing whenever possible. This inevitably leads to contests for the ball that develop spontaneously after each tackle. Understanding what happens after a player has been tackled is at the core of developing a thorough knowledge for both fans and players.

The key to being a good rugby player is to understand the strictures governing each particular part of the game, and then have the skills to excel in those areas. The key to understanding the game as a fan then, is to be able to recognize what is happening as a match progresses, and why the referees make the decisions that they do.

In this chapter, we'll start where the game begins, with kickoffs and restarts, then give further details on the seemingly complicated activity that accompanies a ball-carrier being brought to ground. That will lead us to a comprehensive examination of the breakdown, followed by a closer look at the laws governing rucks and mauls. (These parts of the game may seem chaotic at first glance, but once they're explained you'll see how organized they really are.)

Getting Started

Starting a match is a facet of the game that has undergone a significant change in the last few years. A place kick was once used to start each half. At some point, somebody clever read the law and saw that it allowed for a tee (approved by the union sanctioning the match) to be used for this purpose. This led to a frenzy of plastic tee designs that ended up looking like traffic cones. The goal was to help get the ball as high in the air as possible to make securing it much easier for the kicking team. Sensibly, the International Rugby Board (IRB) stepped in and mandated that all kicking restarts would henceforth be *drop kicks*, which are kicks that are dropped from the hand and hit the ground before the kicker's foot comes into contact with it.

Kickoffs to begin each half

A kickoff is the first opportunity for both teams to contest possession of the ball. Before the game, there's a meeting of both captains and the referee, where a coin toss is made and the winning skipper chooses either to kick off or defend an end. (If the captain decides to kick off at the start of the first half, the other team will do so at the start of the second half.) The choice of ends is especially important when the wind is a factor.

Kickoffs are taken from the center of the halfway line (check out the "What do all those lines mean?" section in Chapter 2 for details about the lines on a rugby pitch). Most pitches will have a half-meter dash line to mark this spot and referees will often direct wayward kickers back to that spot if they attempt to go astray. If the ball is kicked from in front of the halfway line, or too far from the center, the referee can order that it be taken again.

Every player on the kicker's team must be behind the ball until it is struck (Figure 7-1 shows the formation of the players in a kickoff). They're allowed to get a running start but their timing has to be right so that they don't inadvertently pass the ball before it's airborne. If they are judged to be in front of the kicker, a scrum is formed in the center of the field with the opposition getting the put-in. This is an inexcusable mistake that drives coaches nuts, because it gives a great attacking opportunity to the other team.

The players on the receiving squad (the team that isn't kicking) must line up behind their own 10-meter line. The receiving team has a distinct advantage over the team kicking because the players are able to lift the locks (see Chapter 4 for more details about this playing position) up in the air to take the ball, while the kicking team has to rely on regular jumping. (Remember, the kicker's teammates have to charge down the field after the ball; the opposition has the ball coming to them.)

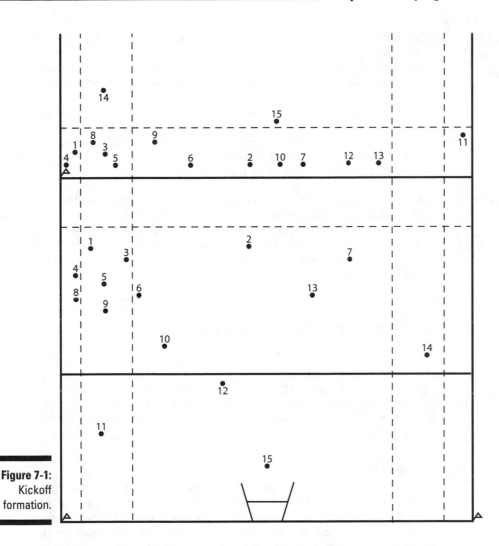

Figure 7-1:
Kickoff
formation.

The ball must reach the opponent's 10-meter line for the kick to be legal. Remember, it's not where the ball hits the ground that determines whether it has traveled the required 10 meters. (See Figure 7-1 for the alignment of the kicking and receiving teams.)

When facing a stiff breeze, if the kick crosses the 10-meter line in the air and is then blown back across the line, it's play on! Even if the kick doesn't reach the 10-meter line, keep playing, because the receiving team can choose to play the ball and you need to be ready to tackle them. If the ball fails to reach the 10-meter line and is not played by the receiving team, the referee will give them the option of having another kickoff, or a scrum at midfield.

Your goal as the kicker is to put enough air under the ball to let your team-mates charge downfield and secure it before the other team can do so. The temptation is to try to kick it exactly 10 meters, but this is unwise because if the ball doesn't go at least that far it's also a scrum to the receiving team.

A ball that is kicked off directly into touch, or out of bounds on the fly, gives the non-kicking team three options. They can have the ball kicked off again, take a line-out on the halfway line, or have a scrum at midfield (with their put-in). A kickoff that goes into the in-goal area and is immediately grounded also produces a choice of a re-kick or a scrum at center.

Unless your team is getting pummeled in the scrums, you should instruct the captain to always take the midfield scrum over another kickoff. The scrum is a vastly superior attacking opportunity for your side because the key back-row defenders are required to stay bound-in while scrummaging, which provides more space for your backs to operate in the midfield. (For all the details about scrums, see Chapter 8.)

Restarts after scores and 22s

In addition to beginning each half, kickoffs are used to restart the game after either team has scored either a try, penalty try, penalty goal, or dropped goal. A great feature of rugby is that when you score, you automatically get another chance to regain the ball because the non-scoring team kicks off to the one that added to their scoreboard total. The same regulations that control kickoffs also apply to restart kicks.

Taking it at the 22

A 22-meter drop-out (a drop kick) is used to restart play after the ball is grounded in the in-goal area by the defending team if the attacking team caused it to go in there. This usually happens if a missed penalty kick is caught and grounded by the opposing team, or if the ball goes over the dead ball line. Another way the ball can end up in the defending team's in-goal area is when an offensive player kicks ahead in general play and loses the race to touch it down.

A 22-meter drop-out can be taken anywhere behind the 22-meter line and, as with a kickoff, everyone on the kicker's team has to be behind the ball. The defense has a little more leeway here and can attempt to block the kick as long as they don't actually cross the 22-meter line in doing so.

If you are the player taking the drop-out, you can prevent your teammates from being offside (in front of the ball) by doing two things before you kick it. First, look both ways to see if any of your teammates are in front of you. If they are, you should wave them back. Once they are all behind the ball, signal that you're about to take the restart before you kick it.

Just like kickoffs, if the ball crosses the 22-meter line in the air and is then blown back, play continues. Similarly, if the ball doesn't reach the 22-meter line, you still need to remain vigilant, as the receiving team can choose to play the ball even if it doesn't cross the line.

If the kicker gives the drop kick a bit too much juice and it goes directly into touch on the fly, the receiving team can take either another drop-out, or opt for a scrum midfield on the 22 or a line-out at the 22-meter line.

Nothing gets under the skin of your forward pack like overcooked restart kicks that go directly into touch forcing them to defend a scrum from a disadvantageous position. So, if you've been entrusted with the kicking duties and want to keep on good terms with the big folks up front, be sure to keep your drop-outs within the field of play.

Another recent strategic development involves players drop kicking the ball a foot or so over the 22-meter line and regathering it immediately. This is perfectly legal because the law only requires that the ball cross the line, one inch or fifty yards are both acceptable.

The Tackle Situation

Unlike football, where the contest comes to a screeching halt after every tackle, in rugby tackles are part of a continuing sequence of play. Without proper regulation, what happens at the tackle situation can degenerate into constant stoppages and continual blowing of the referee's whistle. The laws have evolved to prevent this from taking place, and to turn the tackle situation into a transitional phase for the next positive use of the ball.

In rugby, a tackle is made when a ball-carrier is brought to ground and held there. (It's also considered a tackle when the ball touches the ground while the ball-carrier is being held, or when the player is being held and is lying on another player.) *Brought to ground* means no longer on your feet, which includes having one knee down. Simply put, if you're held and don't have both feet on the ground, you're tackled. Being knocked to the ground without a tackler holding on is not a tackle, and you're free to get up and run some more. But if you're held, a different set of laws take over and you've got some serious responsibilities to take care of.

The tackled player

The ball-carrier who is brought to ground is known as the tackled player. The first requirement of the tackled player is to immediately make the ball available. The tackled player can place the ball in any direction, but the best choice is to direct it towards supporting teammates and away from opponents.

The key is to release the ball under control, so that your side has the best chance to recycle possession. If able to do so, a tackled player can also pass the ball at once. In practice this means that as soon as the ball-carrier comes to a stop on the ground it's time to release the ball.

The most important thing to remember is that once you've been tackled, you can't hold onto the ball, especially if someone on their feet is trying to take it from you. The continuity theory in effect here is that if a player isn't on his feet he can't play the ball anymore so he has to make it available for other players to use.

The error that most new players make in running with the ball is that they don't plan for being tackled. A good player avoids tackles whenever possible but prepares for their eventuality by positioning his body so that when he is brought down, he has control over the outcome. This means securing the ball on the way down to stop it from being ripped away, using strength to go to ground with his body between the tackler and the ball, and placing it so his cohorts can control possession.

The tackler

The tackler is also charged with making sure the ball is immediately available for other players. The tackler's first act after going to the ground must be to let the tackled player go so the ball can be freed. A player cannot wrestle the ball-carrier for possession while they're both on the ground. Holding the ball-carrier tight on the ground will draw the referee's whistle just as quickly as not releasing the ball.

The second duty is to get away from the ball. Letting go and then using the body to cover it up or slow it down is both illegal and dangerous because it will draw unfriendly boots to the tackler's prone figure.

The tackler is also restricted from any contact with the ball until he is back on his feet. Getting back up is the best course of action as it allows the tackler the chance to pick up the ball. Unlike subsequent players that enter the area, the tackler is free to play the ball from any position as long as he has regained his feet. This advantage usually only lasts for a short time, until players from both sides arrive and change the nature of what's happening.

Just because your feet are on the ground doesn't necessarily mean that you're "on your feet" for the purpose of playing the ball after the tackle. If any part of your body is supported by someone on the ground, it's the same as if you were flat on your back — you're not allowed to play the ball.

Stealing the ball after the tackle is one of the most effective ways to create turnovers in general play. Teach all of your players, from fullback to the front row, how to quickly get back on their feet after making a tackle. Then demonstrate the low body position they'll need to reach in with both hands and steal the ball off the ground. Make sure they understand that as other players arrive and the ruck forms, they need to obey if the referee yells, "ruck formed, no hands" (we will cover the rucking rules shortly).

What happens next?

In a perfect world, there would never be any need to stop play at a tackle situation because tacklers would release tackled players immediately, the ball would come free, and play would continue. It isn't always that cut-and-dried on the pitch, however, and the laws outlining what happens next reflect that reality. The term *breakdown* is a catch-all for the multitude of things that can happen from when the ball-carrier is brought down, to when the ball is next played.

Breaking Down the Breakdown

Whenever the ball is on the ground after a tackle it's a free ball and both teams have full rights to it. The events at the breakdown are the hardest to adjudicate because everything happens so fast and the referee's vision is routinely obscured by players flying in and bodies piling up on the turf. More penalties are called at the breakdown than in any other part of the game. The key to successful work at the breakdown is for players to be well coached, self-disciplined, and fully cognizant of the applicable laws.

When we first started playing rugby, the breakdown was a complete mystery. Not knowing the law made it impossible to distinguish between times when behavior was legal and when it was seriously wrong. The easiest way to improve your overall game is to learn the tackle, ruck, and maul laws. Knowledge is power. More energy is wasted at breakdowns by players who don't know what they're doing than in any other area of the game.

Tackle, Ruck, or Maul?

Every rugby spectator, and we mean *every* rugby spectator, has at some stage become befuddled and bemused figuring out the difference between a tackle, ruck, or maul. Don't worry — you are not alone. We didn't pick this one up for at least five years!

A tackle is something that starts with two or more players on their feet, one of them carrying the ball, and ends up with them on the ground. As soon as a tackle happens, however, a new phase usually takes its place. This depends on what happens to the ball once it's released or passed. Tackles more often than not end up morphing into rucks as more players arrive at the breakdown.

The difference between a ruck and a maul is that in a ruck, the ball is on the ground, while in a maul, the ball is off the ground in the hands of a player. To put it simply: off the ground — maul; on the ground — ruck.

Roughing It in the Rucks

A *ruck* is formed when two or more players, at least one from each side, are on their feet over the ball in physical contact with each other after a tackle has been made or when the ball is on the ground.

The player who has been tackled with the ball is allowed to place it on the ground, or push it towards his teammates. He must do this immediately after going to ground. The referee allows his momentum to come to a halt, then the ball must be released. The tackled player can usually get away with one good rollover but a second one is likely to be penalized. If the player hangs onto the ball too long, perhaps to allow his teammates time to catch up or to prevent a defender from poaching the ball, the referee blows his whistle and awards a penalty to the defending side.

The first players to arrive at a ruck have to bind to each other or the opposition, as shown in Figure 7-3. The players grab each other around the shoulders or waist, or whatever body part is handy, and then try to step over the ball. The players on both sides of the ruck can attempt to drive the opposition back and away from the loose ball but under no circumstances can they play the ball with their hands.

Launching your body into a ruck like a Scud missile is illegal and dangerous. Good form and body position are more important than brute strength at ruck time. You need to stay low and balanced, keeping your shoulders above your hips and your head up as you go over the ball to secure possession. A well-placed, concentrated shove is vastly superior to the head-down charging rhino technique.

When the ruck is formed, the prime aim is to remove the ball. Players can only use their feet to rake the ball back to a waiting teammate and are not allowed to touch the ball with their hands. Alternatively, the attacking group of players can drive forward, stepping over the ball and clearing defenders away from it, making the ball available for the waiting scrumhalf, who decides how the team attacks next.

Figure 7-2:
Forming a
ruck.

 Players should not make deliberate contact with an opponent's body that is on the ground unless that body part is blocking access to the ball. Kicking or *raking* an opponent who may have fallen down is not tolerated, and can result in the referee sending the offender off. This is called *stamping* and is dealt with harshly. It is legal, however, to use your boot to clear away the part of the body that is directly covering the ball as long as a backwards motion is used. The exception is if a player's head is slowing down the ball's path of egress.

The ball is won from the ruck when the attacking players successfully bind together, drive forward over the ball, and it becomes available for the halfback at the back of the ruck, who then distributes it. Good rucking means quickly providing the ball to the scrumhalf, which in turn allows the backs to attack before the defense can realign. If the opposition is denied time to realign before the next attacking wave, it's likely to have holes for your backs to exploit.

Rucking rules

Attacking from the ruck can be highly effective and sometimes devastating. But it is also an area where countless infringements occur. The scope for foul play in a ruck is enormous and referees strictly enforce the rules. The whistle is blown if players who join a ruck:

✔ Come from an offside position. The offside line at a ruck is the hindmost foot of the last man in the ruck.

✔ Come into the ruck from the side. Even if you are onside you still must enter the ruck from behind the last man's foot.

✔ Loiter at the ruck. If you are not part of the ruck you must retire behind the offside line.

✔ Use their hands to mischievously get the ball back to their side.

✔ Use their legs to pick the ball up or prevent it from being played.

Players are not allowed to kick the ball back into a ruck, because once the ball comes out the back of a ruck, it must leave that area. As the ball is coming out of a ruck, no player is allowed to fall on or over it.

One of the most common ruck infractions is when a defensive player gets his hands on the ball before the ruck is formed but can't quite rip it away. After the ruck is formed the referee will usually shout out, "It's a ruck, no hands" or something to that effect. It then takes a lot of discipline to let the ball go and avoid the whistle.

Kick the ball, not the man

In rugby, the term "mountaineering" is used to describe the act of players unnecessarily attacking an opponent with their feet and usually involves a situation where players stomp all over an opponent who has fallen and is lying near the ball. (However, since players are not allowed to lie all over the ball an opponent can attempt, within reason, to get another player out of the way with a well-aimed boot.)

A player must strictly ruck for the ball and not ruck the man. If you are attempting to free the ball using a raking motion where your boot is moving primarily backwards, as opposed to straight down, you probably won't get into trouble with the referee. If your boot is aimed at the ball and it unintentionally collides with a body lying near the ball, you'll usually get away with it. But if you strike an opponent with your boot and he's a long way from the ball, you could find yourself in a lot of trouble. Stamping directly down onto the legs, body, or worse, on the head of an opponent who's lying helpless on the turf is unsportsmanlike.

Remember, there's no place in rugby for malicious acts, so keep your rucking technique within the spirit of the game. The Ruck Law is interpreted differently by referees throughout the world; some countries are more lenient than others in what they allow players to do at the ruck.

Stay on your feet

Perhaps the most important law is that players joining or forming a ruck must have their heads and shoulders no lower than their hips because otherwise it's dangerous. At rucktime, the goal is to stay on your feet, and entering with your head down decreases your strength and may lead to serious injury.

Players in a ruck must be on their feet and they must endeavor to stay on their feet. A player cannot deliberately:

- ✔ Fall or kneel in a ruck
- ✔ Collapse a ruck
- ✔ Jump on top of a ruck

Rucks can be unsteady and sometimes collapse, especially when players use the wrong technique, causing them to lose their feet. For a ruck to be successful, players have to be well drilled, well coordinated, and disciplined — and know the laws.

Directing the ruck

The most important player at the ruck is the scrumhalf, who directs proceedings by telling his forwards exactly where to go. The scrumhalf is usually the only person who can actually see where the ball is, how many opposing players are committed to the ruck, and where the defense is positioned. He can then decide if more of his forwards are required at the ruck, whether the ball should be released or retained, and exactly where his teammates need to concentrate their efforts to ensure they get the ball back.

After the ruck has been formed, the scrumhalf is basically the foreman, telling his forwards where to go, what to do, and whether they are being successful in getting the ball back to him. An experienced scrumhalf focuses the forward's energy and attention on the area where it's needed most.

Working the pick-and-go

A successful attacking strategy from a ruck is called the *pick-and-go*. In a pick-and-go move, the ball-carrier strategically places the ball some distance back from his prostrate body. Hot on his heels are several teammates, who step over the ball and quickly drive their opponents off it.

Another attacker, who now has a clear run to the ball, bends down, picks it up, and charges ahead until being tackled, setting up yet another ruck or another pick-and-go. This tactic, if done properly, can be carried out over and over, allowing a team to gain ground and keep the defense off balance.

The danger of too much TV

In 1999, New Zealand All Blacks flanker Josh Kronfeld was one of the world's best ball stealers. He could uncannily anticipate where the breakdown was about to occur and used his tremendous strength and commitment to consistently steal the ball off the deck before the ruck could form. His willingness to give up his body to poach the ball was awesome and, being a flanker myself, he was my personal hero. Whenever I played, I imagined that I was Josh roaming the field, searching for a tackle so I could swoop in and steal the ball before anyone else could get there. In my first game as "Josh," I repeatedly turned-up at the tackle situation and reached in to grab the ball off the deck. To my surprise, the referee, who obviously didn't know I was Josh, blew his whistle and pinged me for hands in at the ruck. I foolishly protested that the ruck had not yet formed and since I was clearly on my feet, it was totally legal for me (Josh) to steal the ball, but to no avail. A couple of phases later, despite my clear laws explanation, a loud blast signaled a second penalty for hands in. Then a third, a fourth, a fifth, a sixth, and a seventh stoppage followed with the referee still wrong (in my book at least) about when hands can and can't be used. After the match, which we lost by three points thanks to my last error, my teammates read me the riot act for giving the match away. The lesson is that no matter who you think you are, you need to play to the referee on the day and adjust your game to comply with the referee's management of the game. And yes, if taken out of context, there can be such a thing as too much TV.

Mastering the Maul

A *maul* is formed when a player who is carrying the ball and is on his or her feet is held by one or more opponents. In addition, at least one teammate must be attached to the player holding the ball. This phase of play is illustrated in Figure 7-3.

Mauls are mostly used as an attacking ploy from line-outs (see Chapter 9 for more details about line-outs). The coordination and cohesion at the line-out is perfect for forming a maul because the forwards involved are all right in the area and ready to bind and drive ahead.

The speed of a maul is not the most significant element. Slow, steady progress where everyone is in sync tends to produce better results than a bunch of forwards with their heads down going at full gallop. Mauls are occasionally created when a player carries the ball into a would-be tackler and then turns to face his supporting teammates in an effort to protect the ball and stop it being wrestled away by an opponent. Teammates can grab the ball-carrier between the waist and shoulders to protect him from the opposition and retain possession of the ball. The goal is to keep driving forward while moving the ball to the back of the maul for immediate use when the scrumhalf deems it's time. This is the one time in rugby when it is legal to be playing while in front of the ball.

Figure 7-3:
Forming a
maul.

A central feature of any good maul is proper binding by all participants. The tighter you are with your teammates, the more force you can exert and the harder it is for the opposition to stop or split you apart. The other indispensable element is communication. Everyone should know where the ball is and where it's going. This maximizes its protection and sharpens the focus of the attacking platform.

Mauling laws

To the spectator, mauls can look totally confusing, like an out-of-control amusement ride. On the pitch though, a well-executed maul can ensure that one team totally controls the game. It requires an enormous amount of dedication and discipline, and a proper understanding of the laws.

An important part of the Maul Law is that players can only join a maul from an onside position. The mauling manual includes other basics such as:

> ✔ Players who are in a maul must endeavor to stay on their feet. Referees regard it to be dangerous play if anyone tries to collapse a maul or jumps on top of it. This is an obvious penalty.

✔ Players are not allowed to remove an opponent from a maul. Dragging an offside player out of the maul is prohibited, it's the referee's job to enforce the law.

✔ While in a maul, the ball-carrier can go to ground, but must make the ball available immediately upon doing so. Players must respond accordingly when a maul goes to ground and it becomes a ruck.

The two main types of mauls are *driving mauls* and *rolling mauls*, which evolve after the maul has been formed.

Attacking from a driving maul

When the attacking team tries to drive through the opposition, the tactic is called a *driving maul.* The ball is usually carried by a player in the second line of the maul to protect it from the opposition. The players in the front line of the maul stay relatively upright, with their teammates behind them, adopting a lower body position so they can get better leg drive and better leverage to push the maul forward. In effect, the maul becomes a driving wedge charging straight ahead, but the big difference is that the ball is being held by one of the players and is not on the ground.

What makes the driving maul so effective is that the defenders not involved in opposing the maul are required to constantly move backwards to stay onside. Backpedaling defenders are much easier for your backline to beat. The key to taking full advantage of maul possession is to have your scrumhalf use the ball before the maul stops moving forward.

In the old days, mauls were allowed to stop and start repeatedly and seemed to go on forever. Then the IRB changed the law, mandating that once a maul stopped, the ball had to be used immediately or it was a turnover. This de-emphasized the use of the maul as an attacking strategy, much to the detriment of the game. Recognizing and remedying the unintended result, the IRB compromised and now allows a maul to stop once. The team in possession then have five seconds to start moving again or produce the ball.

This is a good change because mauling is an important component of a team's physical presence on the field. If your side can regularly drive forward using a controlled maul, your opponent will be physically taxed and mentally demoralized because it takes much more energy to stop a maul than it does to attack from one.

Using a rolling maul

A *rolling maul* occurs when the attacking team transfers the ball into the hands of a player on one side of the maul where the opposition appears weakest or has the least number of players. His teammates roll around to that side, pushing the player with the ball forward in a fairly good imitation of a cyclone. This type of maul resembles a spinning top, with one player rolling onto another, enabling the maul to move forward as the ball is transferred from one player to the next.

When executed properly, a rolling maul is a powerful attacking weapon because it is so difficult to defend against (especially when the team in possession changes its direction, going from one side of the field to the other). Most of the time the opposition has its work cut out just trying to stop the rolling maul from advancing, and has no real chance of getting the ball back. Whoever is currently holding the ball watches for the moment when the opposition defense in front of him is in disarray. He then peels off and takes the ball into the open field once again.

Directing the maul

As with rucks, the scrumhalf acts as the coordinator at mauls. He doesn't get directly involved in the maul but stands behind, right next to the action. The halfback looks for opportunities, decides where the opposition defense is weakest, urges his forwards on and tells them where to go. He advises his teammates where they should join the maul, and who needs support to ensure that the maul keeps moving in the desired direction.

Stopping the maul

A good maul is difficult but not impossible to stop. When trying to stop a maul, the first thing you should do is try to turn the ball-carrier or tear the ball away and gain possession for your team. (This is easier in mauls that occur spontaneously rather than planned ones from line-outs.)

When the maul is near the sideline, the best option is to try to concentrate your opposing shove at an angle to force the attacking side out of bounds. It is also legal to burrow your way into the opposition's maul through the front as long as you remain on your feet and don't come from an offside position. This has to be attempted right away though, because once the ball starts being funneled to the back it is impossible to get to.

If you can't get the ball, or drive the maul over the sideline, then you have to stop its forward progress. This can be done by hitting the leading edge of the maul with full force, at an angle lower than the opposition players who are driving at you. Be careful not to lose your feet and drag others down with you — that can cause the maul to collapse, which will result in a penalty and possibly a trip to the sin bin. A strong back and superb body position are required to stop a maul that already has momentum.

BROWNIE SAYS

The motorhome

I used to own a 1973 Dodge Brougham motorhome. It was the old boxy style, 19 feet long, and incredibly heavy. One Summer in Cleveland it broke down in a no parking zone and had to be pushed to safety up a slight grade or it was off to the impound yard. When I first tried to move the behemoth, I found it impossible to budge until I used the mauling position I had learned at rugby training. The idea was not to push it from up high but to get under the weight, into a body position where all the force possible could be directed into the bumper and then slowly inched forward, step by step. This technique, with hips lower than shoulders and a straight back exactly duplicates the method for stopping the driving maul. I don't recommend pushing a motorhome by yourself, but it's helpful to imagine that's what you are doing during mauling practice. The women that I coached at Occidental College probably grew tired of hearing this story, but I've yet to find a better real life illustration of the unnatural act of stopping a maul.

Chapter 8

The Art of Scrummaging

The scrum is rugby's signature element because it is unique in the world of sport. It is an easily identifiable part of the game, involving more than half the players on the field, two packs of eight battling for possession of the ball. Nothing comes close to the sheer power generated by eight players bound together as one with a singular purpose. Maximizing the combined force of all the forwards is the most technically challenging part of the game. It is also the most physically demanding, as the exertion required to compete in repeated scrums drains the life out of your body faster than any other aspect of play.

Since every game has numerous scrums to restart play after minor infringements, it is considered absolutely vital that a team be able to consistently win their own scrums. Scrums are often described as the engine room of rugby, delivering a team's prime power source. If a team is dominant in the scrum, it usually means they are well on their way to a win, because what happens in this area of the game affects so many other aspects of the match.

In this chapter, we demystify the scrum by providing an inside look at the heart of rugby's least understood phase, so you can compete safely and win the battle up front.

Scrum Is Not Synonymous with Mayhem

If you watch other sports on television, you may hear the occasional commentator refer to a spontaneous pile of disorganized bodies on the ground as a scrum. Nothing could be further from the truth. The reality is that a scrum is a very well organized and synchronized activity where every player involved has a specific set of skills, roles, and responsibilities. For a scrum to be successful in restarting play, all players must remain on their feet. Scrummaging takes strength, technique, aggression, and courage — it certainly isn't a haphazard melee.

We cringe every time we hear or see uninformed announcers and sportswriters use this term inaccurately because it reinforces negative stereotypes about the game and belittles one of rugby's most intriguing features. Scrummaging is an esoteric art form, practiced out of the limelight but thoroughly appreciated and respected by knowledgeable coaches, fans, and the other participants on the field.

The most technical part of the game

Scrummaging is an intense, precise endeavor, where technique reigns supreme over brute strength. Your pack can boast eight incredible hulks, but if they can't work together in a coordinated fashion they'll be well and truly beaten by a side of average-sized players that have their act together.

My first time packing down

I first played rugby at Occidental College in 1987 under the guidance of Coach Michael Godfree. Like many coaches who were backs in their playing days, the scrum was somewhat of a mystery to Michael. He knew immediately that I was a prop of course, but was somewhat vague on what I was supposed to do when it came time to scrum down. My total instruction in propping consisted of another player directing me to "get in there and push." With one week of training under our belts (where we were mostly introduced to basic skills like passing and tackling) the many rookies on that year's Oxy squad faced off on a Saturday against Long Beach State, then a Southern California powerhouse. I played tight-head prop and came up against an Australian guy with a full beard who must have been about thirty years old. Every scrum was an adventure in survival. He lifted me in the air, bent me in half so that I was kissing my knees, twisted me like a wet towel, and hit me so hard on every engagement that I'm sure I ended up several inches shorter. None of this would be legal now but at the time it was considered the price to pay for being a rookie front-rower. My day ended with a split cheek that required eight stitches — suffered in a tackle, not a scrum — and the next day I was sore in more places than I had ever been in my entire life, but I was also hooked on propping and still am to this day. It is the most directly confrontational position on the team and requires heart, strength, stamina, and a desire to not get individually beaten. Learning how to do it right is a long journey of experimentation and setbacks, but in the end the ability to confidently prop up a scrum is the most satisfying of rugby pleasures.

A scrum formation is like a battering ram: The front row (made up of three players) is reinforced with five more players strategically placed behind them in positions that best stabilize the formation and push the opposition backwards. In order to make this configuration work, every player has to have proper alignment and balance, sufficient expertise to adapt to pressure and movement, and be strong enough to withstand the force generated by eight individuals working as a unit to mercilessly smash them.

Becoming a good scrummaging team takes countless hours of repetitive drilling together as a unit. This can be done against either a scrum machine or an opposition pack. Training should be broken up into two types, each with different goals. The first is concentrated on correct binding, foot positioning, leg angles, balance, and spine alignment. Every player is unique in the power they can generate from their body shape, so figuring out how to feel comfortable in the scrum while maintaining maximum effectiveness is the priority in these sessions. The second type of workout involves repetition in engaging hard, pushing as a pack, breaking up and running to a spot, then reforming as quickly as possible to simulate the activity in a match. Undertaking this kind of physical conditioning is useless though, if the proper techniques and muscle memory haven't been sufficiently developed.

Sections of the Scrum

The basics of scrummaging include learning how to correctly bind together as the scrum is formed, using good body positioning prior to and after the engagement, winning the ball, and providing a solid platform for launching the attack (Figure 8-1 shows the formation of a scrum). The best way to explain the scrum is to go through the individual positions, describing how the players are arranged and what their responsibilities are.

The front row

The formation of a scrum starts with the hooker (number 2), who is the central figure of the whole affair. After the referee marks the spot where the scrum will take place, the hooker moves there and raises his arms, enabling the two props (numbers 1 and 3) to bind onto the hooker. The props then slide their inside shoulders under, up, and through, so that they end up in front of the hooker's shoulders. The hooker then binds onto the props, by gripping each of them by their rugby jersey, with his arms across their backs so that the three are closely bound together (see Figure 8-1 for how the front row binds).

Figure 8-1:
Binding
together:
The front
row gets
ready for a
scrum.

The front row is where the scrum is usually won and lost. A bad front row cannot be saved by a good second row. A good second row, however, can make a good front row into world-beaters.

It is extremely important that the members of the front row are solidly bound together at the shoulders and hips because the opposition's goal is to split them apart. The force exerted on the front row from the players behind them and the opposing scrum is enormous and any weakness in binding will be ruthlessly exposed and exploited. Practicing correct scrum formations should be part of your team's training routine. Strong scrums mean fewer injuries and more chances to beat the opposition.

Once they are all linked up, the three front-row players bend their knees, sink their hips, and rock backwards so that they are properly prepared to withstand the pressure when the second row and back row bind-in behind them. They also look directly into the eyes of the opposition's front-rowers in readiness for the battle ahead.

Playing in the front row requires specialized skills, so each player must be suitably trained for the position. For safety reasons, not just any reserve can come off the bench and slot in up front. Without proper instruction and experience, the front row can be a dangerous place. If you are learning to play prop it is best to be able to play on both the tight- and loose-head sides because you never know when you might be called upon to do double-duty in a match.

The term "hooker" is not a pejorative one but instead refers to the action undertaken by this player when the ball is put into the scrum. He hooks it with his foot to be channeled to the back of the scrum for use by the scrumhalf or number 8.

The props derive their names in the same fashion, because they "prop up" the hooker. The terms "loose-head" and "tight-head" refer to the placement of their heads when the scrum comes together. The loose-head is just that: loose on the outside. The tight-head has his noggin sandwiched in tight between the opposition loose-head and hooker.

The second row

While the front row is getting ready, the two locks in the second row (numbers 4 and 5) place their inside arms around each other, gripping onto their jerseys at waist level. They bend forward and place one shoulder against the back of the hooker's upper leg just below the buttock and the other in the same spot on either the tight-head or loose-head prop, depending on which side of the scrum they're on. Once the locks' shoulders are properly positioned, their heads should poke out between the props' and hooker's hips. Their heads should be slightly raised so they have full vision of the ball as it travels through the scrum.

The lock then thrusts his spare arm (the one that isn't holding on to his second-row colleague) between the prop's legs and grabs onto his waistband. This bind has changed over the years — the locks used to put their arms around the prop's hips. It was also common for both locks to go down on one knee before engaging, but this too is becoming a rarity at the highest levels.

Most international locks now get into position behind the front row without going down on one knee. As a lock, you can try this new style by keeping both feet on the ground, and bending deeply at the knees and the waist before you bind to the front row. The advantage of this technique is that as the scrum engages, your feet are already planted and ready to lock out, and you don't have to reposition them after the engagement.

The back row

After the second row is bound in, the two flankers (numbers 6 and 7) bind onto the second row. They reach across the backs of the locks with their inside arms and grab a handful of the locks' jerseys while using their inside shoulders to apply pressure to where the props' buttocks meet their hamstrings.

On an offensive scrum (where their team has the put-in), the two flankers are responsible for keeping the ball from escaping out the sides as it is being channeled back and for keeping the props in tight to the hooker. On a defensive scrum they are more involved in pushing forward and their angles at engagement change to reflect this.

In attack, the flankers need to always keep their eyes on the ball until the scrum is over so they can support the number 8 if he picks up the ball, the scrumhalf if he darts around the fringe, and the backs if they crash back toward the forwards. On defense, the breaks need to focus on where and when the ball is coming out of the scrum, so they are ready to immediately disengage from the scrum and be there to stop the ball-carrier if necessary.

The last piece of the back-row puzzle is the number 8. This player slots in at the back of the scrum, driving forward with both shoulders against the backsides of the two second-rowers. To help stabilize and hold the locks together, he binds his arms around the outside of their hips and puts his head between their bodies.

The number 8 has more to do at the end of the scrum than at the beginning. He must coordinate with his scrumhalf as to what their plan is for each ball he receives. If the scrum is moving forward, then the task is much easier, but if it is static or moving backwards the difficulty level rises. Whether he is picking the ball up from the back and taking it on himself, passing to his scrumhalf, or giving his scrumhalf protection, he must be sure-handed and a quick decision-maker.

He is also charged with controlling the ball with his feet at the back to keep it from emerging too early or in an untidy fashion. This ability to manage the ball at the base of the scrum with his feet is a skill unique to the number 8 position. (Figure 8-2 shows a pack of forwards ready to engage in a scrum.)

The ninth forward — the scrumhalf

Because the scrumhalf is responsible for much more than just putting in and removing the ball from scrums, and despite the fact that he's technically a back, forwards will sometimes pay the little guy a huge compliment by referring to him as the ninth forward.

The scrumhalf is crucial for effective attack and defense from scrum set pieces. This player is the direct link between what happens at the scrum and how the ball is delivered to the backline. If a scrum is barely holding off the opposition's push, the scrumhalf must adapt and be faster in distributing the ball. If the scrumhalf's team has the upper hand, the player can vary the attack and take advantage of opportunities off the edges of the scrum.

On defense, the scrumhalf first puts pressure on his opposite and the other number 8 to prevent them from easily clearing the ball. He's also called upon to make tackles when the offense targets his side of the scrum for attack.

Communication with the number 8 is vital to successfully transfer the ball from the back of the scrum to the backline. This transition from set play (scrums or line-outs) to general play depends upon how well in sync numbers 8 and 9 are in all situations.

Engagement

By this stage, the eight forwards should be bound together into one powerful unit. The players in the front row crouch relatively low, with their shoulders slightly above hip level. The opposition forwards get into scrum formation in exactly the same way. The two groups now face each other in readiness to come together.

Before a scrum can begin, the referee makes sure the scrumhalf has the ball and the front rows are no more than an arm's length apart. The referee then calls, "Engage," which is an invitation rather than a command. The two teams charge into each other so that the heads of the front-rowers interlock with those of their opposite numbers (see Figure 8-3 for an example of this).

Figure 8-2:
The two packs engage to form a scrum.

Next time you watch a match, listen carefully when the scrum engages and you'll hear bodies colliding and players grunting as they exert themselves to the limit. Sometimes, you'll also hear the pack calling out a cadence in unison to coordinate their shove.

Following the engagement, all 16 players in the scrum flex their legs forwards and keep their backs straight.

The area on the ground that is formed between the two packs is called the *tunnel*, and is where the ball will be put in by the scrumhalf. If the scrum rotates or moves off the mark too far, and doesn't immediately stabilize, the referee will usually reset the scrum. Until the ball leaves the halfback's hands, the scrum must be stationary and neither team can push until the ball is inside the scrum.

The put-in

Holding the ball in both hands, the scrumhalf prepares to throw it into the tunnel. When he is ready to begin, the hooker signals for the number 9 to deliver the put-in. When the scrumhalf gets the signal, he puts the ball in play. The throw-in must be done right away, and if the scrumhalf delays putting in the ball, the defending side is awarded a free kick. The ball must be thrown in with a single forward movement, without any spin on it. Trying to trick the opposition with a fake put-in is strictly prohibited.

This is a case where what's written in the law book and what happens on the pitch is very different. The law says that the ball has to be put straight down the middle of the tunnel, but in practice this almost never happens. As long as the put-in is not too far on the side of the offensive team the referee will usually let play continue. This makes it very difficult for the defensive team to steal possession at scrumtime.

The contest for possession

The scrum begins when the ball leaves the scrumhalf's hands. Once the ball touches the ground in the tunnel, any front-rower may use either foot to win possession of the ball. What is not allowed is for any front-rower to have a foot in the tunnel before the ball is put-in by the scrumhalf.

Hookers develop individualized styles of winning the ball but the key is having a quick strike and soft touch on the ball, so that you maintain good control of where it goes. Play around with different styles to see what feels the most comfortable to you. Once you find a technique that works for you, practice to perfect it — you should find it easier to win the ball when your movements are deliberate, not spontaneous.

After the ball has been hooked, the ball is then channeled backwards between the two second-rowers, towards the number 8 who then holds it in the scrum with his feet until he or the scrumhalf decides to play it.

Whatever happens in the scrum, no one is allowed to touch the ball with their hands until the ball has been cleared. A scrum is over when the ball comes out in any direction (except out the tunnel), or when the number 8 unbinds from the scrum and picks up the ball.

Laws at Scrumtime

The laws governing scrums are constantly being tinkered with in the interests of producing a fair contest for the ball and ensuring safety. First, we'll give you some of the general restrictions and then we'll move on to more specific rules.

When a scrum is called after an infringement, it is set wherever the infraction occurred (unless the infraction happened within 5 meters of the touchline or the tryline. In such cases, the scrum begins 5 meters in from those lines).

A full scrum has eight players from each side, but is legal with as few as five participants. There is no requirement for the opposition to reduce their numbers to match the other team when players have been sent off or because of injuries.

Binding and releasing

Every player in the scrum is required to bind onto a teammate with at least one arm until it ends. When any player binds onto a teammate in a scrum, that player must use the whole arm from hand to shoulder to grasp the teammate's body. Placing only a hand on another player is not satisfactory binding. This prevents flankers from disengaging early from a scrum, enabling them to gain a defensive advantage.

Props are the only players who are permitted to grab an opponent. Loose-head props bind onto the opposing tight-head props by placing their left arms inside the right arms of the tight-heads and gripping the back or side of the tight-heads' jersey. The loose-head must not grip the chest, arm, sleeve, or collar of the opposition tight-head. Loose-heads must not exert any downward pressure. This is designed to keep the scrums from collapsing. (See the next section for more details about collapsing.)

Tight-head props bind onto the opposing loose-head props by placing their right arms outside the left upper arms of the opposing loose-heads. Using their right hands, tight-heads must grip the loose-heads' jerseys. They're also not allowed to grab anywhere else or force the scrum down. All other players in a scrum have to bind onto a lock's body with at least one arm. Everyone has to stay bound until the scrum is over.

Collapsing

If a scrum collapses and goes to ground, the referee must blow the whistle immediately to ensure that players stop pushing. This is a safety precaution and is one of the few situations where advantage can't be played. (See the "Advantage Law" section of Chapter 6 for when advantage can be played.)

There are a few rules that focus on preventing scrums from collapsing. Front-row players must not:

- Twist or lower their bodies
- Pull opponents, or do anything that is likely to collapse the scrum, either when the ball is being thrown in or afterwards
- Fall or kneel in a scrum

There is a lot of leeway here between what is actually written in the law and what happens in most scrums. As long as it doesn't collapse and the ball comes out, most referees won't spend too much time scrutinizing everything that goes on in the front row. They will, however, strictly penalize any voluntary collapsing of the scrum because of the dangerous nature of this act.

You can't spend too much time working on your front-rowers' scrummaging technique. Regardless of the laws, opposing players will employ a variety of tactics that can result in a collapsed scrum. Your players need to know how to counter these moves and remain on their feet.

Driving in and up

Front-row players are prohibited from lifting an opponent and can be penalized for doing so deliberately. Regardless of who's responsible, if a player in a scrum is lifted in the air or is forced upwards out of the scrum, the referee must blow the whistle immediately to stop players from pushing.

Lifting an opponent in the air during a scrum is now illegal. It has been banned by the International Rugby Board (IRB) because it can cause serious injury. Sometimes though, players pop out of their own accord because they are under too much pressure. This can also be penalized.

Feeding

The scrumhalf is supposed to throw the ball straight down the middle of the tunnel between the two front rows but this almost never happens. On the infrequent occasion when a scrumhalf is penalized for this infraction it is called *feeding* and results in a free kick to the opposition.

Lax enforcement of the law against feeding has made stealing a put-in at the scrum a rarity. When you successfully hook the opposing team's throw in, that's called a *tight-head*, or *taking one against the head*.

The scrumhalf is also prohibited from *dummying*, or faking a pass, once the ball is ready to be removed from the scrum. If the scrumhalf reaches in and puts his hands on the ball to take it out, then emerges without it and fakes a pass, he can be both tackled and penalized.

Strategic Scrummaging

In addition to securing possession, the scrum can be an outstanding weapon. The primary goal of any pack is to at least be able to win your own scrum put-ins and provide a good platform for your backs to use the resulting possession. This is why most coaches will tolerate a prop that isn't the most effective player around the park if he is a good scrummager. Losing your own ball on scrums is a recipe for disaster on any team, and is certain to be ruthlessly exploited by the opposition.

The scrum can become a multi-faceted attacking platform in different positions and situations. The key to using the scrum effectively is having your pack players be well versed in a number of different techniques and options depending upon what you are trying to accomplish.

Attacking from the scrum

What makes a scrum the ideal set piece to launch an attack from? First, the opposition's best defenders, their back-rowers, must remain bound to the scrum until it is over. This limits their range because it takes them longer to get into the open field. It also gives the offense the element of surprise because they can probe with either backs or forwards. Second, because the offensive backline of the team with the put-in is much closer to the point of attack on a scrum, the defense has less time to react to planned moves.

The best attacking position is a scrum in the middle of the field. This forces the opposition to split their backs because they don't know which side the thrust will come from. Ideally, your scrummagers will push the opposition backwards during the scrum, which puts them into reverse and makes defending even more difficult. Any team worth its salt should be able to win almost every one of their own scrums throughout a match, which gives an air of confidence about starting the offense at scrumtime.

A scrum set near the sideline creates a natural attacking avenue down the *blindside,* or the short side, of the field. The reason why teams target the blindside is that it's less congested with defenders than the wide side of the field. Typically, the blindside is guarded by the weak-side wing, which is left all alone to stop the advance. Teams look to create a mismatch down the blindside, with a back-row forward charging at a wing. Nothing is more tantalizingly tasty to a back-rower than a lone wing isolated one-on-one between you and the promised land.

Wheeling the scrum

Purposefully turning a scrum by a concerted effort of your pack is called *wheeling.* When the other team has the put-in, wheeling is a way of creating a turnover. If you can wheel the scrum past 90 degrees (so that the tunnel has passed beyond a position parallel to the touchline) it has to be reset and this time your team gets the put-in. (See Figure 8-3 for an example of wheeling the scrum.)

There are also situations where a team would want to wheel their own scrum. When close to the goal line, wheeling causes one of the flankers to be rotated further away from the point of attack. Remember, they have to stay bound until the scrum is over, and are thus at the mercy of the wheel.

Another time to use the wheeling technique is when you attack down the blindside. The main pack defender in this circumstance is normally the blindside flanker (who is closest to the short side of the field). If the flanker's shoulders are allowed to remain parallel to the tunnel of the scrum the player is in perfect position to stop a scrumhalf or number 8 who charges down the short side. As the scrum wheels around, the player is forced to go with it, making the tackling angle more difficult.

Wheeling can be used to create turnovers at key times during a match. For example, if your opponent has the put-in on their 5-meter line (that is, near your tryline), turning the scrum past 90 degrees gets you the ball in an excellent attacking position with little risk involved. Late in the match when defending under your posts, attempting to wheel their scrum is a risky choice, but if you have confidence that your pack can work the wheel, you might get the ball and prevent the opposition from getting a try.

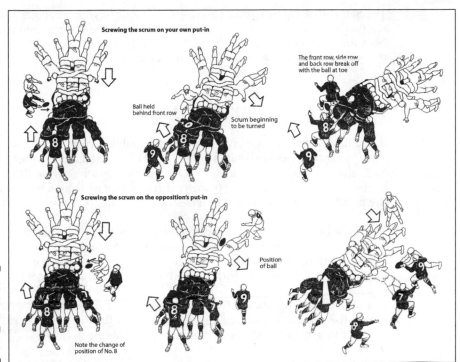

Figure 8-3:
Wheeling
the scrum
past 90
degrees.

If your scrum is getting repeatedly wheeled, you can counter by having your front row step sideways in unison against the direction of the wheel. The motion looks like a crab walking sideways, which is why it's called *crabbing*. Instead of the scrum continuing to rotate on its axis, crabbing causes the scrum to move sideways, stopping the wheel.

Getting a shove on

If your team can achieve the power and skill to win every one of your put-ins, the next step is to strive for physical domination of the opposing pack. This will help immeasurably in the prosecution of your goals and in all other phases of play.

Initially your team should attempt to push the opposition off their ball at every opportunity in the scrum. Even if your players are unsuccessful at winning the opposition's ball, driving the other team backwards is an important defensive tactic. Doing so forces the opposing scrumhalf and number 8 to play the ball more quickly and under more pressure, often leading to rushed passes and mistakes in getting the ball to the flyhalf. It also causes their entire backline to edge backwards while yours can be moving forward, thereby stifling the opponents' attack.

The same idea can be used as an offensive tactic. If your team can consistently shove the other team's scrum back, it puts the opposition's defenders on the *back foot*, meaning that they have to retreat to stay onside. This opens up more attacking options and demoralizes the opposition.

Pushing it over the edge

If you have a scrum near your opponent's goal line you can attempt to score a *pushover try*. After the ball is hooked and channeled back under the number 8's feet, the scrum slowly advances toward the tryzone, while the number 8 keeps the ball in, controlling it with his feet. Once he thinks he can make it, the number 8 picks it up and crashes over the line to ground the ball.

Scoring a pushover try is rare at the international level but much more common in club matches, where the scrums are more likely to be one-sided. There's nothing more uplifting than completing a pushover try — and nothing more demoralizing than being driven back into your own in-goal area.

In a physical sense, domination at scrumtime boosts your forwards and drains the other team's. This means less energy for them during rucks and mauls, further enhancing your conquering capabilities.

Chapter 9

Line-outs: Restarting from Touch

*I*f you appreciate the aerial artistry of basketball, you'll love the line-out. It features the timing and technique of a jump ball with a twist unique to rugby — the jumpers are allowed to be lifted to even greater heights by their teammates. This results in a visual treat where players are hoisted high into the air and a competition for possession takes place a dozen feet off the ground.

Line-outs are the primary method of restarting play after the ball has gone over one of the touchlines (and therefore out of bounds). Line-outs always take place on a touchline and they are instantly recognizable by the two parallel lines of players who face the sidelines waiting for the ball to be thrown-in. (See the "What do all those lines mean?" section in Chapter 2 for full details about the touchlines.)

For most of rugby's history, line-outs were a confused jumble of bodies that usually ended up producing more stoppages than quickly usable balls. The introduction of legal lifting has made the line-out one of the more entertaining parts of the game where true competition for possession flourishes. In less than a decade, the line-out has been transformed from an unsightly phase that favored one-dimensional players, to a dynamic display of athleticism, strategy, and teamwork.

This chapter will unlock the secrets of this highly competitive part of the game. We'll give you a full description of the line-out, detail the variety of roles played by those involved, and explain the rules that the players must follow. Plus, we'll provide insight into the tactics that make the line-out a thing of beauty, and finish up with an examination of prohibited behaviors.

When Does a Line-out Occur?

The line-out is used to get play going again after the ball has gone over the sideline and into touch (out of bounds). It doesn't matter how or why the ball went over one of the sidelines; if it goes out of bounds, play is restarted with a line-out (but there is one exception that we explain at the end of the chapter). That means that if the ball is kicked out, carried out, driven out, or simply rolls unattended over either of the touchlines, a line-out is the prescribed way to re-ignite the action. That part is easy, where it gets more difficult is in determining when a ball actually has gone into touch, thus necessitating a stoppage in play.

Line-outs and the Touch Law

So how can you tell if the ball is out of bounds? The touch judges are the arbiters of this question. If they deem that the ball has gone into touch, they raise their flags to indicate this fact to the referee, who then blows the whistle.

Basically, the Touch Law states that any time the ball, or a player carrying it, comes into contact with the touchline or the ground beyond it, it's in touch. If the ball crosses the touchline in the air and is then blown back or caught by a player in the field of play, it's not in touch.

Where Does a Line-out Take Place?

Line-outs always take place on a touchline. The exact location varies depending on factors such as where the ball went out of touch and how it got there.

In cases where a player is bundled into touch with the ball or an errant pass trickles over the line, it's easy to figure out where the resulting line-out will ensue: at the place where the ball crossed or came into contact with the line. The touch judge will then stand at that exact spot with a raised flag and not move to either side until the line-out is over.

But where it gets more complicated is when the ball is kicked into touch by a player on either team. When the ball is kicked out, the spot for the line-out is determined by where the ball was kicked from and how it went out of play. (See Figure 9-1 for a diagram explaining touch and throw-in location.)

Directly into touch

When the ball is kicked out of bounds and it doesn't touch the ground or another player on its way out, it has been kicked straight out or *directly into touch*. The location of the kicker determines where on the sideline the line-out will be held.

- ✔ If the player who kicked the ball out of bounds is on or behind his own 22-meter line, the line-out is formed where the ball went over the line (see Chapter 2 for an explanation of the 22-meter line). This is a strategically profitable kick because it gains territory.

- ✔ If the kicker is in front of his own 22-meter line when the ball goes directly into touch (kicked out *on the full*), the line-out is taken from where the player made the kick. This means the team doesn't gain any territory — and the kicker loses friends. (Tired and emotional forwards hate having to run back to where a player has kicked the ball out on the full.)

- ✔ If the player kicks the ball out of bounds on a penalty kick (to gain territory and set up an attacking line-out), it doesn't matter where the ball is kicked. The line-out takes place where the ball goes over the touchline.

- ✔ If the player kicks the ball directly into touch from a free kick, but is in front of his 22-meter line, the team does not gain any territory. The line-out is taken from where the player kicked the ball — so make sure you know the different signals for a penalty kick versus a free kick (see chapter 5 for all the referee signals).

Indirectly into touch

When the ball bounces infield or hits any part of a player before going out, it has been kicked *indirectly into touch*. When this happens it doesn't matter where the ball was kicked from, the line-out is taken at the point where the ball crossed the line.

If you have at least one foot either on or inside the 22-meter line, you are considered to be behind the 22-meter line. If you catch the ball outside your 22-meter line, and then take it back behind the line before you kick it, you won't gain the territory. You can, however, pass the ball to a teammate who is behind the 22 and still gain ground from the kick.

On a penalty kick, where a player opts against kicking for goal and instead kicks for touch to gain yardage and set up an attacking line-out, it doesn't matter where the kicker is standing on the field. The line-out takes place where the ball went over the sideline. (See Figure 9-1 for examples of touch and the place for the throw-in.)

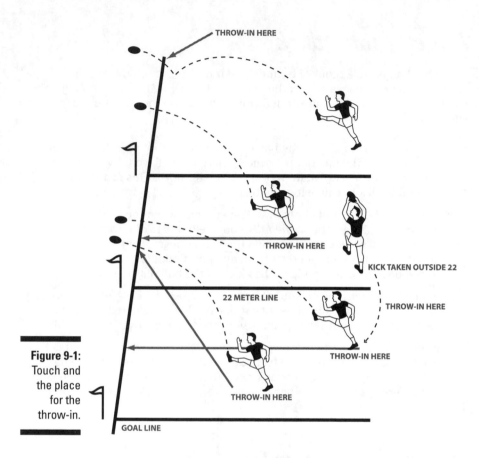

THROW-IN HERE

THROW-IN HERE

KICK TAKEN OUTSIDE 22

22 METER LINE

THROW-IN HERE

THROW-IN HERE

THROW-IN HERE

GOAL LINE

Figure 9-1:
Touch and
the place
for the
throw-in.

Who Gets the Throw-in?

The law determining which team gets to throw the ball in at the line-out is straightforward. Whichever team last kicked, touched, or was in possession of the ball before it crossed the touchline, loses possession. A member of the other team will get the honor of throwing the ball to the players in the line-out. (The team awarded the throw-in at a line-out has the advantage because they know where the ball is going.)

It isn't always easy to tell which player was the last to have contact with the ball, so the touch judges are required to keep up with play and follow the progress of the ball as it makes its way up and down the pitch. When the ball goes into touch, one of the touch judges will signal by raising the flag and pointing with his free arm in the direction of the team that will throw the ball in at the resultant line-out.

The exception to this law is when a penalty has been awarded. In this case, the non-offending teams know that they will get the throw-in. (Remember, players can kick the ball directly into touch during a penalty kick and take the line-out where the ball leaves the playing area, gaining territory for their team.) This is especially common when a team is backed up in their own end and want to advance the ball, or when they're near the opposition's tryline and need to score more than three points. (See "Understanding the Scoring System" in Chapter 2 to learn about the point system of rugby.)

When you carry or kick the ball into touch, it amounts to a *turnover*, since the other team gets the throw-in. This enables tacklers to use the sideline as a sixteenth defender, by driving the ball-carrier into touch whenever the runner is near the sideline.

One of the most common errors for inexperienced ball-carriers is not being conscious of where they are in relation to the touchline. When coming into contact with a defender within 5 meters of touch, your players should lower their body position and lean infield to prevent the defender from driving them out. This is easily practiced with a ball-carrier, a defender or two, and a sideline.

Lining Up for a Line-out

In its simplified form, a line-out consists of two straight rows of designated players from each team who line up facing the sideline. The ball is thrown in between the two lines and the players attempt to secure it for their side to use. When the two groups get into position for a line-out it looks haphazard and casual, but the exact opposite is true. Every move and placement, from the initial location of each individual to the spacing between them and where they end up, is choreographed with attention to detail.

A line-out doesn't officially begin until the ball is thrown in, but the process starts as soon as the ball goes into touch. First, the line-out has to be correctly formed, then a decision on each team's strategic intent is internally taken. This is followed by the actual execution of the play and the distribution of the ball, all without running afoul of the law. A line-out is not over until the ball is passed or run out of the area between the 5- and 15-meter lines (except when a ruck or maul forms after the ball is thrown in, then the line-out isn't over until that phase has cleared the initial line-of-touch).

Forming a line-out

A line-out is considered formed when at least two players from each team are lined up at the spot where the ball went into touch. The players from the competing teams face the touchline in two straight rows, with a space of 1 meter between them. Like in a scrum, this area is called the *tunnel* or *gap*. The middle of the tunnel should be at the spot where the ball went out, called the *line-of-touch*.

The line-out exists in a contained area. The front boundary is 5 meters from the touchline and is marked by the 5-meter line. The rear limit is designated by the 15-meter dash lines, giving each team a total of 10 meters to work with. Every player that is part of the line-out must stand between these two points. Two players who are exempt are the one throwing the ball in and the receiver, who stands behind his line of players. The defense is also allowed a receiver, plus a person to mark the thrower, usually the opposing hooker. He can stand between the sideline and the 5-meter line. (Figure 9-2 illustrates a typical line-out formation.)

The number of players that take part in the line-out is determined by the team that has the throw-in. The number varies depending on personnel and strategy. (In the 1999 World Cup, Ireland used a 14-man line-out against Argentina!) A standard line-out has seven players in the line and one player throwing the ball. A line-out formation with fewer than the standard eight forwards is referred to as a *short line-out*.

On offense, each team decides the best tactical way to win their line-out and can vary their numbers throughout the match. The opposing team can choose to have fewer players in the line-out, but they cannot have more.

On the offensive team, once a player is part of the formed line-out, he cannot leave it. The defense has a little bit of leeway here. If they send seven players to the line-out and the offense puts fewer in the line, a corresponding number of defenders can leave without being penalized, provided they do so in a reasonable amount of time.

Figure 9-2:
Throwing-in
at a line-out.

BROWNIE SAYS

Breaking the code

For the first several years of my rugby career, I played for Occidental College and the Oxy Olde Boys. Because there was significant interchange between the two teams we used the same line-out calls. A series of words and numbers would be shouted out by the hooker but it was the second digit of the second number that determined where the ball was going. Very simple and not too tough to grasp. As I played for other clubs I was exposed to more complex coding systems that I adapted to without too much trouble. Eventually though, I ran into problems during my years playing in Latvia, especially in training with the national team. Their calls were a mix of Latvian and Russian numbers interspersed with slang. I never could keep them all straight, so ultimately the lock I was lifting, Wilmars Sokolovs, would wait until the calls were done and then he'd tell me in English where the ball was going! Problem solved, since he and I were usually the only English speakers on the pitch.

A few years later in Northern Ireland I ran into other issues while training with Ulster and Portadown. The Ulster code was complex and involved using calls that began with the letters from three key words. For example, let's say the three words were "front," "middle," and "back." If the call began with one of the letters from the third word, the throw was going to the back (so if the call was "blue, yellow, green" the ball would be thrown to the back because the first letter of the call begins with the first letter of the third code word). Most of the time I'd get it right but occasionally I'd find myself lifting the wrong man or being in the incorrect spot. This perplexed me until a discussion with the other prop revealed that I had one of the three words slightly wrong because the player who explained the calls to me had a pretty thick accent that I thought I had figured out.

The Portadown club used countries, beers, and banks to signal where the ball was going and after numerous training sessions I thought I had everything memorized. During the first match though, I ran into trouble with a call I'd never heard and I guessed had to be a country. Scotia, however, turned out to be a bank. By the time I started coaching the Oxy women's team I took the easy way out and had my players make dummy calls with the hooker indicating where the throw was actually going by holding the ball in either her left, right, or both hands.

Calling the play

Just like a quarterback in football calling an audible at the line of scrimmage, a certain player (it varies from team to team and could be the hooker, the receiver, the captain, or anyone else in the line-out) is given the important task of making the calls. Timing and coordination are key aspects of successful line-out play so it is absolutely vital that everyone involved knows exactly what the plan is on each throw-in.

Before every line-out, the attacking team decides who the ball will be thrown to and what they'll do after winning it. For example, a particular call might mean that the second jumper will receive the ball and then everyone is supposed to form a maul and drive forward. The line-out caller uses a code system to let everyone on his team know what is about to happen while preventing the opposition from knowing what they are up to.

At training under the coach's direction, the line-out players work on a system of codes for various plays. It may involve numbers or code names, but it has to be understood by everyone to avoid confusion. A throw can be short, long, looping, or bullet-like, depending on the signal or code words used. Some teams are even more sophisticated and have more than one player calling signals to confuse the opposition. Only they know which calls are real and which are decoys. Your code should be simple but flexible enough to accommodate all of your line-out schemes, without requiring that your team be loaded with secret code breakers — you want to confuse the opposition, not your own players!

Throwing in the ball

The throw is usually made by the team's hooker, but anyone on the side can restart play if necessary. To be effective the hooker has to have the ability to vary his throws from quick, hard ones at the front, to higher ones in the middle, and more lobbed ones to the back of the line. For a throw to be legal it has to travel at least 5 meters and straight down the middle of the tunnel. The thrower cannot step onto the field of play before releasing the ball. The referee will normally allow a throw that is slightly off center, but not a throw that blatantly favors the receiver's side. The ball leaving the hooker's hands signals the official beginning of the line-out.

The player who throws the ball in must be consistent and precise in his delivery so he can hit his jumpers with regularity. Timing is of the essence to prevent the opposition from getting their hands on the ball. Mastering the technique of throwing in can be very difficult. The skill requires excellent hand-eye coordination and a good sense of spatial anticipation. The thrower needs to visualize the apex of the lifted player's hands as the target and throw to that spot before the jumper actually gets there. The beginner will miss the mark most of the time and provide the opposition with a chance to steal it. This can be extremely frustrating, even for professional players, who go from hero to zero from one week to the next on the strength of their throwing accuracy.

Hookers need to practice throwing at every training session. They should start with both feet about half a meter behind the touchline, so they can step forward on their follow-through without stepping onto the field. Work on hitting all the spots where your jumpers will be using varying amounts of loft and zip to avoid defenders. The thrower needs to be in tune with each jumper's technique and preferences. If the wind is up at training, rejoice and take advantage of the inclement weather to have your hooker work on adjusting his throws to account for the force of the breeze.

Aspiring hookers can never get enough throws at training and since it's unrealistic to recruit a pack of forwards to come over for a few hours while you play a one-sided game of catch with them (at least without a well-stocked cooler), the best thing to do is find a wall or set of goalposts to throw at. Make marks at different points on the target that approximate the varying maximum heights attainable by your jumpers and then alter your distance from them to simulate their different positions in the line, then throw until hitting them all becomes routine.

Taking the throw

To help a jumper get as high as possible in the line-out, his teammates can lift him heavenward. The catch is that they are also responsible for bringing him safely back to earth.

The best result in a line-out is for the jumper to cleanly catch the ball. This isn't always possible so the next best thing is to tap the ball back to your side in hopes that the receiver or another line-out player will be able to secure it. When they are up in the air, line-out jumpers can use either their inside arm or both arms, provided they're over his head, to grab or redirect the ball. Once the ball is taken, the jumper should turn his body on the way down, so that he's facing his teammates when his feet touch the ground. This allows the other forwards to bind-in around the jumper to protect the ball from the opposing pack and also provides a good mauling platform.

The opposition's jumpers try to figure out where the ball is likely to go and then try to launch themselves to the right place to win the ball. Defensive lifting is even more challenging because the lifters never know where their jumpers will take off from. Contesting the line-out works best when you have instinctive leapers with excellent timing.

Starring Roles in a Line-out

The line-out requires an array of unique skills that must be performed with precision to successfully compete. Just like casting for a theatre company, the line-out performers must be able to play various parts and be versatile enough to switch roles when the situation demands. The players involved in line-outs are almost always forwards, and they're usually required to fulfill multiple duties at various times during the match. (It might be useful to review the "Fearless Forwards" section of Chapter 4 for details about the positions of the players discussed in the following sections.)

Jumpers and lifters

Before players were allowed to lift one another in the line-out, each player had a designated position that rarely varied. The advent of lifting led to more strategic line-outs and now most teams will lift at least three different jumpers in various places up and down the line. To confuse the opposition they may also switch around the roles of players and use jumpers as lifters.

Winning squads used to be the ones with the tallest players who had the longest arms. Now the dominant teams are the ones with the most accurate throwers and best coordination between jumpers and lifters.

Jumpers

Line-out jumpers are still usually the two locks and the tallest of the back-rowers. Whoever they are, they have got to possess balance in the air and good hands. Jumpers should have good footwork so they can quickly move into several different positions in the line. Part of their craft includes faking jumps to draw their opposite off the ground, and also not giving away their true intentions when they're going to get the ball.

The responsibilities of the lifters are as important as those of the line-out jumper. One lifter is positioned in front of the jumper and one behind him. They must work in tandem and be perfectly coordinated to ensure that the jumper reaches the top of his leap a split second before the ball gets there. Figure 9-3 shows a jumper being assisted as he reaches for the ball.

Lifters

Lifters need to be strong and able to confidently lift some of the biggest players on the field. It's not easy to hoist a 240-pound man more than six feet in the air and then hold him there until he catches the ball!

There are two similar techniques used to lift a jumper, depending on whether you are in front of him or behind. When you're the front lifter, the key is to stay low and close to your jumper with your knees bent and your butt lowered. You should support the jumper by gripping the thighs just above the knees so you can attain the maximum lift possible. The lifting power needs to come from your legs and not your arms or back. After the player jumps, extend your arms straight over your head and use your legs to push the jumper up even higher. When he reaches the zenith of his jump, your arms are locked-out straight over your head.

While the basic technique of lifting with your legs and extending your arms is the same for the back lifter, your contact point with the jumper is different. The back supporter should grasp the jumper's legs, just beneath the buttocks. The back lifter has the primary responsibility of providing the initial thrust to help get the jumper airborne.

Figure 9-3:
Getting a lift
as the ball is
thrown in.

The receiver

The receiver position has traditionally been filled by the scrumhalf. This makes sense because once the ball is won, he's the best person to distribute the ball to the waiting backline. Recently though, teams have successfully expanded the role of the receiver by making him into another line-out jumper. From his position behind the players in the line-out, the receiver is allowed to enter the line before the throw-in.

Even if the receiver is not going to enter the line, he still has to be a player with great hands because he is invariably called upon to consolidate loose possession. When the receiver is a forward, teams will also use him to attack right away after a line-out or provide a critical shove to get the maul moving forward once the jumper comes down.

Movement in the line-out

The concept of movement in the line-out is also a relatively new one that has flourished since the introduction of lifting. Movement of jumpers and lifters up and down the line is used to prevent the opposing jumpers from settling

Keystone Kops

Not all modern line-out developments have been good. Some coaches and players have become too fond of trying to outsmart each other by devising complex and elaborate line-out tactics — and sometimes they outsmart themselves. Wacky line-out maneuvers that have players running this way and that (some making dummy runs and others being used as decoys), can appear comical. In the end it looks like a totally out-of-control Keystone Kops routine where everything goes wrong and the opposition wins the line-out ball. There's nothing worse than running through a series of moves and then having the referee blow the whistle to penalize your side for delaying the throw. The best strategy is to keep unnecessary movement to a minimum, making it sharp and accurate with a definite purpose.

in one particular place to contest the throw-in. When a team's jumpers are on the move it's harder for the opposition to steal the throw because they don't know when the movement will end or where the ball is going.

A moving jumper can reach greater heights than a stationary one. It takes a lot of practice to coordinate a moving jumper, two lifters, and the throw-in all converge on one spot at the same time, but when it's done right it looks effortless and is an incredibly graceful display of power and athleticism.

Talking Tactics Down the Line

The line-out has become an elaborate action-adventure, with designated jumpers, special jumps, decoy moves, and more subterfuge than a James Bond movie. The basic aim, though, remains unchanged. Every team wants to set up a good platform to launch their attack. The key is to be able to execute different forms of incursions equally well, so as to keep the opposition off balance. Once the jumper has his mitts on the ball, the options are limitless.

The element of surprise is one of the best weapons available to a team at a line-out. If the defenders are unclear about what form the assault will take, it's tougher to position themselves appropriately. Just when they get ready to counter one tactic, you throw another one at them, thus increasing the overall effectiveness of both moves.

Peeling off

One effective line-out play involves the jumper tapping the ball down to a moving (or *peeling*) forward. The peeling player has to stay within a meter of the line-out until receiving the ball, but can then cut upfield around the front or rear edge of the formation. The key here is to get past the line-out defenders quickly and thrust immediately into the backline. Timing is essential to pulling this move off, but because the peeling player is already moving and the defenders are static, it can lead to clean breaks.

Throwing to the front

Hitting a non-jumper at the front of the line is an option when your traditional jumpers are having trouble securing the ball. For this to work, the defenders must be concentrating on the jumpers, leaving the man at the front unguarded. The opposing hooker will generally be able to tackle this player as he goes down the blindside so the real benefit comes from the man who receives the ball being able to pass to his hooker who is all alone with room to run.

One cheeky variation for throwing to the front of the line-out involves the front lifter getting in position to support the front jumper, but then just as the ball is thrown he turns around to face the hooker and receives the ball via a quick low throw. The key to pulling this off is having the player taking the ball position himself slightly infield, to make sure the ball travels at least 5 meters before he moves forward to take it.

Setting up the maul

Line-outs are a particularly good time to initiate a driving maul (see the "Mastering the Maul" section of Chapter 7 for details of the maul) because all the required players are in close proximity and the defense is preoccupied with stealing the throw-in. As soon as the ball is taken and the jumper is returned to earth, the other forwards bind-in to form the maul and start pounding ahead with concerted effort. It is important to get the ball out of the jumper's hands and moved quickly back so that the opposition has no chance to take it away.

An effective variation on this tactic is to get the maul going (which sucks in defenders) and then immediately spin the ball wide. This gets the defense moving in the wrong direction and creates chances for your backs to break through. An extra benefit of successful mauling from the line-out is that teams will sometimes stop contesting the throw-in and concentrate exclusively on stopping the maul.

Quick off the top

The standard method of distributing the ball from the line-out is to bring it down, consolidate it, and then have it ripped off the jumper and transferred to the scrumhalf. For a speedier way of getting the ball to the backline, the jumper can toss the ball directly to the scrumhalf as soon as the catch is made, saving valuable seconds. This requires a jumper with excellent balance in the air and a deft passing touch. If the jumper can't cleanly take the ball with two hands, the ball can also be redirected using one hand (either way this move is called a *tap down*).

Every one of these tactical moves has a multitude of variations that can be adapted to your team's strengths. Don't try to pull off stunts that your players can't effectively perform. Get the basics right first and then experiment with adding more options.

Things you can't do

More than any other area of the game, the line-out is all about being controlled in your behavior. The Line-out Law is the longest one in the book, detailing a laundry list of prohibited actions.

The primary focus is on the thrower's responsibilities. For a line-out to be legal the ball must be thrown straight down the tunnel, travel at least 5 meters, and the hooker can't step into the field before he releases the ball. The opposition cannot prevent the ball from going at least 5 meters.

Attention then shifts to the other players in the line-out and what they can't do. As a general rule they are not allowed to hold, push, grab, or in any way make contact with the opposition across the line of touch. It's okay to contest the ball but you can't do so by taking out the other player in the air. When the jumper is in the air, leave him alone! The same goes for the other lifters, they have to be left alone until they bring their jumper down. Using an opponent to gain leverage for a leap is also on the banned list of techniques.

Other violations involve the offside lines at the line-out. Before the ball is thrown, the offside line is the middle of the tunnel, afterwards it's the ball itself. A line-out is not over until the ball is passed or run out of the area between the 5- and 15-meter lines. When a ruck or maul forms after the ball is thrown in, the line-out isn't over until that phase has cleared the initial line of touch. For players not in the line-out, their offside line is 10 meters back from the line-of-touch, and they can't advance until the line-out is over.

Taking It Quick

At the beginning of this chapter, we said that there was one exception to using the line-out to get play going again after the ball goes out of bounds; it's called *taking it quick* (when a player opts to quickly throw the ball back into play instead of waiting for a line-out to form).

A quick throw can be used to restart play when the ball has gone into touch, but there are several restrictions governing this practice. A player on the team who will get to throw the ball in at the line-out can instead opt to throw it in quickly from anywhere behind the line-of-touch as long as the line-out hasn't already been formed. The thrower has to use the exact same ball that was previously in play and it can't have touched anyone on the sideline, including touch judges, ball boys, photographers, spectators, etc.

The beauty of a quick throw is that it allows you to re-ignite the attack right away without letting everyone get realigned. Defenders often use the time after the ball has been kicked out to rest and regroup, making it a perfect time to launch an unexpected foray. (So after a long clearing kick, the first concern of the chasers should be preventing a quick throw-in. This is easily accomplished by following the ball downfield and marking the player who picks it up.) The only danger of a quick throw-in is that you can't count on support from your teammates unless you advance the ball to where they are.

Taking it quick also has a unique aspect in that players can throw the ball in to themselves as long as it travels the required 5 meters. Quick tosses also have to be straight (but for some reason this is mostly overlooked by the majority of international referees).

Taking it quick can be a good decision when the kicking team has out-kicked their coverage. This occurs when either the kicker really nails the ball and it carries beyond where the player's teammates can cover, or when the chasers fail to get downfield to play defense. You should only take it quick if you have ample time and the right opportunity presents itself. Otherwise, since the majority of line-out balls are retained by the team with the throw-in, you're better off letting the forwards do their thing and take the moment to catch your breath.

Chapter 10

Individual Skills

In established rugby countries, learning the game starts at a very young age. The skills necessary to become a complete player are introduced and developed over time, building a solid foundation onto which tactical acumen can later be added. Coaches with a lifetime of experience guide youngsters through the essential steps to rugby proficiency as they grow and mature.

In North America we tend to pick up the game later in life, and coaches lack the deep reservoir of knowledge relied upon so heavily by nations where rugby is an imbedded part of the sporting culture.

Instruction in our part of the rugby universe runs the gamut from extraordinary to almost non-existent, and when it is offered, ends up necessarily being more concentrated into a short time span and is heavily reliant upon trial and error while playing. As a result, sometimes even the best players who excel on superior athleticism tend to lack complete skill sets.

Rugby is a game where everyone must possess basic skills regardless of position. Players are expected to instantly switch from offense to defense and vice versa throughout a match. There's no place on a rugby team for one-dimensional players deficient in fundamental running, passing, kicking, or tackling skills.

In this chapter, we'll explain the basics of how to run, pass, kick, and tackle so you can understand the different techniques that players use. We will also provide you with plenty of tips so you can fill in any gaps in your game and perfect your rugby craft.

Running Rampant

Running is an integral part of the sport, essential to playing both offense and defense. While there's certainly nothing wrong with speed, if you can't adapt your running style to handle and pass the ball properly, you'll actually hurt your team more than help. Some of the best rugby players are not the fleetest of foot, but they fulfill their positional responsibilities by practicing good form.

When carrying the ball, you need to be constantly thinking of where the defenders are and what your supporting players are doing in relation to your movements. On top of all this, you should always be mindful of your primary goal — not to lose possession of the ball.

Running in an upright position might work on the track, but try it in a rugby game and you'll get seriously thumped. The best running position for rugby is to lean forward for balance and effective weight distribution. The rugby running style enables you to adapt to whatever is going on around you. You need to be able to quickly react to the situation at hand; you must be able to change directions, accelerate, slow down, and move in all sorts of ways, which a lower body position facilitates. Lowering your center of gravity allows you to react more quickly on the fly.

Running at full pace with the ball will take a little practice before you feel entirely comfortable. When running in the open field, you should hold the ball in both hands in front of your body. This allows you to pass to either side of your body and keep the defense guessing. If you have to get ready to pass the ball, it's usually too late to do so.

When you can't avoid being tackled and there's no one to pass to, the ball should be shifted into your outside arm and held tight against the side of your body. Tacklers will often target the ball in contact, with the goal of dislodging it from your grasp, so you need to hang on to the ball, to keep the bad guys from stealing it.

To preserve possession throughout the tackle situation, practice running into contact while carrying the ball under one arm. This skill requires the ball to be tucked or cradled between your arm and rib cage or armpit, where it will be protected from the opposition's defending players. Carry the ball in the arm furthest away from the defender and you can use the other arm to either fend off your opponent or push away from him when he attempts to tackle you. As you make contact, keep your body between the ball and the tackler. Once you're brought to ground, you have to release, but remember that you're entitled to place or immediately pass the ball, so don't relinquish it too early.

Receiving a pass on the run

Receiving a pass is difficult at first because so many things are happening at the same time. Once the elements are broken down and methodically practiced with precision, ball-handling errors will be dramatically reduced. The receiver should catch the ball while maintaining awareness of the defenders in order to choose the best option.

Whenever you're running in support of a ball-carrier, you should be thinking about where space might be created and how you can exploit it if you get the pass. This is a very subtle and elusive skill that comes from game experience and watching world-class players. Because humans can only look in one direction at a time, your sense of the defensive team's presence and where the gaps are likely to be, is primarily gathered through your peripheral vision.

Prior to receiving a pass you should look at the passer and verbally communicate that you're ready for the ball to be delivered. Before the ball is passed, reach out with both hands to provide a target for the passer, and to get ready for the ball's impending arrival. As the ball nears, extend your arms to meet the ball and catch it with your fingers, while watching the ball into your hands.

When a teammate passes to you, don't take your eyes off the ball until after you catch it. One of the most common mistakes is momentarily losing sight of the ball at the last second to sneak a peak at the defense. Changing your focus too soon may cause you to knock-on and then get knocked silly as you attempt to regather your fumble. (See Chapter 6 for full details about the knock-on.)

Side-stepping the tackler

A *side-step* occurs when a ball-carrier heading in one direction suddenly changes course and heads off on a different path. This move is one of the easiest and most effective ways of getting past an opponent. A good time to use a side-step is when you're running with the ball and a defender lines you up for a one-on-one, open field tackle.

To set up the side-step, run directly at a would-be tackler, which will cause the player to slow down while preparing to make the tackle. Just before the collision, slow down a bit and tuck the ball under one arm for safety (see Figure 10-1a). If you want to side-step to your right, drop your body weight onto your bent left leg, planting the foot firmly on the ground, drop your shoulder to your left, and then drive hard off your left leg and push away in a sideways direction to your right (see Figure 10-1b). (To add to the deception, before you push off towards the right, feint with your upper body to make your opponent think you are about to go left.) Once you have side-stepped around your opponent, accelerate to full speed and continue your run. The key is to slightly reduce your pace before you make your move and to explode off the driving leg to create as much distance as possible between you and the defender.

While the side-step may sound a bit like a fancy move from an eighties disco movie, it's a great skill in rugby because, if it's done well, the defender in front of you looks pretty foolish grabbing thin air as you cruise by.

Figure 10-1:
Stepping out with the side-step.

Curving into the swerve

If you have the pace and space to run around your marker, the swerve is the move for you. The *swerve* is similar to the side-step, involving the ball-carrier initially running directly at the defender then curving away just before contact. The ball-carrier usually makes only a slight swerve of the body, and if done at high speed, it can be very effective in getting past a defender.

To swerve to your right, first bob to the left with a slight turn of the shoulders as your right leg moves forward. Then take a long stride across the running line with your left leg and move your body away to the right as your right leg comes through. The key is to swerve as close as possible to the tackler, to force them to commit, reducing the player's reaction time to adjust and make the play.

Fending off forcibly

Occasionally, despite our svelte physiques and blistering pace, even your esteemed co-authors sometimes fail to completely evade all 15 defenders. When contact becomes inevitable, you can use the tackler's momentum to your advantage by using your arm to push the tackler away, which is called *fending off*. This is a move common to both the rugby pitch and the football field.

To fend off, carry the ball in one arm, then just before the collision, turn your body so that your free arm is facing the direction where the contact is coming from. As the defender attempts to make the tackle, thrust your free arm directly at the closest part of the defender's body, usually his head or shoulders (see Figure 10-2b). The ball-carrier pushes the tackler away and down to stop his momentum (see Figure 10-2c). This action gives the runner leverage and pushes him off the defender, so he can pick up speed and accelerate away before the would-be tackler has time to recover. (See Figure 10-2 for more detail about the tactics described here.)

Figure 10-2:
Fending off a would-be tackler.

Going into a hit and spin

In the *hit-and-spin* move, the ball-carrier commits to contact and then bounces off and spins out of harm's way. You should run at the tackler, get lower than your soon-to-be victim, and drive your shoulder hard into the player's upper body while keeping your feet under you. As you bump-off the tackler, spin or roll away. The spin is made by quickly twisting, swiveling your hips, and turning your back on the tackler.

The more space you create with the initial bump-off, the easier it will be to spin away from your opponent. The key here is to keep your arms free so that the ball can be distributed if the tackler is able to hang on and stop your progress.

Doing the goose step

The *goose step* is when the ball-carrier takes three or four quick steps, lifting his legs with his knees locked straight (as shown in Figure 10-3). If done quickly, it leaves the defense totally bamboozled and hopelessly off balance. The goose step is a tricky, fairly advanced move, that requires a very high level of athleticism to pull off.

Australian legend David Campese was the master of the goose step and left many otherwise solid defenders scratching their heads wondering, "Which way did he go?" If you think this move sounds easy, try it at full speed on the pitch.

Notable running styles

The greatest single example of running rampant in recent memory was New Zealand's rugby colossus, Jonah Lomu, knocking over everyone in sight to score repeatedly in the 1995 World Cup. Lomu simply ran through, straight over, or around everyone and everything.

Players, both past and present, use guile and brilliant changes of pace and direction to make them extremely dangerous when they have the ball in hand. Since very few are blessed with

Lomu's size, strength, and agility, the key to successfully running the ball is to use your head to beat the tackler. Smashing the tackler but losing control of the ball is a victory for the defense. You can't expect to make every defender miss, but if you are mindful of your body position in the tackle, are able to maintain possession, and provide recyclable ball for the next phase of attack, you've done your job as a ball-carrier.

Figure 10-3:
Goose-
stepping
your way
around the
opposition.

Throwing the dummy

A *dummy* is simply a fake pass. By throwing a dummy, you lead your opponent to believe that you are going to pass the ball to a teammate, but at the last minute (just as your opponent changes direction to follow the ball), you pull it back and continue running.

This move involves faking the pass with your eyes, arms, and body, while maintaining awareness to see if the defender bites on the misdirection. Once the tackler takes the bait and commits toward the receiver, pull back the ball and cut upfield. If you don't do a good enough job of selling the dummy, get ready to be hit hard by the tackler.

Passing with Panache

Passing the ball is one of the most elementary of rugby skills that should be the first one taught to all newcomers. The goal of passing is to provide a ball that is easily caught by a teammate who is in a better position to continue the attack.

When preparing to make a pass, hold the ball upright in both hands, with a hand on either side of the ball, fingers spread wide with the thumbs-up to ensure control and balance. When you're ready to pass, swing the ball across your body in the opposite direction of the target. (So if the pass is going to the right, first swing the ball to the left side of your body.) Then swing your arms and shoulders back towards the teammate you're passing to and release the ball. The ball should leave your hands quickly and with a snap. (See Figure 10-4 below.)

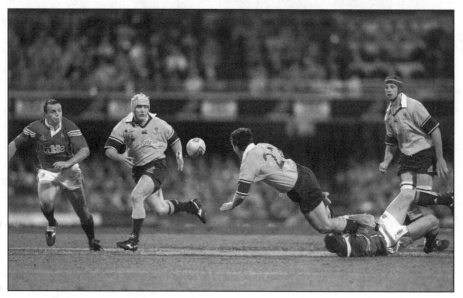

Figure 10-4:
Passing the
oval ball.

Making a good pass means you involve your whole body and are well coordinated. Other factors that are critical to a good pass are the following:

✔ **Accuracy:** Accuracy is vital. When you throw the ball to your teammate, don't throw it directly to him, throw it just slightly in front of him so that he can run on to it and collect the ball at pace. It's much better for him to have to speed up to catch the ball than to have to slow down. A good pass travels on an upward arc that he can catch somewhere between his waist and his chest. If he has to bend over or leap to get the ball his stride will be broken and the defenders can more easily close on him.

For better accuracy and distance, increase the rotation on the ball by bending your arms and turning your wrists slightly as you release it. Your two pinky fingers should be the last in contact with the ball.

- ✔ **Velocity:** Speed is important. Throw the ball with some velocity to ensure that it maintains its height and does not drop before reaching the player who is going to receive it. A pass that is headed downwards is twice as hard to catch as one that is going up. When passing in tight spaces, don't put too much mustard on that hot dog, or the receiver will struggle to control the ball.

- ✔ **Tactical awareness:** Only pass when your teammate is in a better position to continue the attack. Passing the ball to someone who is surrounded by defenders is not only pointless, it's dangerous. A good rule to think of is that you're responsible not only for your pass but also for the next one as well; don't pass the ball if the player you're passing to won't have the opportunity to pass it on, unless of course, they're streaking down the sideline for a try.

Bringing tactics into play

Once you've learned how to pass, the next step is understanding when to do so. One of the most basic tactical skills is drawing the defender and then passing before you get tackled. *Drawing the defender* means getting the tackler to commit to you, which prevents him from covering other attackers.

If the player with the ball passes it too early, the defender might have enough time to change direction and chase down the receiver. To avoid this, lure the defender to commit by running at him. Then before you reach the defender, who is preparing for the tackle, you pass the ball to a teammate who is in a better position to continue the assault.

The ball can be passed much faster than players can run across the field. To demonstrate this principle, challenge your fastest player to run the width of the pitch in pursuit of the ball, while it is being passed along the backline. If your passing skills are adequate, the ball will always beat the man. This is also known as *letting the ball do the work*.

Spiral pass

A *spiral pass* is made when you put some spin on the ball, causing it to rotate as it moves through the air. The hand furthest away from the direction in which the ball is about to be thrown moves up over the ball as it is thrown, which makes the ball spin. (If the ball is being passed to the left, the right hand comes up over the ball, giving it a counter-clockwise top spin, as shown in Figure 10-5.) The advantage of a spiral pass is that it flies straighter and flatter because it is aerodynamically superior to a ball which doesn't have any spin.

Figure 10-5:
Spinning out
with a spiral
pass.

Cut-out pass

When you pass the ball out along the line and deliberately skip the receiver next to you, it's called a *cut-out pass* (as shown in Figure 10-6). The pass travels right in front of the adjacent player, but instead of reaching out and taking the ball, he fakes grabbing it and lets it fly by to the next player in the line. The phrase *two-man cut-out* means that the ball-carrier has thrown the ball past the first two players next to him in the attacking line, sending it instead to the third man in the line.

For example, the flyhalf may pass the ball beyond the inside center and outside center, and straight to the wing (see Chapter 4 for an explanation of where each player lines up on the field). This is usually a predetermined move, but can be executed spontaneously if the passer sees the space outside.

If you are the player being cut-out, do your best imitation of someone expecting to get the ball in order to deceive the opposition. The pantomime includes having your hands ready for a pass and running in your usual position in the backline. At this point, the ball-carrier should make a fast spiral pass, because speed ensures that the cut-out is effective. The ball has to be thrown quickly and accurately so that the outer backs have the maximum amount of time to do something with the ball before the defense can react.

Figure 10-6:
Making a
cut-out pass.

Lob pass

A *lob pass* is a high, looping pass which goes just over the outstretched arms of the opposition. This type of pass is used when you are on attack and find yourself crowded by defenders who are running in the passing lanes between you and your support. The only way to pass in this situation is to lob the ball over the defender's heads to one of your teammates.

Pop pass

A short floating pass in close quarters is called a *pop pass*. It's a versatile transfer where the pass is carefully weighted to allow the receiver to easily take the ball without breaking stride. The ball is passed using one or both hands. Start low and lift your arms and wrists to pop the ball up to the receiver. This should not be a bullet or flat pass, and should have a little loft under the ball so the receiver can catch it between his waist and shoulders.

If you find yourself caught in the tackle but your hands are still free, you can utilize a pop pass to deliver it to a teammate who's running close by in support. The goal is to make the pass as easy as possible to catch, as your receiver is likely to be charging through a tight gap and needs to focus on where the defenders are coming from, not on reaching for a wild pass. Scrumhalves often use the pop pass off the fringes of rucks and on tap penalty plays to transfer the ball.

Dive pass

When you dive forward and pass the ball from underneath your body with a scooping motion, it's called a *dive pass*. This pass is mainly used by scrumhalves when they find themselves under pressure from the defense, usually at the back of the scrum, and need to get the ball away very quickly. Because you're diving away from pressure when it's made, the dive pass also creates a little distance between you and the nearest defender.

Scrumhalf pass

The *scrumhalf pass* is the standard type used by the number 9 to distribute the ball. The essential elements for this pass are that the scrumhalf has his feet behind the ball and his weight initially over it. By staying on his feet and taking a step towards his target, the scrumhalf builds momentum without a time-consuming backswing. When executed properly, the ball goes straight to the target, quickly and with a nice trajectory, making it easy to catch.

The scrumhalf should be your team's best passer. He's responsible for passing it from set pieces and distributing it out of rucks and mauls.

Through practice, scrumhalves learn exactly how to get the ball to their closest teammates. The skill is acquired through hours of training, where the scrumhalf throws the ball to the flyhalf, centers, and wings without looking to see where they're positioned (rugby telepathy, if you like). Scrumhalves have to be the master of every type of pass because they are often forced to improvise when getting the ball out of tricky situations.

Kicking Cleverly

Despite the fact that rugby emerged as a handling game from soccer, kicking still plays a central strategic and tactical role. Kicking in the oval game takes a variety of forms and is used primarily to gain territory, restart play, or score points. While all kicks are similar in that you launch the ball with your boot, they diverge greatly in technique depending on what you're trying to accomplish.

If you are just starting to coach youngsters or beginners, you can do your team no greater service than making sure every player has fairly good kicking skills. You can guarantee that sometime, somewhere in a game, every player is going to be called upon to kick the ball. Nothing is more pleasing than seeing a tight forward forced into a situation where his skilful footwork is suddenly called upon in a desperate circumstance and he delivers flawlessly. It might be the only time he ever puts boot to ball, but when it comes off it's a thing of beauty.

An adept kicker is an asset to any rugby team and, like every other basic skill, learning how to kick effectively requires heaps of practice.

Spiral punt kick

The *spiral punt* is an all-purpose kick that is usually the first one you learn. The basic skill looks just like an NFL punter kicking it away on fourth down. The best method for punting the ball is to make it spin off your boot (shown in Figure 10-7). This corkscrewing action is extremely effective because as the ball leaves your boot, it goes the longest distance and is very accurate.

When you want to kick the ball deep into opposition territory with a *clearing kick* (a kick that clears the ball out of your end), the spiral punt is the best kick to use. It is also easy to learn. Here's a step by step approach to doing it right (see Figure 10-7 for more details):

- ✔ Hold the ball in both hands well out in front of your body, with the ball at an angle so it can spiral off your foot when kicked.

- ✔ Drop the ball at an angle of about 30 degrees towards the center of your body (see Figure 10-7a).

- ✔ Shift your weight onto your non-kicking foot, which should be aimed at the target, while drawing the kicking foot back (see Figure 10-7b).

- ✔ Swing your kicking foot straight through so that it strikes the ball along its long axis. Point the toe of your boot out as you make the kick.

- ✔ Adjust the flight of the ball by changing the angle of your foot and the point at which the ball is struck in its fall.

- ✔ Extend the arm on the opposite side of your body for balance.

- ✔ After the ball is dropped onto your foot, your boot should move slightly across the ball, somewhat like a corner kick in soccer. Watch the ball move all the way onto your boot, and then follow through.

If the kick is done properly, the ball will spiral off your boot. The spiraling effect makes the ball go farther and straighter than the usual punt kick (which usually floats in the air with less distance gained). A right-footed kick will cause the ball to spin clockwise from left to right, and vice versa for a left-footed kicker.

Just like a good golf swing, you don't want to kick the ball too hard. Through trial and error you'll quickly discover just how much force you need to accurately propel the ball the full distance. Once you have the right technique and can regularly hit the ball's sweet spot, you'll be amazed at how far a rugby ball can fly.

Figure 10-7:
Kicking a
spiral punt
for distance
and
accuracy.

Up and under

An *up and under*, or a *Garryowen*, is similar to the spiral punt but is modified for a different purpose. The kicking technique is the same except that the ball is held in the hands so the point and not the side of the ball is facing down. On impact, your boot makes contact with the pointed end of the ball. The goal is to keep it in play and put it high enough to provide hang time for your chasers to contest the ball as it returns to earth. The strategy behind an up and under is that it tests the nerve and concentration of the recipient's fullback and forces the opposition's forwards to retreat.

When making an up and under you have to weight the kick so that the ball comes down just outside your opponent's 22-meter line. That way, the player trying to catch the ball has to deal with tacklers and pray for support from forward teammates. If the ball goes inside the 22-meter line, the receiver can call for a *mark*, like a fair catch in football, which stops play and gives the opponent a chance to kick the ball away.

Chip kick

A short punt kick that's calculated to go just over the head of an advancing defender, is called a *chip kick*. The goal of a chip kick is to regather the ball in the open space immediately behind the opponent.

Figure 10-8:
Testing the opposition with an up and under.

Taking a chip kick on the run is particularly difficult and requires a deft boot, but that's when the option usually presents itself and is hardest to defend against. Chip kicks work because the laws prohibit a defender from impeding any player who has just kicked the ball in his efforts to regain possession.

When chipped with just the right touch, the ball will often be caught by or bounce up for an attacking player to re-gather and continue the attack. Chip kicks are used when the defense is up flat with superior numbers, because once you kick the ball, they've got to leave you alone.

Grubber kick

A short punt kick that travels low across the ground is known as a *grubber kick*. The goal is to create top spin on the ball, causing it to quickly roll forward on the pitch, end over end (as shown in Figure 10-9). This is a good tactical kick when done properly, because the ball scoots along the ground and can bounce in any direction at any moment. Chasers have the advantage of gathering the ball because they are reading the bounce as they follow it and are less likely to be thrown off by an unpredictable hop.

To make a grubber kick, drop the ball and strike the back half of the ball just before it hits the turf so it skips low along the ground (see Figure 10-9a). This kick is an effective tactic when the opposing defensive players are coming up fast and you want to put the ball in behind them.

Figure 10-9:
Rolling out a
grubber kick.

Drop kick

Attempting a field goal during general play is called taking a *drop kick*. Slotting a drop goal is rare, but it gives your side another scoring option when you're near your opponent's goal line and can't break through to score a try.

To take a drop kick, move forward with the ball in both hands, plant your non-kicking foot and draw back your striking leg as you drop the ball onto the ground. It should land on the pointed end and bounce straight back up a couple of inches. The place to drop the ball for a right-footer, is about the width of your hips to the right of your planting left foot.

The object is to contact the ball with your boot a split second after it rebounds off the ground. Timing the kick and being able to control the dropping of the ball takes a very long time to perfect.

For the past couple of seasons, before training started and while everyone else was getting their kit on, we've developed a little fantasy game where we simulate the final drop goal from the Rugby World Cup 2011 . . . the Eagles are down by two, it's the last movement of the match, and the 40-something ageless wonder, out of nowhere, gets the ball and squares-up for the match-winner, strikes the drop, the jam-packed Rose Bowl crowd holds its collective breath, and it's good! The Eagles win the Webb Ellis Cup! (We can dream, can't we?)

Goal kicking

Goal kicking involves placing the ball on a kicking tee, making your approach to the ball, striking it, and following through. Contests between evenly matched teams are usually won by the side with the more accurate goal kicker. Having a reliable goal kicker in your team is a necessity, not a luxury. Goal kicking is a specialist skill, so usually only a few players can handle the responsibility. It's important to have more than one kicker so that if the main guy is injured a suitable replacement is already on the field.

While in Brian Vizard's day back in the 1980s there might have been a few straight ahead kickers left, it's an ancient technique that's gone the way of the dodo bird. Virtually all kickers in the modern game use the round the corner style for kicking goals. The main elements are a measured approach, (or *run-up*), planting the non-kicking foot, striking the ball, and following through. As shown in Figure 10-10, this requires the following step-by-step approach:

1. **Position the ball on the kicking tee.** The usual way to place the ball for a kick is to stand it on end, angled forward towards the goalposts you are aiming for.

2. **Walk back from the ball.** Take about four paces backwards and then take two paces to the left, for right-footed kickers. (If you kick with your left foot, take two paces to the right.)

BROWNIE SAYS

1 for 1 lifetime

In my junior year at Occidental College I became obsessed with the drop kick. It began with the Santa Barbara tournament the previous year where I heard that a drawn match would be decided by five players from each team taking drop kicks from the 22-meter line. Wanting to be ready to help my team if I was ever called upon in this unlikely situation I began practicing drop kicks before and after almost every training session for the next two seasons. Drop kicks are not easy and my success rate at first was pitifully low but eventually through trial and error I found the method that worked best for me. With a lot of practice I actually got pretty good at slotting the ball through the uprights (without any opposition of course and usually off a good patch of grass).

Late in my senior year, after blabbering endlessly to my coach and teammates about how I knew I could make a drop goal in a match, I finally got my chance. We were playing UC Riverside and as I was late arriving at a ruck (not an uncommon occurrence) our captain Dave Hodges, later skipper of the USA Eagles, told me to get ready to drop one so I took my place at first receiver. We won the ball, our scrumhalf passed it to me, I banged it through from about 30 meters out, and the referee blew the whistle and awarded us three points. To this day I've never attempted another in a game but still fantasize before and after training about winning a match with a long drop. If the situation ever arises, I'll be ready.

3. **Approach the ball in a slight arc, in a slow relaxed manner, with your eyes focused on the part of the ball you intend to impact.** Coming at the ball in a slight arc gives the required curl to the run as you approach the ball from the left (if you kick with your right foot). The curl to your run-up creates a slight right-to-left action on the ball when it's in the air, helping its trajectory and keeping it on line. The curl also improves the distance of the kick.

4. **Push your hips forward with the final stride, plant your non-kicking foot, and extend your arms for balance.** The last stride with your non-kicking foot must be the longest, with your planted foot ending up slightly behind and the width of your hips away from the ball. The plant foot should be aligned with the toes pointed at the goalposts.

5. **Swing through and kick the ball.** Your kicking foot should strike the ball on its end where the four seams come together. The top of your foot (near the big toe and instep) contacts the bottom of the ball driving it forward and up. Your foot should be extended as you swing your leg through, pointed in the direction of the target. Your chest should be facing the target at impact.

Goal kickers can come from any position (see "The kick that won the game" sidebar for an example), so if you think you've got the knack for it, practice your goal kicking — you never know when you might be drafted into the role.

Figure 10-10:
Goal-kicking
technique.

Getting into goal-kicking form

Goal kicking requires hours and hours of practice to get right. So get a ball, go down to the local park, and experiment until you are comfortable with a goal kick that suits you. Concentrate on the ball until after the moment of

The kick that won the game

Australian rugby seems to revolve around last-minute kicks. One of the most famous last-minute kicks occurred in 2000 when the Australian Wallabies met the New Zealand All Blacks in Wellington. Wallaby captain John Eales was only given a few seconds to compose himself before taking a kick that would determine where the Bledisloe Cup would end up. (The Bledisloe Cup is an annual trophy with great historical and emotional significance for the competing nations, Australia and New Zealand.)

Five minutes into extra time, New Zealand was leading 23–21 when All Black replacement prop, Craig Dowd, was penalized for an infringement at the breakdown. Eales assumed that the team's regular goal kicker, Stirling Mortlock, would take the shot, until he was informed that Mortlock had left the field a few minutes earlier with severe cramps. So it was up to the skipper to select a replacement goal kicker. Having been the Wallabies kicker in the past, he didn't hesitate to indicate to the referee that he would take the fateful kick himself.

Eales had the onerous responsibility of kicking a penalty goal about 25 meters out from the goalposts and 15 meters in from the sideline, in a swirling, fluky breeze, to determine the outcome of the match. A poor kick and the Cup would be lost to New Zealand.

Rising to the occasion with ice water coursing his veins, Eales casually slotted the ball straight through the goalposts, prompting scenes of ecstasy among the Wallabies as they celebrated the tightest of victories over their fiercest rivals.

impact by keeping your head down and eyes on the ball. Always remember to follow through when kicking for goal. The follow-through ensures that the balance and coordination needed to put the ball through the goalposts is maintained.

If you carefully watch the world's leading goal kickers, you'll notice that they each have their own particular style. From teeing-up the ball to approaching it, from striking the ball to following through, there's a myriad of techniques that work. The one thing leading goal scorers have in common is that each time they kick for goal, they display the exact same routine and a relaxed kicking motion. So encourage your players to experiment and develop their own style to make kicking for goal routine.

Tackling Tough

In football, the object of tackling is simply to bring the runner to the turf by whatever means necessary, because that immediately stops play. In rugby, taking down the ball-carrier is only first part of a sequential contest for possession that begins with the tackle itself.

Since the rugby tackler's job only starts with bringing the runner down, players must always be mindful of body position throughout contact to increase the team's chances of creating a turnover (stealing possession of the ball). This difference is particularly significant when trying to coach former football players, who tend to opt for the big hit, rather than being focused on winning the ball.

For a beginner, the prospect of having to tackle someone is often daunting. When you join a rugby club, great emphasis should be placed on teaching players how to tackle properly. *Tackle bags* (large, vinyl-covered bags filled with foam) are used to help players perfect their techniques without getting hurt and to ensure that they get it right before they actually have to tackle in a match.

The key to teaching and learning how to tackle is to break down the activity into its basic elements and then work slowly to build a progression of drills that simulate the skill. Even though you'll start out on your knees, you need to walk before you can run when it comes to tackling training. Once you have a solid understanding of the basics and confidence in yourself, tackling can become one of the more enjoyable parts of the game. Bear the following in mind:

- **The fear factor:** You can overcome the fear of injury. While it is natural to think that trying to stop a rampaging forward who is charging straight at you is going to inflict damage on your person, the reality is that you won't get hurt if you tackle correctly.

- **The focus factor:** To be a good tackler, you must possess the ability to block everything else out of your mind as you prepare to make the tackle. Tackling is a precise battle of mind over matter.

The real secret of tackling tough is to convince yourself that you can do it. Once you overcome that hurdle, you'll discover that it really doesn't matter what shape or size you are — you can effectively tackle any opponent and not get hurt.

When tackling, don't be cautious or half-hearted about it. Those who do not tackle with 100 percent commitment are the first to get hurt; those who trust their instincts become great tacklers and a vital asset to the team.

Developing a good tackling technique takes time, but it's not difficult. Once you've acquired the skill, you can improve it at training sessions — even the best players regularly return to the tackle bags to keep their tackling techniques up to scratch. As with running, passing, and kicking, there are different types of tackles, which require different techniques.

Front-on driving tackle

A *front-on driving tackle* is used when a ball-carrier is running directly at you. To make a front-on driving tackle correctly follow these steps:

1. **Assess the situation as your opponent approaches.** Figure out the best type of tackle for the situation, which shoulder you are going to use to hit the opponent, then convince yourself that you are going to be successful.

2. **Lean forward and use one of your shoulders to aim at the spot where you want to hit your opponent.** As you prepare to tackle, push forward with your shoulder, targeting the spot where you want to hit, as shown in Figure 10-12. You are not allowed to tackle above the line of the shoulders and should aim between the hips and the knees.

3. **Use your legs to drive into your opponent.** It is important that you launch your tackle from a balanced, low position with both feet on the ground to generate as much power as possible when you drive your shoulder into your opponent. Good tackling begins with the lower body and is finished with the upper body.

4. **Keep your head aimed to the side of your opponent's body.** Your head position is very important. Your chin should be tucked in on your chest, which has the effect of hunching your shoulders, while your back should be straight. By choosing a shoulder to tackle with early on, and by placing your head to the side, you will avoid flying knees and elbows that you would have taken if your head was in front. You should never use your head as a weapon like in football.

5. **Drive into your opponent, grabbing him tightly around the waist.** Drive hard into the ball-carrier to push him backwards and upwards. Wrap your arms tightly around him and hold on (see Figure 10-11b). It's not crucial in rugby to smash the opponent, it's more important to make sure you bring him down, even if you get dragged a few meters.

Figure 10-11: Making a front-on driving tackle.

6. **Try to get the ball from your opponent.** Keeping a strong hold on your opponent so he can't get out of the tackle, try and get some part of your hand, arm, or body on the ball, because that can help to dislodge the ball from his grasp.

7. **Try to regain your feet and win the ball.** Once you are both on the ground, you must release the ball-carrier and immediately attempt to regain your feet and try to steal the ball before anyone on the other team arrives at the breakdown.

You should start beginners off slowly by kneeling, standing, stepping, walking, jogging, and then finally running into tackle drills (see Chapter 18). This allows them to grasp the elements of the tackle slowly and build their confidence.

Side-on tackle

When the ball-carrier is trying to run around you and turns slightly sideways, you'll want to use a *side-on* tackle. A *side-on tackle* is made when you aim your shoulder at the ball-carrier's hip, just below the waist, and place your head behind or alongside the player's inside buttock. After hitting the ball-carrier with your shoulder, put your arms around the player's thighs and squeeze tight. Keeping a strong grip on the thighs has the effect of dragging your opponent down.

When making a side-on tackle, never put your head across the body of the runner, as you're likely to catch a driving knee or thigh on your noggin. If you've played football, you've been coached to put your head in front of the player and you'll need to adapt your tackling technique for safety. Your head should be safely behind the ball-carrier and away from danger.

Tackle from behind

Another variation of the driving tackle is the tackle from behind. When chasing the ball-carrier from behind, the tackler targets the area just above the knees, as shown in Figure 10-12. The tackler's arms encircle his opponent's thighs with a firm grip, which effectively traps his legs and drags him down.

Figure 10-12:
Diving in to
tackle from
behind.

Ball and all tackle

When you tie-up the ball and prevent the runner from passing in contact, it's called a *ball and all tackle*, or *smother tackle*. The advantage of this technique is that you slow down the runner's progress while hindering their ability to recycle the ball. The objective is to at least prevent the ball-carrier from quickly passing the ball to anyone else.

The technique can be made from the front chest to chest, from behind by wrapping your arms around the runner, or any other way you can pin the ball in the tackle. A successful ball and all tackle will prevent the ball from being passed by your opponent so it can only be transferred to another player after you both go to ground and he releases it.

Stationary tackle

The *stationary tackle* is similar to the ball and all tackle, but here the ball-carrier is running right at you while you are stationary. By preparing yourself for the front-on impact and, when it comes, holding on tightly, using the ball-carrier's momentum you can topple your opponent forwards and over your body.

Use the stationary tackle if you are a smaller player confronted by a large forward. If you hold on doggedly and vigorously, you can upset your opponent's balance.

Ankle tap

Even if a ball-carrier has blown by you, it is still allowed to hit his feet with your hand in an attempt to trip him from behind. This is a last ditch effort to bring him down.

An ankle tap takes perfect timing and an effective tap, but it does work. Usually the defender makes a diving attempt at the ball-carrier and tries to disrupt his stride by smacking one of his ankles inward, so that it collides with the other leg and trips the runner. When you ankle tap a player it is essential that you get right back to your feet and pursue him because as soon as he regains his feet he can take off running again.

Chapter 11

Tactics and Teamwork

• •

• •

*I*n North America, we have plenty of athletes; what we struggle to develop are instinctual rugby players. Even when the basic skills are mastered, we lack the key decision-makers in critical positions that other countries produce in abundance. For example, the tactical awareness of a 15-year-old New Zealander is typically miles ahead of a 25-year-old North American, because we start playing the game so much later in life. This places an extraordinary burden on our coaches to open their players' eyes to the tactical possibilities available to them.

As a coach, you need to fully appreciate what your players can and can't do and then develop a style of play that best suits your strengths. Conducting a brutally honest appraisal of your side and a balanced evaluation of the opposition before each game will assist you in developing the most appropriate game plan for every match.

We're not going to promote a particular type of playing style in this chapter because we'd rather give you the information to make an informed decision based on what kind of talent you have at your disposal. In this chapter, we'll provide you with a framework for establishing a game plan, talk about adapting to the elements, detail how to put points on the board, and give you a structural way to defend against all comers.

Creating a Game Plan

The most important element in any rugby team is that all of your players have a solid grounding in basic skills. Planning complicated moves and intricate defensive systems is useless if your chargers can't pass, catch, and tackle.

Once the essentials are taken care of, then it's time to move on to strategic concerns. (See Chapter 10 for full details about running, passing, kicking, and tackling.)

The burden of choosing a particular strategy rests with the coach. Implementing a sophisticated game plan will only work if the time is taken to explain all aspects of it to the players so that they understand the concepts they'll be asked to carry out on the pitch.

The most important first step in attack and defense is to devise a good plan. Everyone in your team must understand the plan and know what is expected of them. Winning teams concentrate initially on working out the best method for overcoming the opposition, no matter what style they play. Plans have to involve the whole team whether they are simple or complex, because any weak link will be ruthlessly exploited by the opposition.

You also need to know which of your players are capable of adapting their game on the fly in case you need to alter the game plan during a match. Your number 8, scrumhalf, and flyhalf should all be able to make in-game adjustments, so keep that in mind when selecting players for those key positions. A game plan doesn't have to be complex to work, so don't feel the need to script every play like a football coach. Keep it simple and stick to what the team does well.

Understanding your team's strengths and weaknesses

The first step in assessing your team's strengths and weaknesses is to look at the size, speed, and fitness of the players. This can be done by testing on the pitch and in the weight room. Simple physical evaluations will give you a good idea of which players are your fastest, strongest, and most fit.

The level of experience of your players will also help in the decision-making process. Maturity and knowledge of the game are vital parts of a successful squad. Once you've got a good handle on your players' physical abilities and match experience, you're ready to select a team and start building a strategic foundation.

Just as every player possesses unique talents, each rugby team has a distinctive character that defines how it will play. To fully evaluate your side's strengths and weaknesses, break their performance down into its various elements. Assess the set pieces, rucking and mauling, how effectively they contest possession, and their overall competence in general play.

When you examine your side, look at both the positive and negative components of its play:

- ✔ Do you have a strong forward pack that usually wins their own scrums and provides good clean ball at the back, or are they being pushed around and barely getting the ball out?

- ✔ Are your forwards adept at rucking and mauling, or is the breakdown a source of frustration, turnovers, and penalties?

- ✔ Do you have reliable jumpers in your line-out that consistently win possession and occasionally steal the ball from the other team, or do your jumpers struggle to win their own throw-ins and concede the opposition's?

- ✔ Are your back-rowers getting to the tackle situation and making an impact there, or are they late, indecisive, and ineffective?

- ✔ Can your flyhalf and fullback read the game and make good tactical decisions, or do they lack the vision to make the correct choices under pressure?

- ✔ Do you have backs with the skills to move the ball quickly who utilize their pace to cross the gain line, or is every trip down the line a retreating exercise waiting for the next knock-on?

- ✔ Do your backs tackle well in the open field, or are they a line of matadors?

Your appraisal needs to be totally impartial. This is a time for clinical observation, where you need to focus on what your players can and can't do. Then, you need to put aside your preconceived notions and institute a style of play that takes advantage of their talent and minimizes their deficiencies.

Winning the set pieces

The best way to guarantee that a team has every chance to beat an opponent is to have a solid forward pack, which means that the forwards must attempt to dominate in all areas of play. At the very least, these players must hold their own in scrums and line-outs, win the ball in tackle situations, and must get clean ball out to the backline.

If your team can't get or keep the ball in rugby, it's impossible to win. Forwards are responsible for winning possession of the ball a majority of the time, so it's logical to build the strongest pack from the best athletes available. A solid but unspectacular backline will perform exponentially better when they are working behind a dominant set of forwards. If the forwards are poor, however, a great backline will be wasted.

The primary focus of any pack is to be able to win their own scrums. This takes hard work, dedication to the task, and countless hours of training time. Short changing scrum practice is a recipe for disaster. Putting out a team of fantastic backs that never get the ball because their forwards are getting steamrolled is one of the most frustrating experiences in the game. To keep this from happening, scrummagers must feel confident that they can win their own ball before moving on to other tasks. (See Chapter 8 for a rundown of requirements for a strong scrum.)

If you have a dominant tight five (two props, the hooker, and the two locks) that consistently drives the opposition off the ball, scrums will be attacking platforms for your side no matter which team has the put-in. On the other hand, if you're being beaten and pushed around up front, you need to adjust your game plan to minimize the damage.

After scrums, the line-out is the next most important set piece confrontation. Timing, teamwork, and accuracy of movement and throws are the key factors to winning the ball at the line-out. Even teams that lack height and gifted jumpers can be productive at the line-out as long as they work together as a unit. (See Chapter 9 for full details about line-outs.)

If you are winning your line-outs with regularity, it opens up a whole host of attacking options. Start with the driving maul, transition to a rolling maul, and when they make adjustments to stop it, try the peel into midfield or down the blindside. (See Chapter 7 for details of driving mauls, rolling mauls, and peeling.)

If you're consistently losing the line-outs on your team's throw-in, you've got a serious problem, and you need to change your approach. Try throwing deep beyond the 15-meter line, or to the front lifter to mix things up. Even if you lose these throws, they aren't likely to make a clean steal. If you're not having any success contesting the opposition's throws, concede the throw-in and concentrate on stopping their mauls instead.

The most overlooked set pieces are kickoffs and restarts. In a normal match there are usually at least four or five opportunities for each team to secure possession in this way. Unfortunately, this is often worked on infrequently, if at all, by many lower level teams. Being ready to contest kickoffs and restarts and having a definite plan for getting the ball and distributing it to the right players during these set pieces will markedly improve your team.

Well before each game, take your captain aside and discuss what options should be chosen in every situation. Do you prefer a scrum, line-out, or a re-kick if the restart doesn't go 10 meters? When you have the choice, do you want to kick for touch to gain territory and restart play with a line-out, or elect to set a scrum to get things moving again? These decisions require a sense of how you expect to match up against the other team and will invariably need to be refined on the fly as the match unfolds. If your captain has the game plan down, making the right choices becomes much easier.

Playing the ten-man game

The *ten-man game* refers to a strategy in which a team focuses play around the eight forwards, the scrumhalf, and the flyhalf. (The backs are usually neglected and hardly see the ball.) The object of the ten-man game is to keep the ball in tight amongst the pack and drive directly through the heart of the opponent's forwards.

Playing the ten-man game is a tactical decision to consider when the players on your team have a clear advantage over the competition up front, but are comparatively weaker in the backline and out wide. This type of game requires a totally dominant pack, a scrumhalf who provides good service, and a flyhalf who kicks the ball accurately, efficiently, and deep. As for the rest of the backs, they are primarily selected for their defensive prowess and ability to prevent turnovers.

In the ten-man game, the forwards usually keep the ball in hand, especially if they can gain territory by using driving mauls and quick rucking. If that doesn't work, the scrumhalf will pass the ball to the flyhalf, who will then either kick the ball towards the sideline to get a line-out, or in front of the forwards for them to chase and contest for possession.

The flyhalf kicks for the sideline, knowing that his team has enough good line-out jumpers to win the ball, even if the opposition has the throw-in at the line-out. Inevitably, through turnovers and good defense, the team can get close to the opposition's tryline and score the tries required for victory.

The tactics are not pretty — the ball is hardly sighted in open play, and watching a big bullocking forward bustle his way over the line from a few meters out isn't exactly a moment of aesthetic beauty. Nevertheless, playing the ten-man game often ensures victory under the right circumstances.

The ten-man game is not commonly used anymore at the international level, although South Africa still practices a version of it. The speed of the modern game and the importance of teams having fast, expressive backs make the ten-man game an anomaly at the highest level. The ten-man game, even though grounded in solid principles, isn't the most entertaining spectacle for the masses, but to those who fully appreciate the subtlety of the battle up front, it's awe-inspiring stuff that can be every bit as riveting as a 100-point tryfest.

The teams that still play the ten-man game do so for important reasons. Teams with powerful packs and reliable line-outs and scrums find it a comfortable way to dominate possession and territory while wearing down the opposition.

Even though the ten-man game is out of favor at the highest levels, it's an effective strategy used by club teams all over the world and deserves inclusion into your array of tactical considerations.

Running from everywhere

At the opposite end of the spectrum from the ten-man game, is the concept of *running from everywhere,* which involves an all-out, attack-at-all-costs style. The goal of this stratagem is to run the ball to gain territory from every situation. Teams that are best suited to this tactic usually have very talented backs and may lack a dominant tight five.

The attempt to run from everywhere on the pitch has to be accompanied by mobile loosies (the two flankers and the number 8) who can support their backs wherever they're stopped by the opposition. The forwards must also be excellent ruckers and ready to run for the full 80 minutes.

In club rugby, you are likely to find that competing backlines can be severely mismatched based on speed, attacking acumen, experience, and combinational dynamics. This is the ideal time to unleash your backs, who can build their confidence by thrashing inferior opposition.

The most successful rugby teams are the ones that take elements from each of these two contrasting styles, striking a balance that allows them to best utilize the talent on offer. The most respected coaches are the ones that aren't married to a particular strategy and can guide their teams based on an evaluation of how their players can be most successful.

Analyzing the opponent

In addition to having basic skills, a successful coach makes a point of assessing the opposition's strengths and weaknesses in advance and then works on devising a strategy to beat that team.

At the professional level, coaches watch videotapes and prepare detailed scouting reports. At the club level, you can at least get an idea of your next opponent's playing style by sending someone from your club out to watch the team play. If the person knows what to look for they can provide a wealth of information on strengths and weaknesses, general tendencies, and any outstanding players or unusual tactics.

Exploiting weaknesses

The first order of business for taking down an opponent is to note any obvious chinks in their armor and take advantage of them. For example, you may notice that the opposition fullback or wings are nervous when the ball is kicked high into the air. If they've struggled with the high ball, test them repeatedly until they either perform successfully or you've gained lots of possession from their miscues. (The same goes for players who are hesitant in the tackle. Target them with strong runners and see if this can give you an advantage in attack.)

A fantastic area for exploitation is in the set pieces. If the other side is having trouble winning their scrums or producing good ball, have your team concentrate on the *eight-man push* (where all eight forwards use coordinated strength to drive the opposition back) and direct your scrumhalf to heighten his aggressiveness in pressuring his opposite.

Anywhere on the rugby pitch where you think your team can legally get the upper hand is a legitimate area to exploit, but be careful in doing so. It is more important that your team stick to the game plan than to try too many spontaneous tactics in the heat of battle. Of course, if your strategy calls for taking advantage of predetermined opposition inadequacies, by all means exploit away!

Containing the stars

In any rugby competition there are certain players who stand head and shoulders above everyone else by dint of their exceptional talent or skills. Even though rugby is a team game, it sometimes becomes necessary to put in place special measures to stop a certain rampaging opponent. Most of the time this means either denying that player the ball or applying additional pressure on him whenever he touches it.

It's not a good idea to rearrange your whole game plan to cope with the speed or power of one individual. What works best is to emphasize basics in tackling and review your defensive goals prior to the match. Containing the stars should always be done within the context of your established defensive pattern and definitely without resorting to cheap shots or illegal tactics.

Sometimes the best strategies for defeating star players are simple. If one of the opposition's jumpers is poaching all your throw-ins, try throwing the ball to a different spot in the line-out. Kicking the ball away from a particular player or cheating a little in spacing to reduce gaps for stars to run through can also be a simple but effective tactic. The best overall strategy is to minimize the impact by denying them opportunities to make big plays.

Selecting horses for courses

Selecting horses for courses is an old-time rugby saying that means the players chosen for a certain match should be determined by the nature of that particular contest. If the opposition has a mammoth pack and you're worried about losing set piece ball, this is a good time to bulk up your own pack, even it if costs you some mobility. Similarly, if the opponent is loaded with pace in the backline you might want to choose quicker, more mobile players in your team to counteract their advantage.

The adage also applies to strategic concerns. When your team is forced to use a style of game that they're not used to (either because of weather conditions or the strength of the opposition) certain players may be better suited for the revised game plan than your regular starters. For example, a flyhalf who specializes in kicking might be a more suitable selection than an attack-oriented flyhalf on a wet, windy day.

The emergence of impact players as substitutes has added another dimension to the horses for courses axiom. Some players are great at coming off the bench and making their presence felt but struggle if they have to play the full 80 minutes. Others can play solid rugby over the course of a match but are very ordinary when they come on as replacements. Recognizing these traits and filling your reserve bench with the appropriate performers is a coaching necessity.

Weathering the conditions

Rugby is a game meant to be played outside in all types of conditions. Gale force winds, sleeting rain, oppressive heat, or freezing temperatures usually won't keep a match from happening but will alter its character. In most cases the conditions on the pitch are the same for both sides. One team might have the wind in one half but the other gets it in the second stanza. Rain stopping and starting affects both teams equally, and humidity drains everyone's energy.

Depending on where your club is located, it might be normal to play in rainstorms or on excessively hot days. The difficulty emerges when you have to play in conditions that are completely foreign or that you are unprepared for. A good coach does everything possible to have his team ready to perform no matter how the elements intervene.

One case where the home team does have a distinct advantage over the visitors is when it comes to altitude. It takes the body at least a couple of weeks to fully adjust to changes in altitude, so unless a visiting side prepares for a fortnight in the opposition's backyard, they will feel the stress of reduced oxygen content sooner than their hosts.

Adapting to inclement weather

Rain is the great equalizer in rugby because it makes the ball difficult to handle and slows everyone down when the ground gets waterlogged. When it's wet out, it's a good idea to keep the ball in hand as much as possible and avoid throwing it around like a giant oval-shaped bar of soap. This strategy calls for more mauling and working the pick-and-go (see the "Working the pick-and-go" section of Chapter 7 for more details), as opposed to passing incessantly (which is likely to produce a multitude of scrums and turnovers).

BROWNIE SAYS

Adaptation

Growing up and going to college in Southern California shielded me from ever having to participate in sports during inclement weather (unless you count smog alerts). My first years of rugby were played in idyllic conditions, with heat being the only real climatic factor. That all changed when I moved to Missoula, Montana, and began playing for the Maggots. Suddenly, I had to be able to adapt on a weekly basis. Late summer snowstorms weren't uncommon and a blizzard in October was considered normal. The idea of not playing just because a foot of snow was falling was anathema to the hearty denizens of the Montana Rugby Union so the games went on as scheduled regardless of the conditions. My atmospheric education continued in Riga, Latvia, where it seemed that only one match out of every ten wasn't played in the rain, and dirt was the surface of necessity until May 1. It was in Riga that I was also introduced to Winter 10's, played in subzero temperatures on a sheet of ice covered in snow for padding. Playing in these conditions I learned that you only get cold when you are standing around, so to avoid freezing to death, you had to keep moving. The biggest shock was when I went to play for Vail, Colorado, in 1999. I had heard about altitude affecting physical fitness, but since I was out of shape anyway I didn't think I'd be a victim. About a minute into my first match in Aspen I was gasping for breath and looking to the sideline for a replacement but there was none forthcoming. By the end of the summer I had acclimated and was warning the newcomers to the Colorado mountains. Finally back in Los Angeles, after experiencing chilly climes all over the rugby universe, I now actually prefer playing in cold, rainy weather and reserve my complaining for when the mercury rises above 75 degrees. Adapting to unfamiliar conditions forced me to focus on basic skills and mental toughness to overcome challenging circumstances.

Many teams opt for a kicking-oriented, positional game when rain becomes a factor. If the weather dictates a radical change in tactics, it's better to put it into place right away, not after an attempt to use your regular style has failed.

A windy day calls for testing the opposition with the high ball, so be prepared for them to do the same thing to you. A strong breeze can also wreak havoc with line-out throws, so it's a good idea to stay away from long ones to the back that will end up being blown not straight or away from your jumpers.

Playing the pitch

Rugby pitches in North America vary from plush carpets of immaculate green grass to concrete-like dirt interspersed with weeds. You have to be able to play on different surfaces from week to week depending on your league. Here are a few tips for being able to play on any pitch:

✔ Always arrive early and inspect the ground by walking around the pitch before the match begins. This includes looking for safety hazards and finding out if there are any noticeable slopes or abnormalities in the field of play or tryzones.

✔ Make sure your players always have a couple of different lengths of studs for their boots so they can swap them if necessary. On a very hard surface, wearing boots with long studs can be like running on an ice rink, but they provide better traction on a soft track.

✔ Figure out in advance where the sun and wind are headed so your captain can make an informed choice during the coin toss. If your defensive confidence is high, playing against the wind in the first half can provide a psychological boost to your team, knowing that you'll have the advantage of the wind in the second half.

Deciding on a game plan

Before the first match, a coach decides which style of play best suits the talents of his assembled charges. As the season unfolds and players begin to gel, injuries take their toll, and what works and what doesn't becomes obvious, the coach needs to adapt. He should employ a dynamic approach to preparing each week's game plan that takes into account the present state of his side and the opposition.

When trying to determine what type of play will lead your team to victory, it may be useful to organize your thoughts by asking yourself a series of questions. Do you expect to win the contest for possession in the forwards? Are your backs superior to theirs? Where along the continuum, from playing the ten-man game to running from everywhere, takes best advantage of your teams' comparative strengths? Once you've settled upon an overall strategy that's calculated for your opponent, you then shift to specifics.

The initial area of concern is *first-phase possession*, which refers to a team gaining possession of the ball from set pieces (scrums, line-outs, restarts, etc.) rather than stealing possession from a ball-carrier from the opposing team. Do you expect to win the set pieces or will you struggle to get the ball from restarts? For example, if you think you'll have a clear advantage in the line-outs, you'll feel more comfortable kicking the ball for touch to keep your opponent pinned in their own end. On the other hand, if the other team is full of dominant line-out jumpers, your team would be better off with a plan that keeps the ball in play through several phases and avoids putting it out of bounds.

The next area to look at is how you match up at the breakdown. On attack, do you expect your loosies to get there first in support of your ball-carriers, or will they be beaten to the spot and have difficulty recycling the ball? If you have the upper hand in maintaining possession, you can implement a more expansive attacking style. If you think the enemy has better ball-ferreting skills, avoid the tackle situation by passing before contact and use kicks to advance the ball.

It's rarely a simple matter of saying we have better forwards or backs and therefore we should adopt one style or another. More often you'll identify areas where you expect to hold an advantage, others that will be even, and some where the opposition will be better. The best game plan utilizes these observations to accentuate your strengths and minimize your weaknesses.

Your game plan shouldn't be written in stone. You need to be able to adjust your strategy as the game unfolds. Watching and analyzing your opponents during a game is critical. The first forty minutes of a match can give a quick-thinking coach plenty of material to rapidly digest and then make changes for the second half.

Attacking Artistically

A successful attacking game plan relies on predetermined patterns and collective goals. Before a team goes into a game, the players should have practiced a variety of attacking moves during training, with everyone clear on their roles and responsibilities.

Attack plans don't have to be overly innovative or elaborate, but they do have to be precisely executed and not easily read by the defense. When the defenders don't know what's going to happen next, they're more likely to hesitate, which creates gaps for your side to exploit. Intricate moves that confuse your own side do more harm than good, so keep it simple at first.

Launching an effective attack

Offensive attacks, where your team has the ball, can be initiated from set pieces, general play, or turnover ball. The starting point for every move is how the ball is presented before the attack begins. If the ball is made available from a controlled platform, it's called *quality possession.* When your attack begins with quality possession, your backline's timing and coordination aren't disrupted, which increases their chance of success.

Quality possession at scrumtime means the ball is delivered cleanly, quickly, and accurately to the backs. Sloppy ball from a scrum that's moving backwards is nearly impossible for a scrumhalf to use positively. Likewise, if you're struggling to win clean ball at the line-out, your scrumhalf will be under tremendous pressure distributing the ball. Since it's rare to score a try directly off first-phase possession, launching an effective attack more often depends on how efficiently you can reset your attacking pattern through multiple phases.

The most dangerous attacking opportunities come from turnover balls that are used quickly. Immediately after turnovers (when possession of the ball moves from one team to the other), the team that loses the ball will be ill-prepared to defend because the players will still be in an attacking formation. The key here is that the team with possession launches their attack before the opposition can assume a defensive posture. Rucks and mauls are the most common launching pads for attacking movements because they provide an excellent base for unleashing your backline. This is because defenders tend to get sucked into the fray at the breakdown, creating space and potential mismatches out wide.

If you can't run through or around the other team, you can integrate attacking with the boot into your game plan. You can kick into open space with the goal of re-gathering the ball, or boot it high to put pressure on the receiver.

Breaking through

Breaching the opponent's line requires a targeted point of attack. If you can beat them out wide, use your speed. If they have a particularly weak tackler, run repeatedly right at him. If they're coming up hard and flat, use deception to draw them out of position. When you can't find a way through, kick it behind them to turn 'em around.

Successful attacking moves rely on correct alignment, running proper angles, and hitting the gain line at pace using a coordinated sequence of movements. Positioning your backline flat and close makes passing easier but provides less time and space to operate in. Placing them deeper and wider gives them more room to move, but allows defenders to cover multiple attackers and diminishes the space out wide.

You should practice a new move over and over, first in slow motion, and then gradually increasing the speed until everyone knows exactly where to be and what to do. Attacking artistically relies on good communication, with your play-maker calling the play and the rest of the team getting into position to run it.

You can usually tell when a set move is about to happen because the play-maker starts talking and gesticulating to his backline.

Defending Devilishly

The ultimate goal of playing defense is to regain possession of the ball. The effectiveness of any defense is dependent on the structure used and the attitude of the players. The objective is to employ an aggressive, pressure-orientated scheme that focuses on stopping the offense and stealing the ball.

The most important defensive attribute is commitment. There is no place for half-hearted attempts to tackle in rugby, as you'll likely miss the runner and hurt yourself in the process.

Coordinating the defense

The keys to team defense are communication, structure, and execution. Playing defense is a fluid activity where you need to constantly react to an ever-changing situation. Communication is vital because as the attack changes, you need to talk to each other to maintain your pattern. The defensive structure relies upon every player knowing where to cover, making good tackles, and understanding what everyone else is doing.

An effective defensive team plan requires working together as a unit, communicating well, and backing each other up when necessary. Walking and talking your team through their defensive system is every bit as important as hours and hours of tackling drills. Be sure your players understand the concepts behind what's expected of them.

Blocking the advance: Defensive systems

Pressure, width, and depth are the three main principles of team defense. Pressure takes time and space away from the attacking team. Width prevents them from running around the outside of the defense. Depth provides additional levels of defenders who can step up and make tackles.

Two basic approaches to applying defensive pressure, ensuring width, and maintaining depth are man-on-man and drift.

- ✔ **The man-on-man defense:** Defenders are responsible for tackling their opposites.
- ✔ **The drift defense:** Defenders drift sideways to cover the next attacker outside them.

Man-on-man defense

In *man-on-man* defense, each tackler's assignment is to contain his opposite.

Figure 11-1 shows the defensive formation at a scrum, with the defenders *marking*, or matching-up against, the attacking team (as shown by the arrows). For example, the defending flyhalf marks the attacking team's number 10. In order to cover the last player in the formation, the defending fullback moves towards the sideline to cover the attacking team's left wing.

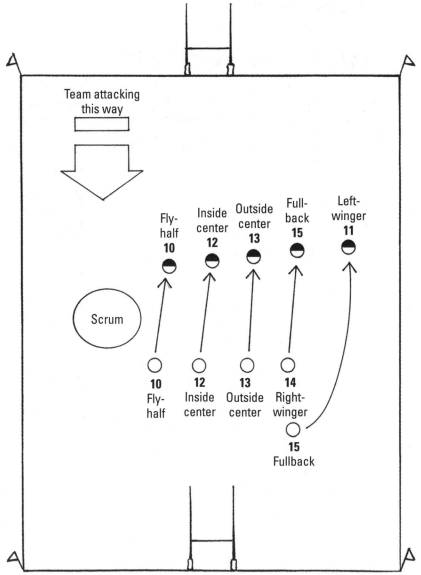

Figure 11-1:
Ready to
mount a
man-on-man
defense.

Drift defense

The *drift defense* involves the defenders all sliding outside in unison to take away the attacking team's ability to outflank them. It is often used after a line-out or a scrum and provides increased width and depth, but lacks the pressure element of the man-on-man defense.

Figure 11-2 illustrates a scrum with the defenders setting-up a drift defense. The normal progression is that the openside flanker takes the attacking flyhalf, while the defending flyhalf pursues the inside center, followed by the inside center being responsible for the outside center, and so forth down the line. The defense drifts across field, cutting off any attempt to come back inside while forcing the ball-carriers toward the sidelines.

When executed properly, the drift defense accounts for an extra attacker being brought into the line. For example, if the extra attacker enters the line between the inside center and outside center, that player would be tackled by the defending inside center.

Commitment and trust

If you look at the best defending sides, they all share a common trait — trust. Developing mutual trust between your players is essential when it comes to team defense. Confidence in your fellow defenders ability and commitment to tackling builds the trust required to stay focused on your individual defensive responsibilities.

The Crusaders

The Crusaders won four Super 12 titles because they excelled on defense. They had an enormous capacity to defend over long periods of time against multiple phase attack without losing their defensive pattern. The Crusaders take great pride in their defense and it's the cornerstone of their entire game plan. They relish the opportunity to make a tackle, always trying to meet the runner behind the gain line and knock him back, so the ball can be turned over. At the fringes of rucks, you'll see Crusader players pointing and calling out to each other while getting ready to make the next tackle, so everyone knows their role well before the ball comes out. As soon as the scrumhalf touches the ball, they become an attacking force on defense, charging up the field to crush the infidels for daring to challenge the men from Christchurch. By sharing self-belief in their collective strength, the Crusaders prevent the attacking side from creating confusion and hesitation amongst the faithful defenders. They all know their mission and believe wholeheartedly in each other's desire to get the job done. Establishing trust is a fundamental part of developing the resolve necessary to maintain defensive solidarity and a critical element in creating a championship culture. Once that trust is established, there's no limit to what your team will endure to achieve their collective goals.

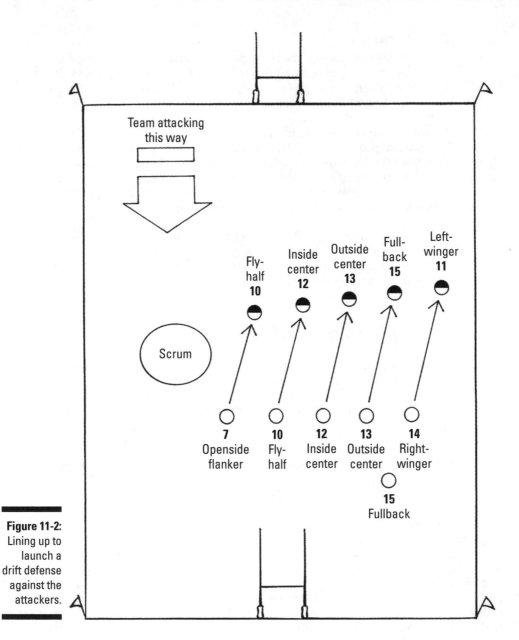

Figure 11-2:
Lining up to
launch a
drift defense
against the
attackers.

Chapter 12

Talented Training

● ●

In This Chapter

▶ Getting ready to run on

▶ Stretching your way to fitness

▶ Conditioning for success

▶ Winning with your wits

▶ Eating right for rugby

● ●

*F*or most of its history rugby was largely an amateur sport where even at the highest-level players had to have a career outside the game to support themselves. Training was usually done after the end of the workday. That all changed with the advent of professionalism in 1995 when modern training regimens were introduced, and the fitness required to excel in the game shot up accordingly. Rugby players at the international level now are on a par with professional athletes in other contact sports, but the approaches to conditioning around the world vary from country to country.

A typical rugby match involves miles of running interspersed with hundreds of bursts of energy when you encounter the enemy. To survive and pass this grueling test of cardiovascular and muscular endurance, you need to be strong and extremely fit. The game has become less stop/start and more fluid in recent years; this requires a more focused approach to physical preparation that develops both baseline conditioning and position-specific fitness.

In this chapter, we describe what you need to do to attain a basic level of fitness, how to mentally prepare for matches, and what to eat for peak performance.

Getting Match Fit

Fitness is acquired in the hours spent running or working out on your own in the gym, not at training. For non-professionals, the limited amount of practice time necessitates a focus on skills and drills and leaves very little room for conditioning. All rugby players should be physically prepared for battle before the season begins instead of the old method of playing their way into shape. Nothing takes the place of hard work.

Before rashly starting any exercise program, think carefully about the physical demands that are made on you in a match. You need to build and maintain a level of fitness that ensures you have plenty of the following:

- ✔ **Stamina:** Since a match is played over 80 minutes you need to develop both aerobic and anaerobic fitness. *Aerobic capacity* gives you the endurance needed to roam the pitch for the entire match. *Anaerobic capacity* provides energy for repetitive bursts of high exertion over the course of the game.

- ✔ **Strength and power:** Because you constantly encounter opposing forces who want to run over the top of you, you need to be strong enough to stop them and reply in kind. You also need muscular endurance to be as tough in the last minute of play as you are the first.

- ✔ **Flexibility:** When you have the ball in your hands, or are trying to take it away from the opposition in all phases of play, you need flexibility to be effective and avoid injury.

Even in the final minutes of the game, you should still be breathing easily. Sprawling face-down in the turf, suffering from exhaustion or cramps, does nothing to help your side and is not a good look.

Focus on exercises that target the parts of your body that you want to strengthen, but be careful not to overdo it — we don't want legions of *Rugby for Dummies* readers turning up at their doctors' offices tomorrow with strains, sprains, and broken bones. Only do as much as you feel comfortable with and increase the intensity of your workout gradually. Fitness can't be acquired in a few days or even weeks, so don't try to speed up the timetable — it will only lead to disappointment.

Warming up and having a good stretch

Before every practice or fitness session, you should start with a well-planned warm-up. Establishing a routine that prepares the body for the higher level of exertion to follow is very important. Jogging a couple of laps, riding an exercise bike, jumping rope, or doing light calisthenics are all acceptable methods of breaking a sweat and warming up.

A good warm-up followed by a stretching routine minimizes the risk of injury. Improving your flexibility can help prevent ligament, joint, and muscle injuries on the big day. Devote at least 10 to 15 minutes to stretching before you start the more strenuous activities. All the stretches that are described in this chapter will help increase your flexibility and get you ready for action.

Only perform stretching if you are absolutely sure you can manage it. It's always a good idea to check with your coach and your doctor to determine if a new program is right for you. This is especially important if you've been injured before, or have any health problems.

Stretching for performance

Stretching is an important part of any training program and should be performed with as much care and enthusiasm as the active part of any training session. The stretching program should be prepared before training starts and have goals and objectives already in place.

Obviously, different training regimens require the use of different muscle groups. The stretching that comes after training should be targeted towards those groups that have carried the biggest workload.

For example, if the session will feature sprint training, it needs to focus on stretching the hamstrings, calves, gluts, and hip flexors. If the workout involves upper body weight training, you need to stretch the chest, back, and shoulders. Other areas still get stretched, but more emphasis should be placed on these target areas. Any stretching session should have goals and guidelines in place.

The goals should be:

- ✔ to prepare for training (dynamic stretching may be used)
- ✔ to maintain flexibility (static)
- ✔ to increase flexibility (developmental)
- ✔ to help recover from injury (may include all of the above)

Stretching can have many benefits including:

- ✔ helping to reduce muscle tension
- ✔ helping to clear metabolic waste (lactic acid) from muscles
- ✔ increasing length of and straightening muscle fibers
- ✔ improving body awareness
- ✔ increasing quality of muscle movement
- ✔ helping with muscle-firing patterns

All of these elements together increase the quality of recovery, thereby allowing players to train with a higher intensity and have less time in the rest/recovery phase or on the physiotherapist's table with an injury. Many a promising player has had his career cut short due to an avoidable injury.

Dynamic stretching has become very popular before activity as it takes the muscles through a range of movement that stretches them the same way they will be during a game. It also helps establish firing patterns within the muscles' stretch reflex and proprioceptors so the correct signals are being relayed at the appropriate time, thus preparing them to go from a slow jog to an explosive sprint without tearing.

Dynamic stretch routine

A stretching routine starts with the usual jog and ball-handling skills, followed by some static stretching to slowly warm up and help with muscle lengthening. As the players get warmed up, they can add dynamic stretching. Once they start stretching dynamically, they shouldn't go back to static stretching. Remember, static stretching slows the muscles down and dynamic stretching wakes them up.

Doing 6 to 10 repetitions of each stretch is recommended, but on a cold day more may be necessary. Ball skills and running can also be added with the dynamic stretching:

- Groin: walking, side step and standing
- Hamstrings and quads: walking and standing
- Waist and lower back: standing and bent at waist
- Back and hamstrings: ground and bent
- Waist and adductors: sitting
- Calves: standing and leaning forward
- Shoulders and upper back: standing

Static stretching after training

Following a training session, it's a good idea to finish with a static stretch. Static stretching returns the muscles to the length they were when they started and is most effective when the stretching is focused on the muscles that were heavily utilized in the session. Work for 5 to 15 minutes and have the players hold the stretch for 15 to 30 seconds each.

A stretching diary is very helpful in keeping focused on the task at hand and keeping some form of order to the stretch routine by writing down the stretches that are specific to a team's needs.

Developing a fitness program

To prepare yourself properly for rugby, you need a fitness program that develops speed, muscular strength, agility, and cardiovascular endurance. To improve your *cardiovascular endurance*, that is, to increase the fitness of your heart and lung system, you need a series of exercises that enhances the body's ability to take in oxygen and circulate it throughout the body to your muscles that will be screaming for more O_2. If you have plenty of stamina, you won't run out of gas or tire excessively while playing or training.

Improving your stamina

When you heart is pumping fast and you're sweating bullets, whether you know it or not, you're working on your stamina. One of the best ways to increase stamina is to run varying distances. A good combination is to do distance work and then finish with some sprinting (which we cover in the next section). For distance work, your ultimate goal is to be able to run non-stop for six miles (as this is roughly the ground you'll cover during an average match). To start off, try running around the pitch for about 20 minutes at a slow but steady rate and see how you feel.

If you are unaccustomed to running, increase the distance slowly. Stay within your comfort zone until you can hold a conversation or sing to yourself while jogging effortlessly. When you can do that, increase the distance in small increments. Once you reach the six-mile plateau, gradually increase your speed, lowering your total running time.

Don't do too much too early, otherwise you may cause muscle damage. Run well within your own limits and stop if you suddenly find yourself struggling. Your distance and speed will improve over time, but not overnight!

Running at full tilt: Sprint training

Rugby involves periods of jogging mixed with flat-out sprinting. So, once you're comfortable jogging, you need to work on your speed by sprinting shorter distances. Try running at a brisker pace from one end of the field to the other, take a 30-second break, and then run back the other way followed by another break. Do this three or four times. You may struggle early on, but within days you discover that the number of sprints you can make before collapsing in a heap will rise remarkably.

Sprint training is an important element in building up speed. During a game, a player often has to accelerate from a standing start and hit top speed within a couple of seconds. To simulate this activity and improve your speed, your training schedule should include a series of sprints, punctuated by prescribed rest periods. This is called *interval training*.

An effective sequence is to run ten 10-meter sprints with a 15-second rest between each one, move up to ten 20-meter sprints with a 30-second rest between them, followed by ten 30-meter sprints with 45 seconds rest, finishing with ten 40-meter sprints with 60 seconds rest between each.

As your cardiovascular fitness increases, you'll find that it progressively takes less time to recover during the resting intervals. Interval training mimics the type of exertion required in a match, so give it your full effort on every repetition and visualize yourself running toward the tryline for the game winner with an opponent hot on your heels.

Sprint training is demanding fitness work and should only be done after you've warmed up properly. If you begin your fitness program without stretching or warming up first, you could cause some serious muscle injuries.

Working on your agility

To improve your agility, construct an obstacle course, involving cones placed at intervals of 4 to 5 meters. With a rugby ball in your hands, weave through the markers and practice bounding off first your left foot and then your right foot, as if trying to get past a defender with the side-step or swerve (Chapter 6 gives full details about these moves). Begin slowly, but challenge yourself by trying to move quicker each time.

You are welcome to try this in your own backyard or at a neighborhood park. You not only improve your agility, you also keep the neighbors entertained. Watch out for small dogs yapping at your heels and local kids trying to figure out what on earth you are doing.

Another good drill is to run at speed through the same obstacle course, throwing the ball up and re-gathering it. Let the ball bounce occasionally, so you get accustomed to picking the ball up from the ground while on the run.

Building up your strength

Increased competition among professionals has raised the physical demands of the sport; the lucky few who play for money have become reliant on lifting weights to improve their strength and power. While weight-lifting is mandatory preparation for the advanced player, it is not essential for prepubescent youngsters, who can build up their strength by going down a different, perhaps safer, path.

A heavy weight-lifting program can cause permanent damage to bones and muscles if the body is not yet ready to accept heavy weights. If you want to lift weights, ask your coach for advice on an appropriate, safe, and effective weight-lifting program.

The Zen Theory of Rugby Fitness

Being match fit is crucial for peak performance over 80 minutes of gut-wrenching exertion. However, if you have the experience and mental powers required, no matter how unfit you are, you can still make an impact over the entire match using the Zen Theory of Rugby Fitness. Under the theory, you conserve energy whenever possible and only exert yourself when it's absolutely vital, picking your spots carefully. The goal is to be the polar opposite of a rookie who chases the ball all over the field running aimlessly like a chicken with its head cut off. This can only be accomplished by wily veterans, who draw upon all their vast reserves of rugby knowledge. The strategy necessitates an uncanny sense of anticipation as to where play is going. If the ball is headed out wide and is likely to come back inside toward you, there's no point in running out there, when you're already perfectly positioned to defend once the pill works its way back inside. As you roam the pitch, look for critical opportunities to inject yourself with a sudden burst of pace, a well-timed clean-out at a ruck, or a crucial tackle that will stop a promising movement cold just before it gets rolling. The key to gaining enlightenment through the Zen Theory is concentration and mentally willing the ball to come back to where you are. You must remain totally focused on preserving what precious little gas you have left in that old rusted-out tank. You need to avoid at all costs the destructive effects of taking an unwarranted quick step, unless the circumstances dictate. The theory is definitely not for beginners, as they lack the rugby IQ to correctly pick their spots. In fact, the Zen Theory of Rugby Fitness isn't really appropriate for anyone, other than gray-haired veterans like me, who occasionally turn out for master's games. But like most things in rugby, explaining the theory makes great conversation over a couple of cold beers at the reception.

Good old-fashioned push-ups and sit-ups are perfect for toning the body and increasing upper body strength. If you begin slowly and gradually build up the number of repetitions, your strength is sure to improve.

Varying your routines

Variation is an important aspect of training. You should regularly change your regimen and not be afraid of attempting different ways to get fit. If you get bored while training, you eventually won't bother, which won't do much to develop your conditioning. It's also very effective to train with a partner, as you'll take turns motivating each other to get into the gym or out onto the track, and push yourselves to achieve more than you might on your own.

Get adventurous: Invent your own drills that involve a rugby ball. The more times you have a ball in your hands, the more comfortable you'll become with it. Before long, the ball feels like a natural extension of your hands.

A simple, fun activity for two people is a kicking game. Start just outside the 22-meter lines on opposite sides of the pitch and try to kick the ball as far as you can over the other player's head. Then your partner has to kick it back to you from wherever it was caught. The goal is to gain ground and drive the other player back toward the tryline. If you're by yourself, kick and chase the ball up and down the field, trying out various styles of kicks and working on re-gathering. The constant kicking and running will improve your kicking accuracy, catching skills, and overall fitness.

Coaches should utilize a balanced approach to developing each player's individual and the teams' collective fitness. Create a plan that addresses their particular and team deficiencies, monitors their progress, and adjusts as need be over the course of the season.

Because there's often wide variation between approaches within a single country, from international down to provincial and club levels, you'll find plenty of different schools of thought on virtually every aspect of getting match fit. The key is to welcome new ideas and make them your own.

Psyching Up for a Stellar Performance

While it's terrific to look good and be able to run effortlessly for 80 minutes, if you lack the right mentality, your physical prowess will not translate into effective play. Getting mentally prepared doesn't mean spending days on a psychologist's couch, or calling the psychic hotline to find out what the stars say about your team's chances in the match tomorrow.

Being mentally prepared means that a player is totally focused on the task at hand and can instantly sum up a situation and work out the best way to handle it on the fly. Rugby is often like a chess game revolving around intricate strategies, with the best players responding instinctively to the variations as they unfold in front of them.

Before each game, take some quiet time and ask yourself these questions:

- ✔ What are my responsibilities in the game plan?
- ✔ What's likely to happen in the game?
- ✔ What do I want to accomplish and what am I expected to achieve?
- ✔ How can I best take advantage of any opportunities that present themselves?

The Zone

Former All Black Murray Mexted, who played in every international match for New Zealand from 1979 to 1986, had a unique way to mentally switch on prior to tests. In the changing room before each match, he would imagine reaching up with both arms to pull down a huge light switch that would put him into what he called "The Zone." Once the switch was thrown, he became totally focused on the task at hand, completely destroying his opposite and contributing in every way possible to an All Blacks' victory. He cleared his mind of everything else so he could focus all his mental energy on the game.

Mental toughness separates the good from the great rugby players. While Murray's light switch method might not turn you on, you should develop your own technique to get mentally focused before each kickoff and stay that way throughout the match.

Get motivated by visualizing yourself scoring the winning try, kicking the winning goal, or leading your team to a memorable victory. Most great players find this an effective way to build their confidence. If it works for them, it can work for you.

Good mental preparation means you are less likely to shy away when a big, intimidating second-rower runs straight at you. Fear is important as long as it doesn't hinder your performance. All players, at some stage of their playing careers, experience the fear of failure or the fear of injury. It's a natural emotion in a contact sport, but you can use it to your advantage by re-channeling the adrenaline flow into controlled aggression.

Eating Your Way to Victory

Gone are the days when rugby players believed that loading up their breakfast plates with steak, eggs, and hash browns was the only way to win. A starvation diet that allows you only one celery stick a day is not the answer either. If you want to be a successful rugby player, common sense has to prevail — eating and drinking in moderation is the only way to go.

Choosing a balanced diet

Nowadays, most professional rugby teams have a dietician hovering somewhere in the shadows who's counting calories and monitoring milk shakes, all under the guise of recommending the optimal diet for rugby fitness. For the elite athlete, dietary modification is a proven method of marginally increasing performance.

For the club player your diet should be dictated by your general level of fitness. While no one single food is likely to make you a superstar, as a rugby player you have more energy requirements than the average Joe walking down the street. Common sense should lead you away from fast food and bingeing on too many pints of Ben & Jerry's.

We recommend you eat a balanced diet that includes proteins, carbohydrates, fats, and fiber, and foods that provide nutrients, vitamins, and minerals. This means taking in measured amounts of food from each of the four food groups. For peak performance, make 60 to 70% of your daily caloric intake come from carbohydrates, along with 15% protein and 15% from fats (and this includes alcohol).

Clearly, the best thing a rugby player in training can drink is not the amber fluid — it's water. Dehydration causes fatigue more than any other dietary factor. Contrary to the prevailing wisdom contained in the Oxy Olde Boys training manual, beer does not, in fact, help you take on water to play the game. So drink plenty of water all week long to replace the water you've lost during training. Two hours before kickoff is too late to guzzle a gallon of water to prevent dehydration.

Taking on fuel

You should never eat too close to game time. Your pre-game meal should be consumed about four hours before kickoff, allowing food to settle in your stomach. The most effective pre-game fuel is high in carbohydrates, low in fat, and low in protein. Loading-up on a couple of double cheeseburgers and a giant bag of fries is definitely not recommended before you play. Instead, opt for a bowl of meatless pasta with lots of vegetables and tomato sauce.

Eating on the way to a game, or just before kickoff, should be avoided at all costs. Nothing is guaranteed to make a player more sluggish than running on a full stomach.

After you finish punishing your body at training, you need fuel to recover, so it's a good idea to eat within an hour following practice. Milk and yogurt are very good for recovery purposes because they contain about 50% carbohydrates and 50% proteins. And if your club assembles for a post-practice chat, it certainly won't hurt to drink a pint of water before each pint of ale.

Choosing your supplements carefully

Professional players that utilize supplements to maximize performance do so under the guidance of dieticians and doctors. In these circumstances, supplements can have a safe and beneficial impact on your play.

If you're a club player and are considering taking supplements, schedule a doctor's appointment to discuss whether they are safe and appropriate for you. Eating right, training smart, and getting plenty of rest are the tried-and-true ways to improve performance. Don't be tricked into thinking that supplements can provide a shortcut to success.

One line of products to avoid are so-called energy drinks. If they contain heaps of caffeine and other stimulants, they are not appropriate for use because they lead to an elevated heart rate and dehydration.

Part III
Welcome to the Oval Planet

The 5th Wave   By Rich Tennant

© RICHTENNANT

Several injuries resulted from this year's running with the bulls event in Pamplona, Spain, involving a European rugby team. The bulls remain in stable condition, while the team members expressed their concern from a local cafe.

In this part...

This part of the book explores the various rugby competitions around the globe. We start our tour of planet rugby with a look at the Rugby World Cup, the sport's crowning jewel, where we offer up all the information you need to know about the quadrennial tournament, including its history and format, plus some of the most memorable moments dating back to 1987.

Next, we take you on a tour of the world's annual international tournaments, including the Six Nations and Tri Nations Series. The inter-provincial scene is next with a glance at the Super 12 and the Heineken Cup, and we conclude our international sojourn with a peek at the leading domestic leagues in New Zealand, South Africa and the United Kingdom.

Closer to home, we discuss the North American international picture and then focus on the heart and soul of the game, the local club. We finish with a survey of the collegiate, high school and youth rugby scene.

Chapter 13

The World Cup

For most of its history, rugby has been an insular game. Development and expansion of the sport was seen as despoiling its traditions and uniqueness. With the exception of a few poorly attended inclusions in various Olympic Games, until 1987 determining a world champion was always an unofficial bit of guesswork, open to interpretation and argument. That all changed in the mid-eighties when the International Rugby Board (IRB) was dragged kicking and screaming into the modern era.

In this chapter we'll give you an overview of what the Rugby World Cup has become in just a short time, tell how it came about, provide qualification details, and look at some other components of the World Cup system.

The Crown Jewel of Rugby

The Rugby World Cup is the pinnacle of achievement for players and coaches around the oval planet. Every four years, touring fans converge on the tournament to display their national pride and revel in historical rivalries, while attending a multitude of social events and enjoying plenty of rugby camaraderie. The pool matches are like the NCAA Basketball Tournament, where longshots get a chance to topple the favorites and pretenders emerge as contenders. The knockout stages culminate with the Cup final, producing a Super-Bowl-like atmosphere with the world's collective focus on one single match. In fact, only the Soccer World Cup and the Olympics command a larger worldwide television audience!

From the first hastily organized 16-team tournament in Australia and New Zealand in 1987, the Rugby World Cup has grown into a quadrennial spectacle that is watched by more than three billion people around the globe. Staging the tournament has become an immense undertaking that involves the resources of an entire nation or region, worldwide corporate sponsorship, and an army of volunteers and paid administrators.

The prize awarded to the winner of the Rugby World Cup is the William Webb Ellis Cup, named after the legendary founder of the game. Lifting the cup in triumph has become the primary goal of the world's leading rugby-playing nations; it's more important than any other rivalry or competition. For years prior to each edition, national unions and their coaches focus on developing players and strategies to bring "Bill," as the trophy has come to be known, back to their shores.

In its current format, which is determined individually during the bidding process to host the next event, the World Cup brings together 20 teams that have qualified either by their performance in the previous Cup or through regional elimination. The participants are seeded according to world ranking and placed in four pools of five teams. Every pool member plays each other and the top two teams advance to the quarterfinals. The eventual finals, victor gets the title of World Champions for the next four years.

The Origins and History of the Rugby World Cup

The World Cup was born out of a desire by the southern hemisphere nations to increase the visibility of the game around the world. From its beginnings, rugby was mostly amateur and all aspects of commercialization were tightly controlled by each national union and the IRB. The more tradition-bound members from the northern hemisphere feared that commercialization would lead to the encroachment of professionalism, which is indeed what happened, albeit a few years later.

In the early 1980s Australia and New Zealand both proposed the idea of holding a World Cup and by 1985, after much study and committee work, they were finally able to force a vote on the issue in the IRB Executive Committee. With backing from France, who had always been more inclined towards moving the game into the professional ranks, and a late decision by South Africa to support the idea, the measure passed and the world's third great sporting competition came into being.

1987 World Cup — Australia and New Zealand

The first World Cup in 1987 involved 16 invited teams and was held in Australia and New Zealand. The tournament was a moderate commercial success but achieved much more in the area of exposure with more than half a million fans attending matches and some 300 million supporters following the game on television.

France, Australia, Wales, and New Zealand made the semifinals, giving the tournament an even north-south distribution. The New Zealand All Blacks were the eventual champs, winning at home in Auckland's Eden Park over the French Tricolors 29–9. Direct competition in a tournament format showed that the southern hemisphere teams had surpassed their northern rivals.

1991 World Cup — Great Britain, Ireland, and France

The 1991 Rugby World Cup took place in Great Britain, Ireland, and France and was again a 16-team affair, but this time the IRB implemented a qualification process, whereby 8 sides had qualified through a regional formula to join the 8 quarterfinalists from 1987. The surprise of the tournament was eventual champions Australia upsetting the defending titleholders New Zealand in the semifinals. Australia went on to beat England 12–6 at Twickenham in the final. The World Cup audience also grew substantially, with over one million stadium attendees and nearly two billion watching over the airwaves.

1995 World Cup — South Africa

In 1995 the World Cup moved to South Africa, whose Springboks competed for the first time. President Nelson Mandela opened the tournament wearing a Springbok jersey, long a symbol of the apartheid era, and appealed for the Rainbow Nation to come together through sport. The tournament was a smashing success from the opening match to the tense final, when in a near-fairy-tale ending, the Boks beat the All Blacks 15–12 in extra time on a Joel Stransky drop goal.

Their victory at Ellis Park in Johannesburg was the third consecutive triumph of a southern hemisphere team. It also marked the end of the amateur era in rugby. With the sport's governing body no longer able to stem the tide of professionalism, the IRB had been forced to acquiesce and allow the game to become a marketable commodity, with paid players and commercial opportunities galore.

The worldwide television audience shocked even the most biased rugby optimists, with more than 3.1 billion viewers around the oval planet tuning in. Rugby had arrived as a worldwide television product just as professionalism was about to take hold.

1999 World Cup — Wales, England, Scotland, Ireland, and France

The 1999 tourney moved once again back to Britain, France, and Ireland, with Wales taking the lead role as hosts. The finals tournament was expanded from 16 to 20 teams and for the first time, included quarterfinal playoffs.

The semifinals were thrilling affairs with South Africa and Australia going into overtime and France shocking the world by knocking off a heavily favored All Blacks side in one of the most exciting Rugby World Cup games ever played. The Wallabies then comprehensively defeated the French 35–12 in the final, becoming the first country to win the Rugby World Cup twice. The 1999 tournament broke all previous records for attendance, TV audience, and revenue.

2003 World Cup — Australia

The 2003 Rugby World Cup was originally scheduled to be co-hosted by Australia and New Zealand, but after a commercial dispute over advertising in stadiums, Australia ended up staging the entire tournament alone. Building on the success of the 2000 Olympic Games in Sydney, the Australian Rugby Union set a new standard for hosting excellence.

The tournament returned to a four-pool format where the top two nations advanced to the quarterfinals. Australians of all backgrounds embraced the tourney and set new attendance marks while showing their true colors in a unprecedented display of international sporting camaraderie.

The final pitted the pre-tournament favorite England against the host Wallabies. In the most riveting World Cup final to date, Jonny Wilkinson booted England to victory at the end of extra time, becoming the first northern hemisphere team to hoist the William Webb Ellis Cup overhead. It was a fairy-tale ending for the Men in White and a fitting conclusion to the best World Cup ever.

In just 16 years, the World Cup had gone from an idea that met stiff resistance to a colossus on the world's sporting stage. In the process, the game itself was changed from an exclusive, clubby activity to a professional game with a worldwide audience. Such is the power of creating an international competition that determines ultimate bragging rights for an entire sport.

Qualification and Finals Tournament

Originally, the World Cup was by invite only. In 1991, the IRB instituted a qualification structure, which enabled teams from all over the globe to aspire to compete on the rugby world's premier stage. The first eight slots in the tournament are reserved for the champion, runner-up, beaten semifinalists, and the losing quarterfinalists.

BROWNIE SAYS

How I earned a cap for Latvia

The first qualifying match for the 1999 Rugby World Cup was in September of 1996 between Latvia and Norway in Riga. Because it was the kickoff match of a tournament that would eventually culminate in a world champion being crowned in Cardiff, the fixture drew journalists from the rugby capitals of Europe and the post-match function was a lively affair. I lived right across the street from the University Stadium, and Uldis Bautris, my club coach for Rigas Miesnieks, was also in charge of the national team squad, so naturally I attended the game and the following festivities. After chatting with various Norwegian team members it became apparent that very few of them were actually Norwegian. Most were expatriates from rugby-playing nations living and working in Oslo who gained eligibility for Norway on residency grounds. That night, at the suggestion of Latvian lock Wilmars Sokolovs, the notion was born that I could become the first foreigner to play for

Latvia. What transpired over the next seven months was a personal odyssey involving a never-before-seen devotion to fitness, twice-weekly training sessions in the snow and rain on dirt pitches, bewildering eligibility paperwork for the Latvian sports ministry, a stint at hooker in both a possibles versus probables match and a friendly against Lithuania, and finally, selection to the Latvian team. Listening to the national anthem with my teammates before we crushed Bulgaria 89–0 in a World Cup qualifier was the proudest moment of my life. Unfortunately, our hopes of progressing out of our pool to the next level were dashed by Croatia the following week. The World Cup is such a powerful motivating force that even to have been involved at all will always be the highlight of my rugby career. I believe that one day Latvia will make it to the World Cup and when they do, I'll be in the stands cheering rabidly for my adopted nation.

RUGBY JARGON

Qualifying is a two-year-long process of more than 100 matches that involves almost every member of the IRB. Ten places go to qualifiers from Africa (1), the Americas (2), Asia (1), Europe (4), and Oceania (2). The last two berths are determined by use of the *repechage* system, or runner-up's last chance, where near-qualifiers are given the chance of sneaking in by knocking each other off in a home and away series.

Qualifying begins with the lowest-ranked nations playing in a regionalized pool system to weed out the least deserving sides and minimize travel costs. Winning a pool allows that country to advance to the next level where they face stiffer competition from more established international teams.

In 2003 the qualifying unions were: Namibia from Africa; Canada and Uruguay from the Americas; Japan from Asia; Ireland, Italy, Romania, and Georgia from Europe; and Fiji and Samoa from Oceania. Tonga and the United States were able to sneak in the back door of the qualification process through the repechage.

Canada in the World Cup

Canada has been competitive in all five Rugby World Cups. The Canadians have won 6 and lost 11 finals matches, including wins over Tonga, Fiji, Romania, and Namibia. Their best showing was in 1991, when they advanced to the quarterfinals, where they lost by a very respectable 13–29 score against New Zealand.

In 2003, Rugby Canada was placed in Pool D with New Zealand, Wales, Italy, and Tonga, comprising the most evenly matched group in the tournament. Going into the tournament, the Canadians had hopes of again making the quarterfinals, but lost first to Wales, were crushed by New Zealand, and played Italy tough in a losing effort; they salvaged some pride with a convincing victory over Tonga.

The United States in the World Cup

Since the U.S.'s back-to-back Olympic triumphs 80 years ago, the Eagles have struggled to field a competitive international side. After winning their opener against Japan in 1987, the U.S. was shut out in 1991, and failed to qualify for the World Cup in 1995. In 1999, the Eagles lost a heartbreaker to Romania and went three and out for the second time. The Eagles barely made the 2003 finals, coming in the back door via the repechage tournament.

The United States was placed in Pool B alongside France, Fiji, Japan, and Scotland. They charged out of the gate against Fiji but a missed conversion denied them their second Rugby World Cup win in 16 years. Against Scotland, the Eagles were brought back down to earth; they rebounded with a win over Japan, before losing heavily to France.

Mammoths and Minnows

For countries that have very little chance of ever hoisting the Webb Ellis trophy, the tournament is an opportunity to measure themselves against the best in the world. Winning a match or even just playing well against a major power is a source of intense pride and a reason for commendation.

Rugby is a sport where there is no such thing as letting up on an overmatched opponent. The way you show respect for the other side is to continue to play as hard as possible against them, no matter how large the lead. This "no let up for 80 minutes" ethos results in some awfully lopsided scorelines.

Even so, a 100-point loss is not a source of embarrassment in the rugby community, but instead a measuring stick of how much needs to be done to become more competitive. So while some of the results may be a bit lopsided, the overall effect is to lift the game of the up-and-coming nations by exposing them to a higher level of play.

The upside of the relative disparity between nations occurs when a country is able to move up the international pecking order. In 1999, Argentina beat Ireland in a quarterfinal playoff match, an unlikely victory that lifted rugby's profile within a soccer-mad country and has since led to steady improvement for the Pumas.

Despite losing 55–19 to Australia in 1999, the USA Eagles came away from that match with their heads held high, knowing that they had competed well. In fact, they scored the only try tallied against the eventual World Champs in the entire tournament!

Great World Cup Moments

Some World Cup matches become part of history because of the moment in time when they took place and others for the pure drama of the battle joined. Over the 185 finals matches played from 1987 to 2003, there have been several contests that rise above the rest.

South Africa versus New Zealand — 1995 final

The most incredible moment happened after the 1995 World Cup final when New Zealand faced an inspired South Africa. With the score tied at the end of regulation, the match went into extra time, and was eventually won 15–12 on a drop goal by South Africa. Without at all minimizing the monumental effort put in by the players on the pitch, what we'll never forget took place at the trophy presentation.

At a time when South Africa was struggling to reunite a nation divided by generations of apartheid, the sight of Nelson Mandela up on the podium in a Springbok jersey, pumping his fists in the air, when Bok Captain François Pienaar lifted the Webb Ellis Cup was truly inspirational. It was a moment when sport transcended politics and a divided nation took a brief respite from the enormous task of nation-building to celebrate as one.

Australia versus South Africa — 1999 semifinal #1

The 1999 semifinals both stand out because of what happened on the field of play. In the first semi, South Africa faced Australia after drop kicking England out of the quarterfinals. The game went into extra time and was won by a drop goal from the Wallabies' Stephen Larkham. The game had all the elements of a classic, smashmouth encounter, punctuated by patches of enterprising play, throughout a seesaw affair that sapped the collective energy from the capacity crowd at Twickenham. After the match, supporters from both sides were so exhausted and emotionally drained from the twists and turns of the match that you couldn't tell which team had won. Everyone in attendance knew they had witnessed something special that would be remembered for years to come and were gracious in victory and defeat.

After the drama of the first semifinal, we all chatted over a few beers and came to the well-reasoned conclusion that Sunday's semifinal couldn't possibly match the drama and excitement of the Wallabies win over the Springboks. The next day, in observing the procession from Twickenham station to the stadium, the All Black fans were relaxed and cocky in contemplating the destruction to come, while the French supporters looked to be on a death march, with heads down and nary a smile among them.

GUTHRIE SAYS

Walking Twickenham

Every now and then, working in the TV business has its perks. After literally living in the windowless edit bay in the basement of Fox Sports World for the round-robin stages of the 1999 Rugby World Cup, my boss approved a classic junket as a reward for my dedication. Being a licensed broadcaster, Fox received a few semifinals and finals tickets as part of the deal. When the top brass passed on them, I played the advantage and asked whether I might be released from my underground dungeon to pop over to London for the semis and then immediately return to L.A. before we taped our studio show.

My "job" was to make sure the pay-per-view signal was all sorted out so the folks back home in the U.S. and Canada could watch live. With a few minutes to spare before kickoff, inspiration struck. It occurred to me that Brown and I had been issued all access media passes and that we were entitled to walk out onto the hallowed Twickenham turf if we so desired. So just before the teams took the field, we marched out of the tunnel and past an array of security guards stationed to keep out the riffraff.

Before we knew it, we were walking the perimeter of the pitch, being careful not to step on the field and stopping periodically to feign a purpose for our perambulation, by pointing up at some imaginary friends that were seated amongst the 50,000-plus who anxiously awaited the impending kickoff. The atmosphere at pitch level was totally and completely awesome. Before we finished our walk around, Brown ran into a photographer he knew from Latvia who asked what possible business we might have walking out on the field before such a huge match. We explained that we had to perform a safety check of the ground just to make sure everything was ready for the match to proceed! Finding everything in order, we marched back up the tunnel and took up our positions in the TV truck. Of course, after our pre-game blessing ritual set the stage, the French team shocked the world with an awesome display of attacking rugby that left the heavily favored All Blacks in tatters. I still get chills thinking about the feeling of looking up at that crowd and the spectacle that followed.

New Zealand versus France — 1999 semifinal #2

The game that followed gets our vote as the most exciting World Cup match
ever played. At a time when a beef row had elevated tensions in the Anglo-
French relationship, a curious thing happened within the mostly British crowd
when the French began their second-half comeback. The crowd suddenly
realized that the French had a chance after all, and virtually every non–New
Zealander in the stands started pulling for the French to win. The Tricolors,
displaying all their Gallic flair, scored 26 unanswered points playing vintage
champagne rugby that left the Kiwis dazed and confused. By the end of the
match, a Stade de France crowd couldn't have cheered any louder for Les
Blues. Their 43–31 victory proved the old adage that any team can win on the
day, and on October 31, 1999, that day belonged to the French.

Sevens World Cup

The sevens game has long been a fixture on the international scene but the first
IRB Sevens World Cup wasn't played until 1993 in Edinburgh. The participants
play for the Melrose Cup, named after the city in Scotland where the seven-
a-side game developed in the 1880s. In the inaugural final, England defeated
Australia 21–17.

The second Sevens World Cup moved to Hong Kong, the venue responsible
for popularizing the game and bringing it international attention. It delivered
a multitude of exciting games and plenty of local color. Fiji, led by their
legendary sevens magician, Waisale Serevi, defeated South Africa in the
final 24–21.

The Sevens World Cup, following the pattern of almost all sevens events,
features consolation brackets. The USA Eagles made an impressive showing,
beating a very capable Japanese side 40–28 in the Bowl Final, to take home
some hardware.

In 2001, the third edition of the Sevens World Cup moved across the Pacific to
Mar Del Plata, Argentina. Sevens is a unique game that allows smaller nations
to become competitive at a much faster rate than is possible in the 15-a-side
game. Qualifying tournaments for the event were held all over the globe and a
total of 91 countries took part. New Zealand totally dominated the tournament
scoring 251 points while giving up only 40 points over 8 matches, including
their 31–12 victory over Australia to win the Melrose Cup.

Women's Rugby World Cup

The Women's Rugby World Cup was not sanctioned as an official IRB championship until 1998, but the first competition took place in Wales in 1991. Twelve countries participated and the surprise winner was the United States, beating England 19–6 in the final, to become the first modern-day U.S. rugby team to be crowned World Champions!

Figure 13-1:
USA Women team photo after winning World Cup 1991.

After the first one it was decided to alter the timing so that the event wouldn't be in the same year as the men's World Cup. Thus, the next tourney was scheduled for 1994 in Holland. Various problems in the lead-up prevented the IRB from giving its approval to the competition in the Netherlands and as a result most national unions pulled funding from their squads. An alternative tournament was organized in Scotland, and it was attended by 12 sides. The U.S. faced England again in the final. This time, however, England knocked them off their perch as World Champions, winning 38–23 in an exciting affair. With scant support from their national union, the Eagle women soared high on the strength of their individual ability and team spirit.

In 1998 the IRB made it official and 16 teams competed in Amsterdam. The Canadian women reached their first World Cup semifinal but lost 46–6 to the United States. The Black Ferns from New Zealand rampaged through the tournament and ended up easily winning the final 46–12 over the Eagles.

Barcelona, Spain, was the site for the Women's Rugby World Cup in 2002. England and New Zealand met in the final and the Black Ferns won their second consecutive title 19–9, firmly establishing themselves as the dominant force in the women's game. New Zealand and England have clearly created a gap between themselves and the rest of the world as a direct result of their unions' vision and investment in developing the women's game.

The Under-21 Rugby World Cup

The Under-21 Rugby World Cup grew out of the SANZAR/UAR Under-21 tournament that began in 1995 involving Argentina, Australia, New Zealand, and South Africa, and steadily added other countries in following years. The cup exposes promising youngsters to a high level of international competition and among today's brightest stars are numerous alumni of the annual event.

The inaugural IRB Under-21 World Cup was held in South Africa in 2002. The Baby Boks continued a South African tradition of winning World Cups on home soil with a 24–21 victory over Australia in the final.

In 2003, the Under-21 World Cup was staged in England. The second edition saw New Zealand and Australia play to a thrilling 37-all draw in pool play, only to meet again in the Final, where the young Kiwis prevailed over the mini-marsupials 21–10.

In the span of just 16 years, the IRB has created four distinct World Cup competitions, giving men, women, sevens specialists, and future stars their own championship to aspire to, where they can test themselves against the best in the world. The challenge for the IRB is to raise the standard of play of the lower-level nations, which will inevitably lead to rugby becoming a truly global game.

Chapter 14

The International Calendar

R ugby fans around the world enjoy a plethora of international and provincial competitions that run year-round. For more than 130 years, until the first Rugby World Cup in 1987, international test matches served as the highest level of the game. Over that period, leagues gradually developed on a regional basis.

In 1996 the rugby calendar changed forever when the three leading southern hemisphere powers, South Africa, New Zealand, and Australia, joined together and created the Tri Nations Series and the Super 12. This established an annual schedule of international matches for each nation and included an interprovincial competition where the leading regional sides from the big three would play 69 matches leading to a winner. The 1995–96 season also saw the Six Nations unions launch the European Cup, the north's version of the Super 12.

Despite these international developments, the heart and soul of rugby is the game that is still played at the domestic provincial level. All of the leading rugby nations have their own leagues where future stars are cultivated amid deep running local passions. In this chapter, we give you a tour of rugby's annual calendar, looking first at the international order, then dropping down to the interprovincial scene, and finishing off with a dab of local provincial color.

The Powers That Be

The first international, or *test match*, was played between England and Scotland in 1871. A test match is a game where caps are awarded by the respective national unions to signify that the players are representing their country.

In the early days, caps were made of wool with fancy embroidery and served as a keepsake for those who were lucky enough to earn one. In the modern game, with a few notable exceptions among the smaller amateur unions, this practice of actually awarding a cap has fallen by the wayside, and the term "cap" simply means that the player has appeared on the pitch in a full international match for his country.

In the 1880s, England and Scotland were joined by Wales and Ireland, and the International Championship began. These four home unions were joined by France in 1910 to form the Five Nations. Although France was thrown out of the competition from 1931 to 1939, the Five Nations served as the world's first and most prominent annual international competition from the early 1900s to 1999, when it expanded to include Italy and become the Six Nations.

While Europe focused on the Five (and then Six) Nations, the southern power-houses of Australia, New Zealand, and South Africa had to be content with organizing periodic tours, as they lacked an annual international set of fixtures. Although New Zealand's first recorded test match was against Australia in 1893, it took the southern giants more than 100 years to organize their own yearly international competition.

Where tradition is king — the Six Nations

The Six Nations is the world's oldest rugby tournament, possessing a rich and colorful history that tracks the regional rivalries and the tumultuous times that Northern Europe has endured over the past 120 years. Over that period, England and Scotland have played 120 tests, each one a microcosm of the unique political and social circumstances prevailing at the time.

Over the course of 12 decades, two historically distinct terms, the "Triple Crown" and the "Grand Slam" have developed in the Six Nations. To take the *Triple Crown*, which was first contested only amongst the four original "home unions" of England, Scotland, Wales, and Ireland, you had to win all three games against those teams. The *Grand Slam* was added into the mix after the French joined. To win the Grand Slam, you must make a clean sweep and defeat every other country. England has won the most Grand Slams and Triple Crowns.

From February to April of each year, the Six Nations occupies the attention of rugby fans around the world. Each nation plays all five of the other teams and the winner is determined by a scoring system that takes into account wins, draws, and points differential for tie breaking. The fans bring with them all the attendant historical regional rivalries that have colored the Anglo-French, Anglo-Welsh, and Anglo-Irish relationships (plus all the other national permutations) over several generations. The Welsh team can lose all their other games, but if they beat England, that makes their entire campaign a success. Such is the nature of the beast in the Six Nations.

North versus south — the SANZAR home tests

When the southern hemisphere unions of South Africa, New Zealand, and Australia joined forces to create SANZAR (SA, NZ, AR) in 1996, professionalism was ushered in with the force of a cosmic Big Bang. Suddenly, the three juggernauts were charged with producing a series of annual rugby events to satisfy the requirements of a mammoth US$550 million television contract.

One part of that commitment included SANZAR's agreement to regularly host touring sides in-bound from Europe, the Pacific Islands and Argentina each June. The International Rugby Board (IRB) sets the fixtures on a rotating basis where England, Ireland, Wales, Scotland, France, Italy, Argentina, Samoa, Fiji and Tonga make tours to the SANZAR countries. For example, in 2003 England played two matches in New Zealand and one in Australia. The previous June, England toured Argentina, in 2001 they traveled to North America, and in 2000 to South Africa. The IRB schedules the games so all of the teams play each other on a rotating basis and the smaller unions get a chance to periodically measure themselves against the best.

The battle of the Big Three — the Tri Nations

The Tri Nations Series delivers some of the world's most exciting and tense rugby action every year. The Series features New Zealand, South Africa, and Australia (the three countries that won the first four Rugby World Cups) in a home and away extravaganza that produces six huge tests a year. Each nation hosts two games and plays one on the road in the other two countries. Since its inception in 1996, the Tri Nations Series has produced some of the finest tests ever played, including the 2000 Australia versus New Zealand encounter, which is regarded by many as the best test match of all time.

Like the Six Nations, the Tri Nations is a natural outgrowth of the traditional rugby rivalries that exist between these three rugby mad behemoths. New Zealand and South Africa's rivalry on the pitch is well established in each nation's collective consciousness, going back to South Africa's first tour of New Zealand in 1921. Since their first meeting in Dunedin, the All Blacks and Springboks have battled each other with a fierce intensity that is rarely matched in any sport. New Zealand holds a very narrow lead in the all-time series, which serves as a testament to how evenly matched these nations have been throughout the years on the pitch.

The greatest test ever

In 2000, Australia and New Zealand played before a world-record 109,874 fans at Stadium Australia in Sydney in what has since come to be regarded as the best test ever played. The World Champion Wallabies had won ten straight tests and boasted the world's most skilled backline, the best scrumhalf combination on the planet in George Gregan and Stephen Larkham, and arguably Australia's best-ever captain in John Eales. The All Blacks went into the match with the burden of sky-high expectations that plague every Kiwi side, plus a boatload of talent, including the most feared attacker in the game, a 6'5", 265-pound monster named Jonah Lomu. The Tongan Torpedo had wreaked havoc at the 1995 World Cup, running over and through everything that got in his path, and after a bout with a rare kidney illness, the big man was again primed for action. The game started magically for New Zealand, with three converted tries and a penalty in the first eight minutes. The Wallabies had barely even touched the ball; it was a dream start for the All Blacks and a nightmare for the Wallabies. Being down 24 to zip, the Aussies could easily have given up, but in his typically icy cool fashion, John Eales summoned his troops under the posts and instructed them to stick to the game plan and told them they were capable of getting back into the match if they just didn't panic. From the ensuing kickoff, the Wallabies controlled the ball and Stephen Larkham broke the line to find Stirling Mortlock, who dotted down for the try. By halftime the Wallabies had scored 24 unanswered points of their own and it was 24–24 at the interval. The second half was a seesaw affair in which the reserve hooker, Jeremy Paul, scored a try with two minutes left and put the Australians up 35–34. The Australian crowd went crazy, as they thought the match was surely won! Then, three minutes into injury time, the All Blacks worked the ball out to Jonah Lomu and the big fella rounded the corner to score the match winner. The final score was 39–35 as New Zealand clinched victory at the death in a breathless match that produced ten tries over 80-plus minutes of heart-stopping action. It was an extraordinary match for the ages that we've watched about a dozen times since and will never forget.

Since the inaugural campaign in 1996, New Zealand has dominated the Tri Nations Series, winning five of eight titles, with Australia having won twice and South Africa only once in 1998.

The *Bledisloe Cup*, which is awarded to the winner of the annual test series between New Zealand and Australia, is the most coveted piece of hardware on offer between these two antipodean nations. Under the current Tri Nations Series format, the two All Blacks versus Wallabies games double as Tri Nations and Bledisloe Cup encounters. The importance of the Bledisloe Cup to Kiwis was emphatically demonstrated at Eden Park in 2003 when the crowd politely clapped as Captain Rueben Thorne lifted the Tri Nations Cup — then roared with approval when he hoisted the Bledisloe Cup for the first time in more than five years. The Cup is by far the biggest prize in any sport within the trans-tasman rivalry.

North versus south — the Fall tests

In October and November of each year, the southern hemisphere teams head north to face the European powers. Similar to the SANZAR tests in June, these matches afford an opportunity to see how the best of the north shape up against the south. Australia, New Zealand, and South Africa, plus occasionally Argentina, and the Pacific Island nations of Fiji, Samoa, and Tonga, make the journey to play against some combination of England, Scotland, Wales, Ireland, Italy, or France. The in-bound sides generally play two or three European nations over a three- to four-week tour.

The British and Irish Lions

The British and Irish Lions are an all-star team composed of the best national team players from England, Scotland, Wales, and Ireland. The Lions assemble every four years and have a long and storied tradition dating back to 1888, when the first representative side from Great Britain made a mammoth five month tour of New Zealand and Australia, playing an incredible 35 matches. Since that first tour, the Lions (or a derivative side from the U.K.) have played 575 matches around the world.

Becroft and Braugh's moment

When the Lions tour they take the game out to rugby's hinterlands. On the early tours, local clubs were competitive — the Lions tied their last match of the 1888 tour against the provincial team from Wanganui, New Zealand. With the onset of professionalism, Lions games against the smaller provinces have become one-sided affairs, with the class, skill, and pace of the Lions proving too much for the amateur sides to handle.

In 2001, the Lions assembled a powerful side to challenge the World Champion Wallabies and opened their ten-match Australian tour in the far western corner of the continent in Perth, against an amateur Western Australia team called the Swans. Within two minutes, the Lions had scored the first of their nine unanswered first-half tries. At the break, it was 57–0, but to their credit the Swans never quit playing. The biggest ovation of the night happened in the 51st minute when Brent Becroft dove over in the corner to become the first player from Western Australia to score a try against the Lions. With the Lions pushing for 100 points, the crowd rose to their feet again when reserve scrumhalf Robbie Braugh scored the second try for the local boys. In the end, the Lions ravaged the home side, notching 18 tries to post their highest ever score, winning 116–10!

Rarely in sports do amateurs get a chance to compete against the world's best. Regardless of the final score, Becroft and Braugh accomplished something historic and totally unique to rugby. No matter what they do in life, they'll always be famous in Perth for the day they faced the Lions and scored a try.

One of the main features of a Lions tour is that they make a point of playing numerous games against the smaller provincial or club sides in the country they visit. This brings world class rugby out to the people around the country and gives local players the chance to get a game against some of the world's best rugby players.

A Lions tour is a huge party for legions of British and Irish fans who take leave from work for a month-long rugby celebration that, in many cases, takes about four years to recover from.

The Lions have been hugely successful both on the field and more recently as a commercial enterprise. They have dominated the Wallabies, winning 9 and losing only 3 times, trail the Springboks in the series 8–12–3 and have struggled against the All Blacks winning just 4 while losing 21 with 2 ties. The Lions teams of 1955 and 1974 earned series victories in South Africa, the 1971 side won their only test series in New Zealand, and the 2001 Lions were the first to lose a series in Australia after four successive triumphs down under.

The Barbarian Football Club

The Barbarian Football Club was created in England in 1890 to foster goodwill and fellowship amongst rugby players around the world. The Barbarians' (also known as the Baa-Baas) creed is "Rugby Football is a game for gentlemen in all classes, but for no bad sportsman in any class." The club is unique in that they are a touring-only side that doesn't have a home field, clubhouse, or membership fees. Players are selected by invitation only and the Barbarians' list of rugby luminaries is loaded with legendary names.

When the Australians toured the U.K. in 1948, the Barbarians played them in a fundraiser to finance the Wallabies' desire to play a match against Canada on their way home. Since that watershed moment, the Baa-Baas have been a regular fixture at the tail end of U.K. tours, promoting a wide-open style of attacking rugby designed to entertain without the pressure of having to win. As a result, the scorelines are normally well above test averages and provide value for money to the paying customers, whose hard-earned money goes to a variety of charitable causes.

The most famous Barbarian victory is the 1973 win over New Zealand. In that match the rugby world's all-time greatest scrumhalf, Wales' Gareth Edwards, scored "The Try" that is regarded by many as the best try ever scored. The Baa-Baas went on to win 23–11 before a hysterical Cardiff Arms Park crowd. In typical Barbarians camaraderie, the moment of the match came after the fulltime blast when the teams gathered at midfield and joined together to sing "Now Is the Hour" and "Auld Lang Syne." There are at least nine Barbarian clubs that have formed around the world to emulate the unique ethos of the original club, including the New Zealand, French, South African, and South American Barbarians.

The World Sevens Series

The IRB's World Sevens Series was launched in 1999 and serves as the annual international competition for the seven-a-side game. While several events had long been a fixture on the annual sevens calendar, including the oval planet's week-long party each March in Hong Kong, the advent of the Series instituted a points system to crown a World Sevens Series Champion. Series points are tallied over the course of the year to determine a winner.

The World Sevens Series has experienced some growing pains since 1999. The Series was launched with ten events and has since constricted to seven events for the 2002–03 season, cancelling three of the stops for security and financial reasons.

New Zealand has totally dominated the Series, winning the title over the first three years, from 1999–00, 2000–01, and 2002–03. The Kiwis also won the Sevens World Cup in 2001.

For the 2003–04 season, the IRB awarded USA Rugby a stop on the World Sevens Series — the USA Sevens. Venued at the Home Depot Center in Carson, California, the USA Sevens is the first-ever multinational rugby event where teams from all the leading nations came to the USA to compete. (For more details about the Sevens World Cup, see the "Sevens World Cup" section in Chapter 13.)

Interprovincial and Provincial Rugby

Positioned just below test rugby in the global rugby pecking order, inter-provincial competition pits the best teams against others within their regions. For example, the Tri Nations countries of Australia, New Zealand, and South Africa also compete at the interprovincial level in the Super 12. Likewise, the Six Nations members compete interprovincially in the European Cup. While international, or test rugby, drove the development of the amateur game over its first 125 years, since the dawn of professionalism in 1996 the Super 12 and the European Cup have had an enormous impact on the way the game is played around the world.

The next level is national provincial action, where traditional rivalries abound amongst the New Zealand, South African, and Irish provincial sides. The heart of rugby will always reside at the provincial level where local rivals compete within a rich tapestry of historical encounters.

The sensational Super 12

The Super 12 annually delivers the world's most exciting rugby action. The competition was established in 1996 and includes 12 franchises. Five teams hail from New Zealand, four from South Africa, and three from Australia. The Kiwi sides include the Blues, Chiefs, Crusaders, Highlanders, and Hurricanes. The Aussie teams are the ACT Brumbies, Reds, and Waratahs. The Bulls, Cats, Sharks, and Stormers are the South African representatives.

The Super 12 season runs from mid-February to late May each year and features 12 weeks of regular season play, followed by the semifinals and the final. In all, there are 69 Super 12 games every year. The sheer number of games and the length of the season make the Super 12 a fan-friendly tournament, as enthusiasts can follow their teams' progress through the course of a long and difficult season. The relative parity among the teams also makes the Super 12 an exciting competition to follow because the race for semifinal berths always comes down to the final regular season weekend.

New Zealand teams have won seven of the nine titles since 1996. The Blues won the first two and again in 2003, the Crusaders won four times, and the Brumbies triumphs in 2001 and 2004 stand as the only non-New Zealand Super 12 Championship. The Super 12 is the breeding ground for the southern hemisphere's stars of tomorrow, as the season directly precedes the selection of the SANZAR countries' national teams for the June tests.

The Heineken Cup overfloweth

The Heineken Cup is Europe's version of interprovincial competition. The tournament was launched in the fall of 1995 by the then Five Nations committee to provide a new level of cross-border play.

Twelve teams competed in the inaugural season with Toulouse lifting the European Cup for the first time. In 1996–97 the league expanded to 20 teams in four pools of five and after 46 matches, the French were singing in the streets of Cardiff, when Brive were crowned Heineken Cup Champions in front of 41,664 at Cardiff Arms Park.

In the 1997–98 season, the format was changed again with pool matches being played both home and away, and the addition of three quarterfinal playoffs, bringing the total number of games to 70. In the final, England's storied Bath club lifted the Heineken Cup after overcoming the defending champs 19–18. Our Man of the Match was none other than USA Eagle Number 8, Dan Lyle, who created Bath's only try of the match.

The politics-driven absence of the English sides in the 1998–99 season prevented Bath from defending their title, opening the door for Ireland's Ulster to defeat Colomiers 21–6 for the first Irish victory on the European interprovincial scene.

In the1999–2000 season, perennial bridesmaids Northampton pipped Munster by a single point to earn the Saints first major cup title in the club's long and tortured history of coming up second best in a variety of competitions. The Leicester Tigers pounced on the Cup in 2000–01 and became the first team to defend their title when they repeated the feat in 2001–02. The 2002–03 season saw Toulouse join Leicester as the only teams to hoist the Heineken Cup twice.

The Air New Zealand National Provincial Championship

The Air New Zealand National Provincial Championship is hands down the best domestic competition in the world. New Zealand is divided into 27 provincial unions that all field representative teams. Although the format has evolved somewhat since the National Provincial Championship (NPC) was established in 1976, the current set-up has the 27 provincial teams organized into three divisions. Teams can move up and down via a promotion and relegation system.

The Ranfurly Shield

The Ranfurly Shield is the most coveted piece of domestic hardware in New Zealand sports. It's contested on a challenge basis, with the holders usually defending the Log of Wood at selected home matches. The trophy was presented to Auckland in 1902 by the Governor General of New Zealand, the fifth Earl of Ranfurly. Since then, the Ranfurly Shield has dominated the thoughts of all New Zealand rugby players and inspired the dreams of countless Kiwi youngsters, imagining themselves making the critical play to win the Shield. One of the things that makes it so special is that even the smallest provinces periodically get a shot at lifting the Shield. When Marlborough upset Canterbury in 1973, the entire town broke into a delirious celebration that will always be remembered as the high point for local pride. For the challenger's fans, Shield week is a glorious time of eternal hope where numerous receptions and prefatory events focus on the upcoming encounter and culminate with a mandatory road trip to the holder's venue for the game. For the holders, each defense comes complete with a defense song and a full compliment of hospitality and shield fervor. For the few players who get the chance to play for the Shield, it's the highlight of their careers and they leave everything on the pitch in pursuit of their place in New Zealand's rugby folklore.

The NPC displays a rich wealth of talent throughout the ten first-division teams. Each of the provinces play a unique style of rugby that developed through adaptation to particular local conditions and coaching styles. Even though the All Blacks' availability to participate in the NPC is limited, it's still loaded with outstanding performers — a testament to the incredible depth of the talent pool in the Land of the Long White Cloud!

Auckland is the dominant provincial team in New Zealand, with the most players, financial resources, and NPC titles, having won 13 times since 1976!

The South African ABSA Currie Cup

Even though rugby-mad South Africans think it's delicious, the Currie Cup is not, in fact a hot Asian dish served over rice, but rather, South Africa's premier domestic rugby competition. The Holy Grail of South African rugby is named after Sir Donald Currie, who first presented the cup in 1891 to Griqualand West. The inaugural Currie Cup Tournament was held in Kimberly in 1892. In subsequent years, the trophy was awarded periodically using various tournament- and log-style formats. In 1939, the first Currie Cup final was played at Newlands in Cape Town and after Transvaal beat Western Province, the trophy was only occasionally on offer, until the return of the annual finals system in 1946.

The Currie Cup format is currently broken into an eight-team Premier Division and six-team First Division. The top two sides from each group meet in a final with the premier finalists competing for the Currie Cup. Western Province has dominated the Currie Cup, winning 29 times, while the Blue Bulls have taken top honors 18 times. Together, the two teams account for 47 of the 61 times the Currie Cup has been officially awarded.

English domestic scene

Until recently, the English domestic game was contested through knock-out play for various cups. Under this model, teams from all divisions would compete in a single elimination tournament leading to an annual English Cup Champion. The establishment of an English League is a recent invention since the launch of the Courage Leagues. With multiple changes in corporate backing, the Courage League became the Allied Dunbar Premiership in the 1997–98 season, and then the Zurich Premiership in 2000–01.

The process of playing a league season with points tables leading to a champion is now an integral part of the English club game. The Zurich Premiership, more than any other domestic league on the planet, contains a huge contingent of foreign players from New Zealand, South Africa, Australia, Ireland, Wales, Scotland, France, and other leading rugby nations. Bath and Leicester have historically dominated the competition, winning six titles each since 1987.

The Celtic scene

With the success of the Zurich Premiership making a British league impossible, the Celtic nations of Ireland, Scotland, and Wales launched the Celtic League in 2001 to raise the standard of their domestic competitions and to provide additional income. The 12 Celtic League teams include five Welsh, four Irish, and three Scottish provinces.

The first-ever Celtic League fixture was held on August 17, 2001. Over the course of the inaugural campaign Irish sides earned three of the four semifinal berths. The final was staged at Lansdowne Road in Dublin with Leinster defeating Munster for the hardware. In 2002–03, Munster erased the memory of the previous final, with a comprehensive 37–12 victory over Welsh side Neath.

The proliferation of interprovincial competitions like the Super 12, the Heineken Cup, and the Celtic League all serve to create an intermediate step in the professional era from provincial to national team play. It's no surprise then that the likes of Australia, New Zealand, South Africa, England, France, Ireland, Wales, Scotland, and Italy have all consistently improved since those competitions were created. The challenge for the Americas is to develop its own framework of provincial and interprovincial leagues to stop losing ground.

Chapter 15

North American Rugby

*U*nbeknownst to all but the most die-hard fans, rugby in North America has a long and storied history. In Canada, the game developed mostly on both coasts and was able to sustain a continuous if low-key presence for the entire twentieth century. From hazy beginnings at the collegiate level, the United States managed to win two Olympic gold medals in the 1920s before the game all but vanished from the American sporting consciousness.

In this chapter we'll give you an overview of the somewhat nebulous history of rugby in North America including the formation of the two national governing bodies, detail the significant accomplishments of both Canadian and American representative teams on the world stage, and look at their current involvement in various international tournaments.

Rugby in Canada

Rugby in Canada dates back to the 1860s when it was initially played by army and navy personnel in British Columbia and Nova Scotia.

The first recorded match was played in Montreal amongst the members of an artillery unit in 1864.

The early desire for standardized play, always a crucial moment in any burgeoning game, was met by Toronto's Trinity College, who published a set of rules for rugby that same year. In 1868, the Montreal Football Club was formed, making it Canada's first official rugby organization. These identifiable firsts point to a growing interest in the sport in diverse parts of the country.

Over the next two decades, as more and more clubs sprouted across the width of the nation, an administrative structure also developed, beginning with the establishment of the British Columbia Rugby Union in 1889, followed by the formation of the Maritime Provinces Rugby Union in 1890, and the Manitoba Rugby Football Union in 1892.

Rugby's development in Canada was slowed considerably by both World Wars, but since 1945, it has spread to every province. Rugby is now a permanent fixture on the Canadian sporting landscape.

The birth of Rugby Canada

The first incarnation of a national governing body for the sport took place in 1929 with the creation of the Rugby Union of Canada. The organization functioned for the next ten years before going into hibernation for the duration of World War II and beyond. Following the war, most administrative issues were dealt with on a provincial level until the re-formation of the national group in 1965. During the 1960s, Canada played test matches only sporadically so there wasn't actually a mountain of responsibility placed on the volunteer administrators.

In 1974 the body that is now known as Rugby Canada was incorporated and took over the day-to-day running of the sport at the national level. This was sufficient until the first Rugby World Cup in 1987. The desire to compete in the tournament prompted Canada to become a member of the International Rugby Board (IRB). (For more details on the IRB, see Chapter 5. For more details on the Rugby World Cup, see Chapter 13.) Since that momentous decision, Rugby Canada has placed a high priority on regular participation at the international level in men's, women's, under-19s, under-21s, and sevens rugby.

The Canadians played their first recognized international in 1932 against Japan, but it wasn't until the 1970s that they began to play tests on a regular basis. Canada has always been known as a tough team who can't be intimidated on the pitch. Over the last dozen years the national team has occasionally competed successfully with the top teams in the world.

In the 1991 World Cup, Canada opened the tournament by beating Fiji and Romania before losing a close contest to France. The two wins, however, were good enough to advance to the quarterfinals for the first time. On a quagmire of a pitch in Lille, France, Canada hung tough against the All Blacks but came up short, losing 13–29.

In 1993 Canada shocked Wales 26–24 at the Arms Park in Cardiff and in 1994 they beat France 18–16 in Nepean. In 2000 Canada continued the tradition of battling strongly against quality opposition by drawing a match 27–27 with

Ireland in Markham, Ontario. Their most recent scalping of a Six Nations side came in 2002 when the touring Scots were upended 26–23 in Vancouver when flyhalf Jared Barker kicked 16 points. Since the game went professional in 1995, Canada has contributed numerous players to the top leagues in Great Britain and France. Unfortunately, this has prevented the members of the national team from training together in a cohesive fashion before big tournaments and has led to some disappointing results. Canada had high hopes of making their second quarterfinal appearance going into the 2003 World Cup, but were able to win only one match against Tonga and failed to move on to the knockout stage. (For more details about the Rugby World Cup, see Chapter 13.)

Canadian women on the rise

Women's rugby in Canada began in the late 1970s in various parts of the country, but there was no organized interprovincial competition until 1983. Four years later the women's national team played their inaugural match in Victoria, British Columbia, against the United States.

Canada has competed in all four Women's World Cups beginning in 1991. In the first tournament in Wales, Canada lost to New Zealand in the opener but drew with the hosts to end up 0–1–1. In Scotland, for the 1994 event, the team lost in the quarterfinals to England, beat Japan in the Shield semifinal, and fell 5–11 to the Scottish women in the final for an eighth-place finish.

The 1998 World Cup in Amsterdam was the first to be officially sanctioned by the IRB, and the Canadian women benefited from increased support from Rugby Canada. The national side reached their first World Cup semifinal in the Netherlands but lost 46–6 to the United States.

In 2002, Barcelona was the site for the fourth Women's World Cup and once again the Canadians were solid contenders. An opening round 57–0 destruction of Ireland was followed by another shutout, this time 11–0 over Scotland. That victory propelled Canada into the semifinals to face England where they were thumped 53–10.

Sevens

The Canadian Sevens team has performed very well in the seven-a-side game. They have a regularly collected hardware on the World Sevens Series, and in 2004, they won two Bowl trophies in Dubai, UAE and George, South Africa, and were beaten finalists in the Plate division in Los Angeles. Some of Canada's stars of the future can be seen on their sevens team today.

Rugby in the United States

Knowledgeable rugby commentators from around the globe often remark that the USA is a sleeping giant. The theory is postulated that as soon as the United States is properly exposed to the game, a vast supply of superior athletes will take the world by storm. Unfortunately, this school of thought totally misses the mark on two key points. The first assumption is that superior athleticism will make Americans world-beaters. This ignores the critical role that learning the game from a young age serves in developing players with rugby vision. Knowledge of the game and finely honed skills are more significant than physical attributes in separating the good from the great players. If the NFL Pro Bowl team lined up against the All Blacks, even with a solid year of rugby-specific coaching, the NFLers would get a massive lesson in tactics, and would struggle to compete at all.

The second misperception is the notion that American expertise in the business of sports will be able to transform our shortcomings on the field with a magic bullet of slick marketing and boatloads of cash. This is false for two reasons, the most compelling being that the U.S. sporting marketplace is incredibly crowded with well-established sports, all competing for a finite pool of television time and sponsorship dollars. This is further complicated by the emergence of made-for-TV sports like the X-Games that are created and backed by the networks themselves.

The second obstacle is that rugby is viewed by most Americans as a foreign game and therefore ignored by mainstream media companies and sports marketers. Americans are notoriously parochial and inward-looking when it comes to sports. The reality is that the United States is not a sleeping giant, it's a comatose one. The good news is that new leadership at the top of the game finally has the country poised to get off life support and back on the right track to catch up with the rest of the world.

Origins and Olympic gold

In this age of all-encompassing media coverage of sports, it is easy to forget that in earlier times games were played largely for fun. Many different kinds of ball sports emerged and flourished on a regional basis throughout the United States without benefit of central governing bodies to codify every rule and legitimize each individual competition. Rugby was one such game that was played in various forms across the country. The origin of the game of rugby in England was deliberately obscured by those who wanted to promote it as an exclusive endeavor. In America, the beginnings are murky because rugby's roots are intertwined with those of American football — and for a while they were one game before splitting into completely separate sports.

It is generally agreed that the first rugby match in the United States, of which a written record exists, occurred in May of 1874 when Harvard University played host to Montreal's McGill University. This contest led to attempts at determining a definite set of rules and inspired collegians in various parts of the country to take up the game. For the next thirty years, rugby was the primary form of football competition in the United States. If you could go back in time to watch, however, the game would bear little resemblance to rugby union as we know it today.

The catalyst that split the game into Rugby and American Football was the attention of President Theodore Roosevelt. Following an outcry over numerous deaths and injuries caused by the then violent nature of the game, reform was demanded and Roosevelt led the charge to modify the more extreme parts of the sport. The end result was that most of the leading colleges latched on to the reconstituted game, which eventually became gridiron, while in certain areas, notably the West Coast, rugby continued to be the dominant version of the sport. In the years before World War I, teams like the All Blacks and the Waratahs, the precursor to the Wallabies, toured from Los Angeles to Vancouver on their way to Britain. Thus, it was no surprise that when the U.S. Olympic committee authorized a team to compete at the 1920 Games in Antwerp almost all of the players were from Northern and Southern California. The rugby competition at the Seventh Olympiad was really just a one-off match between the United States and France, which the Americans won 8–0 to earn the gold medal.

Figure 15-1:
1924 USA
Olympic
Gold Medal
Team.

The 1924 Games in Paris were far more dramatic but still featured only the United States, France, and Romania. After the Americans and the French both dispatched the Romanians, who were awarded the bronze medal, the two sides met in front of a 50,000-strong, heavily partisan crowd at Colombes Stadium. The Frenchmen in the stands had come to see their countrymen win a gold medal — and when the match swung decisively in the visitors' favor, the audience took on the characteristics of a mob. A 17–3 triumph by the Americans only inflamed the assembled spectators. The poor behavior is sometimes pointed to as one of the reasons why rugby was never again contested in the Olympic Games. Any momentum for the sport gained by winning two consecutive gold medals quickly ebbed when subsequent Olympiads failed to include rugby in their program of events.

The Dave Hodges story

Dave Hodges is the captain of the U.S. National Team and has led the Eagles into battle 27 times over his 51 test-match career. Since his debut in 1996 against Uruguay, Dave has been a mainstay of the Eagles program, delivering a fully committed performance each and every time he has taken the pitch. He's a humble, soft-spoken, blue-collar skipper who puts in the hard work and leads by example. After six years' playing professionally for Llanelli and Bridgend in Wales, Dave has transformed himself into a complete rugby player, but that's not the game he originally intended to play.

Being a football player from an early age, Dave aspired to play in the NFL. He was a three-time all-league outside linebacker at Occidental College earning Division III All-American honors in 1989. After Oxy, Dave played football professionally for the Hamburg Blue Devils in 1993–94. When he returned from Europe to Los Angeles following his stint with the Blue Devils, the Oxy Olde Boys were in the middle of our summer sevens season and we welcomed Dave back into our side for the Sunsplash Sevens in Long Beach. We went undefeated thanks to a last movement match-winning try from Dave in the final. He was clearly the MVP of the tournament. At the reception, the coaches from Belmont Shore and OMBAC both made a concerted effort to recruit him to play for their sides. Knowing that he needed first-division exposure and experience to have any real chance of making the Eagles, Dave chose OMBAC and was selected to play for the national team soon after. The key factors that enable Dave to excel at rugby are his intelligence and raw athleticism. As a conscientious student of the game, Dave was able to rapidly assimilate rugby's intricacies, to make up for lost time and become a solid professional despite his late introduction to the highest level of the game. Dave's success proves that if you have the physical attributes and are willing to commit yourself to learning the game, becoming an international rugby star is not an impossible dream for North Americans.

Figure 15-2:
3-time past President of USA Rugby, Bob Watkins (left), and USA Captain Dave Hodges.

Formation of USA Rugby

In response to the need for a centralized national structure, the United States of America Rugby Football Union (USARFU, later renamed USA Rugby) was formed in 1975 to serve as the game's governing body. The formation of the national union was essential to coordinate test matches with the IRB and its member unions. The Eagles' first test under the USARFU banner was played against Australia on January 31, 1976, in Anaheim, California.

Although the Eagles lost 24–12 in their inaugural flight, they played the Wallabies close and had landed quite respectably on the world stage. Later that summer, a bicentennial-inspired group of Eagles pushed the then Five Nations runners-up France to the limit, scoring two fabulous tries before finally being vanquished 33–14. The early Eagles sides were renowned for their fearless and aggressive American football-style tackling technique. What they lacked in skills they made up for in commitment. From 1976 to 2003, the Eagles played 120 tests, winning 33 percent of them. Although they've yet to take the scalp of a founding IRB country (England, Ireland, Wales, Scotland, France, New Zealand, Australia, or South Africa), over the years they've defeated Canada, Fiji, Samoa, Tonga, and Japan.

The current structure of USA Rugby comprises 7 Territorial Unions and 37 Local Area Unions that compete for regional and national championships. The national office is run by paid staff, including the union's first-ever Chief Executive Officer, Doug Arnot. With the appointment of Arnot as CEO, USA

Rugby finally has a qualified professional running the organization — one who understands the business of sports development and appreciates what rugby needs to do to find its niche within the crowded sporting marketplace of the United States.

Soaring with the Eagles

The Eagles represent the United States around the world in international play. USA Rugby fields eight national teams — Men's and Women's 15s and sevens, the Under-23 Women's, Under-19 Boy's and Girl's, and Men's Collegiate All-American teams. Being chosen to play for one of the U.S.'s representative sides is an honor bestowed upon only a select few players each year.

For the aspiring male or female player, there are a variety of pathways to become an Eagle. Those fortunate enough to get started early can compete to make the Under-19s, Under-23s, or Collegiate All-American sides. For the club side player, being chosen for your union's representative team can provide exposure to the national coaching staff at the annual National All-Star Championships. For the senior men, starring for one of the 16 USA Rugby Super League teams can provide a fast track to the national team. Players who soar high enough on the international stage in the Eagle jersey, might earn professional rugby contracts overseas. Several of the current Eagles are fully professional players who ply their trade in the U.K. and elsewhere in Europe.

Eagles atop the world — women's rugby

The United States women's national team program was very successful right from the outset. Since their first match in 1987 against Canada, the American women have amassed an impressive 30–16 record, winning 62 percent of their tests. The Eagles won the first unofficial Women's Rugby World Cup in 1991 over a heavily favored England 19–6. The Eagles continued to be one of the world's top teams throughout the 1990s making the Women's World Cup Final in both 1994 and 1998. Suffering from internal strife going into the 2002 event, they were eliminated at the quarterfinal stage.

Unlike men's international rugby, which started 132 years ago when England first played Scotland, women's tests are a relatively new phenomenon. Since the United States was one of the first nations to play women's rugby, they have been able to compete at the highest level right from the beginning, without having to play catch-up like the men.

The Eagles' early success was a result of an increased emphasis on women's sport within the United States, and a reluctance of the established rugby powers to get behind the women's game. Women's sporting participation in the U.S. grew dramatically in the 1980s, and with the unique allure of rugby's full contact action and special camaraderie, the game spread quickly across the country on collegiate campuses. This occurred during a time when women's rugby was largely ignored by rugby unions around the world. And so in the early days of women's international rugby, the U.S. had a larger pool of gifted athletes to draw upon and were thus able to compete at the highest level quite well.

Since 2002, the USA women have struggled to keep pace with other countries that have made the decision to support the women's game, winning just two of six test matches. If the United States is successful in getting more development resources and corporate sponsorship, the Eagles have a chance of soaring to the top of the women's game.

North American internationals

One key to improving performance on the international scene is to regularly play matches against quality opposition. In the last decade there have been a variety of attempts to provide Canada and the United States with the opportunity to play in annual tournaments that will serve to raise their level of competitiveness. One such effort, the Super Cup, was spearheaded by the IRB in 2003. The tourney includes Russia, Canada, Japan, and the United States.

The Churchill Cup is another international tournament that made its debut in 2003. Named after the British prime minister, the festival features both the men's and women's teams from Canada, England, and the United States. England swept the honours at the inaugural event, held initially in Vancouver. The Churchill Cup is a partnership between the Rugby Football Union, Rugby Canada, and USA Rugby that seeks to foster advancement of the game in North America not just through direct competition but also by including coaching and youth clinics as part of the overall program. On the men's side of the draw, England is in another class entirely than the USA and Canada so the Rugby Football Union sends a squad of younger elite players which helps all three nations in their development. The women are a different story altogether, with England, the United States, and Canada currently ranked as second, third, and fourth in the world behind the Black Ferns of New Zealand! In 2004, the New Zealand Maori men and the Black Fern women joined the competition, making it a four-team affair for both sexes.

The Pan American Rugby Association (PARA) puts on a bi-annual tournament that has been played intermittently since 1995 involving Argentina, Canada, Uruguay, and the United States. The most recent edition in 2003 was thoroughly dominated by the host Pumas in Buenos Aires, who won all three of their fixtures by commanding margins.

Sevens

With only seven players per team playing on the same size pitch as a 15s match, sevens rugby offers a spectacle of non-stop action where speed, skills, and athleticism rule the day. In contrast to the limited accomplishments of the United States in the 15-a-side game, the Eagles have had some minor successes in sevens rugby. The Eagles have competed well at the Hong Kong Sevens, winning the Bowl Final in 1997 and occasionally making the Plate semifinals.

The Eagles compete in the IRB's World Sevens Series each year, where the best men's teams in the world battle it out for the annual World Sevens Series championship. Fiji and New Zealand have dominated the Series from its inception. The USA Sevens kicked off in February 2003 at the Home Depot Center, marking the first time the United States ever hosted an official IRB-sanctioned international sevens tournament. With a worldwide TV audience and 16 national teams converging annually in California, the USA Sevens promises to boost rugby's profile within North America.

Chapter 16

Amateur Rugby in North America

. . . .

In This Chapter

▶ The Canadian club scene

▶ The Rugby Canada Super League

▶ The USA Rugby Super League

▶ Club rugby throughout the United States

. . . .

The rugby club is the heart and soul of the North American game. It's where new players are introduced to the sport, where lessons are learned, and where rugby's unique camaraderie and love for the game is nurtured. In contrast to the professional game around the world, the North American club scene still embodies the amateur ethos of the game. The local club is the place where anyone can show up and become part of the action. Inclusiveness distinguishes rugby clubs from most other sporting activities. No matter where you come from or when you arrive at a rugby club function, you'll immediately be welcomed into the family as the bonds of the game supersede race, religion, sexual preference, politics, and any of life's myriad trivialities that might otherwise divide us.

North American rugby clubs are all amateur and organized in a series of tiers. At the top of the heap are the Rugby Canada Super League and the USA Rugby Super League. The club structure is further divided into several divisions, which serve to offer meaningful championships for teams of varying size, gender, and skill levels. In this chapter, we focus on the backbone of the North American game — the clubs.

The Canadian Club Scene

There are over 400 rugby clubs in Canada, which serve 20,000 registered players throughout the entire country, from British Columbia to Newfoundland. The clubs are governed by the ten provincial unions and play in a variety of championship leagues and formats. The three largest unions — British Columbia, Alberta, and Ontario — also have sub-unions that run the sport on a regional basis. Each provincial union is responsible for selecting its own representatives for competition in the Rugby Canada National Championships.

Like rugby countries the world over, Canada's clubs range from huge organizations fielding numerous teams at different levels to small ones that only put out two men's teams each weekend.

As can be expected, players from provinces where rugby is less ingrained in the sporting environment were often overlooked when it came time for national selection and honours. To help even the playing field and provide for nationwide exposure and competition for all, Rugby Canada and its member unions helped to found the Rugby Canada Super League in 1998.

The Rugby Canada Super League

The Rugby Canada Super League will enter its seventh year of competition in 2004 when 12 teams will compete for the national men's championship. The Super League was formed with the ultimate goal of raising the general level of Canadian play by exposing more athletes to higher standards of competition on a regular basis. The dozen teams that compete in two divisions are regionally based and draw players from clubs throughout the provinces where they originate.

Figure 16-1:
Calgary
Mavericks,
2003
Canadian
Super
League
Champs.

Prior to the formation of the Super League, Canadian selectors had few opportunities to see all of the talent on offer across the nation. As a result, individuals from less prominent provinces had a harder time making the national team than those from rugby hotbeds like British Columbia and Ontario. Now the best players in the participating provinces have the chance to showcase their wares on a weekly basis against other top teams.

The 2003 RCSL championship final was held in Calgary and the West Division winners, the Calgary Mavericks, upset the East Division champions, the Toronto Extreme 40–24. The match was part of a televised doubleheader that also featured the Canadian national team facing off against the New Zealand Maori. As the competition grows in stature through increased visibility, making it onto one of the Super League teams becomes a necessary first step in earning a spot on the men's national team.

Canadian National Championships

Rugby Canada holds national championships in five categories: Senior Women, Under-21 men, Under-19 women, Under-18 men, and Under-16 men. In previous years, Rugby Canada held the various competitions in different parts of the country, but in 2003 the event was consolidated into a National Championship Festival in Winnipeg, Manitoba. Over 1,000 athletes took part in the inaugural affair.

Figure 16-2:
Ontario Under-21 Men, 2003 Rugby Canada National Champions.

BROWNIE SAYS

Maggotfest

I can proudly say that I'm a Maggot and have been since 1994. No, I'm not a terrible person, I just happen to belong to one of the finest rugby clubs in the world, the Missoula All-Maggots. The Maggots are by charter dedicated to playing hard rugby and having fun, and to that end they have hosted a unique festival on the first weekend in May every year since 1977. The Maggotfest gathers together 28 men's and 8 women's sides from throughout the U.S. and Canada for what can only be described as a celebration of the ideals of the sport and a spur to the inclinations of those who choose to play it. The party kicks off on Thursday afternoon when a specially selected "hosted team" arrives early and plays an opening match against the home side at Maggot Park. A raucous party soon follows and eventually spills into downtown Missoula. Early the next morning both teams board the Maggot Bus for a long ride into Idaho for a white-water rafting trip down the Lochsa River. Survivors who make it back to town are treated to the Friday night arrival bash at a local watering hole, where the other 34 teams make their first appearance and begin vying for the weekend's honors.

In a normal rugby tournament, wins and losses are the measure of success. At the Maggotfest,

overall team spirit on and off the pitch is the most highly revered quality. A good showing on Friday night can put a team in the running for the most coveted of awards, that of "Most Honored Side." The rugby gets going and the beer starts flowing at 9:00 on Saturday morning. Fixtures are determined with an eye towards producing interesting match-ups between sides with similar skill levels and tendencies. After a long first day of competitive rugby, the Fest really hits its stride with the Saturday night party. Held in a cow barn at the Western Montana Fairgrounds, it's part Mardi Gras, part Halloween, and all rugby camaraderie extraordinaire. Teams dress thematically or not at all, and a thousand people infused with the rugby spirit dance to the band, drink beer, throw beer, and generally have a smashingly good time. Sunday features one more match for each club and the awards ceremony. There is an award for "Best Play on the Pitch," but it is wholly secondary to the "Most Honored Side."

The real winner at Maggotfest is the community of rugby devotees who live for the one weekend a year when the game and lifestyle they love and cherish is celebrated with whole-hearted devotion.

Combining the championships into one festival setting served to make the event into a major happening on the Canadian sporting landscape. In addition to family members and enthusiastic rugby spectators, the festival drew national selectors, executive board members from participating unions, and staff from Rugby Canada. The future stars of Canadian rugby had a chance to strut their stuff in front of the very people they'll want to impress and work closely with in the future.

Clubbing with the Yanks

Club rugby in the United States is played solely for the love of the game. The players compete for the joy of the contest, the administrators organize club activities on a volunteer basis, and everyone involved shares the common kinship of commitment to the rugby lifestyle. This participant-based focus, where the main goal is to make sure that next week's game comes off, has resulted in rugby developing very quietly across North America over the past 130 years. There are more than 59,000 registered players in the U.S., which play for nearly 2,000 clubs from Alaska to Arkansas and New York to Los Angeles.

The development of the game in the United States has been largely driven by initiatives at the club level. Prior to the formation of USA Rugby in 1976, there were pockets of rugby activity on the east and west coasts and a few spots in between. The leading clubs played a critical role in spreading the word about the sport and providing a means for rugby people to enjoy their chosen game.

Ever since the birth of USA Rugby, there has been a very palpable tension between the clubs and the national office. The clubs have viewed the national administration as posers and control freaks working largely for their own personal profit, while the clubs rightfully have seen themselves as the embodiment of the true ethos of the game.

GUTHRIE SAYS

How I became president of the Oxy Olde Boys

After my triumphant return to Los Angeles following a short, ill-advised stint in Boston in 1992, I was keen to get fully stuck back into rugby with the Oxy Olde Boys RFC. Although a relatively new convert to the game, I enthusiastically welcomed and relished the physical challenge and camaraderie that my newfound game provided. Since I was a young lawyer and not afraid to speak my mind about how things should be run at the club, it was suggested that I consider running for president at the upcoming annual elections. Unfortunately, the elections were being held while I was in the heat of a major trial, which prevented my personal attendance. So to make my case for the office, I offered the following statement of my platform to be read aloud to the membership by proxy: "If elected as your president, I promise to faithfully uphold the social tradition of the Oxy Olde Boys, providing two kegs at all receptions and I will make sure that our bar tab at the Big-O is always paid on time. Yours in Rugby, Guthrie." By all accounts, the assembled electors rose to their feet and I was thrust into office by acclamation. The lesson here is that becoming a rugby administrator is not particularly difficult (and sometimes happens even if you're not there). The tricky part is making sure that you do your mates proud once you've taken on the responsibility.

Traditionally, the United States club model includes an administration consisting of a club president, vice president, secretary, treasurer, and other crucial appointees. The club officers are usually current or former players whose age and leadership skills have cursed them into taking on an organizational role. The *fixtures chair* is responsible for making sure the pitch is ready and the *social chair* has the all-important job of looking after the third half, the mandatory reception following each home game. Add to that a coach and a slew of willing players, and voila, you've got a rugby club.

The USA Rugby Super League

The USA Rugby Super League represents the top tier of club rugby in the United States. The league was launched in 1997 to address the need of the country's top clubs for a higher level of competition week in and week out. Before the Super League was created, the top teams would only play one or two regional rivals of similar standard before the national playoffs each year. The concept behind the Super League was to create a competition where the best teams in the country would play against evenly matched opposition throughout the season, and then compete for the national championship.

Figure 16-3:
Belmont Shore attacking versus OMBAC in 2003 USA Rugby Super League Final.

Like most good things in USA Rugby, the Super League was started by a group of leading club visionaries who, being unable to persuade the national office to address their need for better regular competition, took matters into their own hands and created the league over the objections of USA Rugby. With leadership from former USA Rugby President Bob Watkins, the Super League clubs joined together in 1996 and signed up Harp Lager to sponsor their first two seasons of play. The benefits of the league were immediately apparent to all, with the best teams being matched against opponents of similar ability every week, the scorelines were much closer and the standard of play was raised for all involved.

After four successful years of operation outside of USA Rugby's control, the Super League was finally sanctioned in 2001 by the national governing body as the top level rugby competition in the United States. The nation's top 16 teams are now divided into Eastern and Western Conferences. The Super League delivers the best club rugby on offer and is strategically positioned in 13 major markets (see www.usarugbysuperleague.com for more on the Super League).

While there are some limited exceptions, most Super League players are unpaid for their services. Most often, if a player is being paid, it usually involves a foreign player who was recruited from overseas to bolster the local talent. Even those being paid are only semiprofessionals at best, as the money is barely enough to live on, with most needing a real job to supplement their income from rugby.

USA club championships

Whether playing for a local social club, or one of the few established national powers, there's a championship for American clubs to aspire to win. The USA club structure is multi-tiered with men's Division I, II, and III all playing off to crown a national champion. The women's club structure includes Division I and II playing to determine annual champions. Regardless of division, competing for and winning a USA National Club Championship is a highlight of any American player's career.

The road to becoming a National Champion is not easy. First, clubs have to advance out of their local area union competitions, which are basically the teams within their leagues. The next level is to qualify for one of the territorial berths that each of the seven territories have for their respective divisions. Depending on the past year's performance, there are two or three openings per territory in the divisional playoffs.

After a club secures its ticket to the big dance, the journey becomes much more arduous, as team members scramble to get time off from work and to cobble together the money needed for airline tickets and hotel expenses. USA Rugby provides the structure, but the clubs are responsible for all the costs. From regional tournaments a quartet of winning teams advance from

PLAYER TIP

Finding the right club to join

The key to finding the right club is to first figure out what kind of rugby experience you want to have. If you're a newbie and don't know what to expect, then you're probably better off hooking up with a second or third division club. They'll be familiar with taking aboard new players and you'll have a better chance of getting playing time sooner at those levels. If you've played a bit of footy already and are looking to improve your skills, focus on first division clubs, paying special attention to how the coaching staff interacts with the players at training. Rugby is unique as a team sport in that you will be immediately welcome at virtually any club in the world as soon as you say that you're a rugby player. Even so, before you join a club, it is absolutely imperative that you go to a training session to meet their players, coaches, and supporters before deciding if they're right for you. Once you go through a practice session and get a chance to chat with the team after training over a beverage, you'll be ready to make the call.

the round of 16 to the final 4. The final four teams play off over a long weekend, with the winning team having to play two matches in 72 hours. Despite these challenges, the joy of being a National Champion is something that remains dear forever as the accomplishment grows in stature every time the story is retold.

Figure 16-4:
Boston Irish Wolfhounds, USA Men's Club Div. 1 Champs '03.

Chapter 17

Collegiate, High School, and Youth Rugby in North America

· ·

In This Chapter

▶ Canadian interuniversity sport

▶ Mini rugby in Canada

▶ The most popular club sport on U.S. college campuses

▶ The growth of high school and youth rugby in the United States

· ·

C ollege campuses were the first home of organized rugby competitions in North America. From the first game in 1874, through rugby's dark years at the end of World War I, to the early 1960s, the collegiate game was the only consistent presence keeping rugby's torch lit in the United States. Even today, for the vast majority of North American participants, playing in college is their first exposure to the game and remains the primary developmental arena for local clubs to stock their teams.

Recently, however, the sport has enjoyed unprecedented growth in high school and youth programs across the United States and Canada. In this chapter, we focus on the three areas that are the future of the North American game: collegiate, high school, and youth rugby.

Canadian Collegiate Championships

In men's rugby in Canada, there is no formal national collegiate championship. Individual provincial unions hold their own competitions to determine their divisional winners. This is partially because greater emphasis is placed on the under-21 national championships, but also results from the multi-tiered nature of Canadian clubs, which feature many age-grade teams.

The women's collegiate rugby national championship is played under the auspices of Canadian Interuniversity Sport (CIS). The CIS is the national governing body for 19 different sports at the university level, including track and field, basketball, and hockey. In women's rugby, 35 teams compete in the Canada West, Ontario, Quebec, and Atlantic divisions for six playoff spots.

The 2003 qualifiers were the Alberta Pandas, the Lethbridge Pronghorns, the McGill Martlets, the St. Francis Xavier X-Women, the University of British Columbia Thunderbirds, and the Western Ontario Mustangs. The reigning five-time champs are the University of Alberta Pandas, who beat the University of Lethbridge Pronghorns 20–3 at Strathcona Rugby Park.

High School Rugby

In the most competitive rugby-playing nations around the world, by the time kids reach high school age they are already steeped in rugby skills and culture because they have been playing and watching since they were very young. In a place like Canada, where rugby is well down the national sporting ladder, many players have their first introduction to the game at the high school level.

Rugby at the secondary level in Canadian schools is organized and run by high school athletic associations in each province, with assistance from the provincial unions. Every province has its own organizational structures to fit its specific needs.

At opposite ends of the country, British Columbia and Nova Scotia have two flourishing programs for high school participants. The Nova Scotia School Athletic Federation counts 29 boys' and 26 girls' teams competing in four regional competitions. From a population base four times larger, the British Columbia Secondary Schools Rugby Union is made up of more than 130 teams split into two divisions. Throughout the country, high school rugby is a valuable introductory component of the sport — its continued growth is essential to the long-term health of Rugby Canada.

Youth Rugby

Youth rugby (or mini rugby, as we call it) is a catch-all term that includes players between the ages 5 and 15. In Canada, the development of young players is handled mostly through individual clubs as part of an overall provincial strategy. The advantages of starting players from as young an age as possible are borne out by the success of rugby-playing nations where mini rugby is taken as the natural order of things. The sooner players begin to amass the basic skills of passing, running, and kicking, the easier it is to develop critical thinking and strategic skills at the high school level.

Mini rugby players start without boots and since it is initially non-contact, they don't engage in tackling. An appropriately sized ball is also used, the better to be passed by smaller hands. The fundamentals are introduced in a non-threatening environment where the emphasis is on having fun and learning sportsmanship, rather than serious competition. Girls and boys play on the same team, usually until about age 10. Like the sport at the highest level, mini rugby is great for all kids because regardless of size or development, there's a place for everyone in the team. (See "Introducing the Players" in Chapter 2 for details on player positions and characteristics.)

The goal of mini rugby is to acclimate kids to the essentials of the sport and then slowly introduce the finer points of the game. Along the way they grasp the beginnings of teamwork, physical fitness, and social skills. A rugby club with a mini rugby program is by definition a family-friendly place.

The American Collegiate Game

On May 5, 1874, Harvard University hosted Montreal's McGill University in the first recorded match of rugby played on U.S. soil. Over the next 30 years, the game evolved through the process of rules codification and modification. These changes culminated in the 1906 legalization of the forward pass, the final deviation that forever divided rugby from American football. So by 1906, most colleges across the country had switched from playing rugby to playing American football.

Figure 17-1: Air Force Academy, USA Men's & Women's College Champs '03.

Bucking the national trend, the West Coast held firm and the University of California at Berkeley and Stanford University actually dropped American football in 1906, setting the stage for later Olympic glory. (See "Origins and Olympic gold" in Chapter 15 for more details.)

In 1910, an All-Star team composed primarily of Cal and Stanford players toured Australia and New Zealand under the banner of the American Universities team. Rugby had become the contact game of choice out West and regularly drew up to 20,000 fans for the annual showdown between Cal and Stanford. In 1912, 1913, and 1914, the New South Wales Waratahs, New Zealand All Blacks, and an All-Britain side toured the West Coast to play the All-Americans.

By the end of World War I, however, American football took center stage on collegiate campuses throughout the country and rugby suffered through a period of stagnation that would last until its revival in the mid-1960s.

Today, rugby is the most popular club sport on U.S. college campuses. With 440 men's teams and 319 women's programs competing in 2003, collegiate rugby is once again flourishing on campus across the United States. USA Rugby awards four national collegiate titles for men and women in Divisions I and II. Like the club-playoff structure, each territory produces a predetermined number of teams to compete in regional playoffs, leading to a national final-four tournament to crown the annual USA Rugby National Collegiate Champions.

Most people's initial impression of collegiate rugby is a bunch of rowdy, beer-swilling frat boys getting naked and having a good old time. And while that reputation isn't entirely unearned, USA Rugby is attempting to implement a new program designed to lift the standard of play and rehabilitate collegiate

Highland High School

If you're looking for excellence in rugby, Utah's Highland High School has set the bar sky-high. In their 29 years of rugby at Highland, Coach Larry Gelwix and his staff have created a model program where rugby is the vehicle used to teach life's lessons of honor, integrity, and achievement. In the 16 years since USA Rugby has held a national high school championship, Highland has won an incredible 12 national titles, placing second three times, and third once. Their mission statement is: "To teach young men to do their best. To excel athletically, spiritually, and in their family lives."

The season at Highland runs from March to May and typically draws from 100 to 120 prospective players at the start of each year. By treating their players with respect and by demanding commitment from them to be the best they can be, both on and off the pitch, Highland serves as a prime example of how rugby, when properly presented, can play a positive formative role for the high school athlete. If you're a parent or high school teacher and want to learn more about Highland's program, visit www.highland rugby.org.

rugby's image on campuses nationwide. The Collegiate Commitment will be one of USA Rugby's key initiatives over the next several years and will be administered by local Game Development Officers who are trained in implementing best practices (see www.usarugby.org for more information).

Meanwhile, the NCAA has placed women's rugby on their list of emerging sports, and with *Title IX* fairness concerns at work (Title IX requires that there be relative parity in the numbers of men and women that participate in NCAA sanctioned sports), we may see the NCAA install women's rugby as an intercollegiate sport under their control. If the NCAA opts to include women's rugby, the result would be a substantial increase in coaching and administrative support for the women's game on campus.

The U.S. High School Championships

The rapid growth of high school rugby is one of the least well known, but biggest success stories in the advancement of the oval game in the United States. In the five years from 1999 to 2003, the number of high school programs across the country more than doubled from 226 to 525. If these high school students stick with the game through college and then join the top clubs over the next several years, USA Rugby's representative sides will improve by having a larger pool of more experienced talent to choose from.

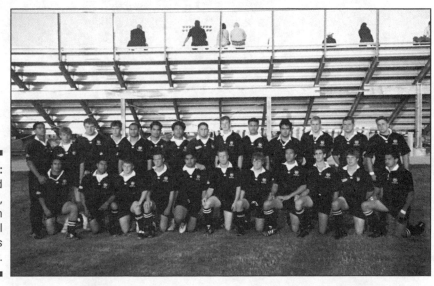

Figure 17-2: Highland High School, USA High School Champs 2003.

USA Rugby introduced the national high school championship tournament in 1985. The tournament now involves the top eight nationally ranked high school teams who play for the USA Rugby National High School Championship.

Youth Rugby in the United States

Developing youth rugby is the biggest long-term challenge for rugby in the United States. From 1999 to 2003, the number of youth rugby teams in the United States has quietly leapt from 240 to 429. Despite this rapid growth, it's also the least understood segment and the sector where recent substantial gains in numbers have mistakenly been attributed to successful efforts of the national office.

The reality of why the youth game is growing is based on two factors. The first is that more and more players are now reaching the age where they are no longer actively playing the game and have young children who are looking for a sport to compete in. This has combined with the increased availability of rugby on television, to give rugby parents a chance to sit down on the couch and show their children the game they learned to love in college. All around the country, new youth programs are being created as the students' demand for the game increases.

Figure 17-3:
Youth rugby.

Youth development

In the United States, the median age that players begin participating in rugby is 19 years old. By the time most Americans have figured out the nuances of the game, they're approaching 30 and beyond their athletic prime. As more and more local rugby leagues pop up across the country, USA Rugby has targeted youth development as a key area for growth. With support from the International Rugby Board (IRB), USA Rugby has implemented a National Youth Development Plan. The strategy involves utilization of local Youth Development Officers (YDOs). The YDOs are trained to provide expertise, materials, and other support needed to launch, maintain, and nurture new youth teams. The program has 15 physical education curriculum lessons, a youth development guide, a coaching text called *Play the Game*, plus videos and other helpful aids. To learn more about youth development visit www.usarugby.org/resources/youth.html.

That said, there is no doubt that USA Rugby's Youth Development Officers (YDOs) are doing an important service in helping to create new teams, but it's very important to realize that it's really a groundswell of demand from kids and parents that is driving the increased number of youth teams, and not the fine work of the YDOs supplying assistance to support these new groups.

Non-contact youth rugby

For children too young for full contact rugby, non-contact or touch rugby is used as an introductory tool. This version of the game eliminates tackling and other contact to minimize skeptical parents' safety concerns. The result has been a smashing success, thanks to the efforts of visionaries like Pat Walsh who has dedicated much of his free time over the past several years to create a thriving non-contact youth league in the Washington, DC/Virginia area.

The main advantage of non-contact rugby is that all players still get to run with the ball and play both offense and defense, but since there's no tackling, rucking, or mauling, the collisions are replaced with a two-handed tag of the ball-carrier. The non-contact game is ideal for boys and girls from six to ten years old. Once their bodies are ready for the stress of the tackle game, they can move on to playing rugby with a local youth side. If you want to find a non-contact team in your neighborhood or start a new team of your own, check out Appendix C for the contact details of your local USA Rugby Youth Development Officer.

Growth Trends of Grassroots in the U.S.

The bad news for the rest of the rugby world is that more Americans than ever before are playing rugby. The good news for all those foreigners shaking

GUTHRIE SAYS

Women's rugby on the rise

Women's rugby is the fastest growing segment of the game in the United States. From 1993 to 2003, women's rugby exploded across U.S. campuses, growing from 125 to 319 teams in ten short years. This unprecedented increase has led directly to a dramatic surge in the number of women's club teams, which saw a 38 percent increase from 88 to 121 clubs over the past five years. Rugby attracts women because it's one of the few full-contact sports where they play by the same rules as the men and can be as physical as they choose. I've coached men and women collegians for a few years now, and while the men are all about bash and crash, the women actually listen at training and are much more technically sound in the basics of the game. Moreover, for most women, playing their first rugby match is like a baptism of fire, as they've never experienced anything remotely close to the physicality of the game, and once they've made it through that first test, they're hooked on rugby for good. Rugby is the perfect sport for an ever-increasing number of confident women who are no longer content with the relative safety of softball, when they can choose to compete in a game where they're able to physically test themselves to the limit.

in their boots right about now is that USA Rugby will need at least another 10 to 15 years to translate this growth into substantial success on the international stage.

In the five-year span from 1999 through 2004, every important sector within USA Rugby has experienced growth, ranging from steady to spectacular. The number of men's clubs increased by 5 percent, while men's collegiate programs saw an 8-percent growth. The biggest overall increase was in girl's rugby, which increased by 153 percent from 38 to 96 teams. Women's clubs also grew by 38 percent, while women's collegiate teams increased by 16 percent over the same interval. The sole area of retraction has been in the number of old farts trundling around paddocks; masters' sides decreased from 90 to 60 teams as the older guys either died off or finally retreated to the couch for good.

These positive trends in participation present a double-edged sword to USA Rugby. How can the national governing body best utilize its very limited financial and other resources to serve a growing constituency? And how should those resources be allocated and prioritized going forward? We believe the key to making the United States truly competitive around the world is to nurture an ever-increasing crop of younger players in order to produce individuals who have the instincts to compete with those who have been playing barefoot since they were five years old.

Part IV
Coaching and Refereeing

The 5th Wave   By Rich Tennant

"I've got a ruck in aisle 5. I'm going to call a scrum unless I see that veil pretty soon."

In this part...

This part addresses the needs of the two key areas for development of the game in North America, coaching and refereeing. We start with the basic requirements needed to become a rugby coach. Next, we examine the false assumptions about injuries in rugby and discuss how coaches can make the game safer for their charges. That's followed by the steps that coaches need to take to become certified in the USA and Canada.

To round off this part, we concentrate on refereeing. We start with a discussion of what it takes to become a referee and then explain the certification process on both sides of the border.

Chapter 18

Coaching

· ·

In This Chapter

▶ Appreciating the qualities of a good coach

▶ Being everything to everyone on the team

▶ Making the coaching decision

▶ Finding yourself a supporting role

· ·

Coaching is not really a profession — rather, it's an obsession, attracting some of the strongest individuals. In North America, since only a handful of lucky ones actually make a decent living from the job, your motivation to coach has to come from reasons other than financial gain.

The hard work that coaching requires is rewarded by the warm feeling of being an integral part of a team. There's an enormous amount of satisfaction when your team achieves greatness, or when a player you have nurtured is selected for a representative side and goes on to be successful. Numerous people rely on you and look to you for guidance. Their success is your success.

The effectiveness of the coach is paramount, because good players without a good coach make a mediocre team. While rugby players often get all the kudos for strong performances, much of the credit should really go to the coach.

In this chapter, we explain the abilities and talents required of a coach. Should you decide that the hot seat is just a little too hot for you, you can choose from a range of other jobs that give vital support to the team.

Grand Obsession: The Making of a Good Coach

Picture the scene: It's the end of the tournament, the winning captain stands there clutching the trophy with a smile as wide as the Grand Canyon, and an interviewer pushes through the crowd and shoves a microphone under his nose, asking him to explain just how his team managed to do it. The inevitable response is, "I'd just like to thank our coach for getting us to where we are today." Cue to rapturous applause, hugs, and kisses all 'round.

While natural talent and a strong work ethic will take you a long way, to make it to the very top in any sport you need the trained eye, dedication, and cajoling of a coach. Someone who cares enough about you to coax, nag, bully, and pester the very best out of you. Someone who is there to monitor your progress at that 5 a.m. training run or to demand you do another 30 minutes on the tackle bag when all you want to do is have a shower and go home. While sometimes you love to hate them, coaches can make all the difference between being good and being great.

It's usually pretty easy to figure out who the coach is at a rugby game — it's the person trotting along the sideline, gesticulating at the players on the pitch and shouting advice. He or she is invariably the most emotionally involved person at the ground.

A coach has three main areas of responsibility. A coach must:

- ✔ Improve a team's skill level
- ✔ Improve the fitness, strength, and power of a team
- ✔ Motivate players so that the team reaches their potential

Improving skill levels

A coach should do everything possible to ensure that the skill levels of all players improve as the season progresses. Obviously, skill levels vary from individual to individual, so you need to adjust your training program to make allowances for these variations. Your main aim, though, is to improve the overall skill level of the team as a unit.

To improve your team's skills, implement a challenging and mixed training schedule that maintains the interest of all the players. For example, you can mix it up by incorporating both skill drills and weight training into the regimen.

Getting your team fighting fit

A good team is a fit team, so it is important that you incorporate fitness routines into your schedule in order to build up stamina. (See Chapter 12 for details on how to devise the best exercise program for your team.)

For your team to succeed, you need to develop a good, simple, and effective training program. Once you have your training program, stick to it.

Motivating your team

Motivating players depends largely on trust — and trust comes through openness and honesty. When you have to drop a player, don't make up feeble excuses or blame your decision on someone or something else. Players will quickly find out if you are bending the truth, so always be honest and up front.

The members of any team will talk to each other and look after each other's interests, both on and off the pitch. If you lose the trust of your players, your future with the team is limited because the players won't be motivated to listen to your advice or instruction. But if you earn the trust of your players they'll do anything for you.

Motivation also involves saying the right words at the right time. You don't have to memorize the speeches of Winston Churchill; being positive during training and in the dressing room gets your players in the right frame of mind to get on the pitch and defeat the competition.

Never underestimate the importance of encouragement. As long as it is not overdone, praise can cure many ills. Guide your players and give them direction and purpose. Whatever support you give them will be returned to you on the rugby pitch. The art is to keep things simple without insulting the intelligence of your players.

A smart coach has to be prepared to mix the message up a bit to avoid the problem of players getting sick and tired of just one person ranting at them. Calling in experts from other fields, or other authoritative voices, will often inspire weary players.

Coaching Safety

Safety is a principle concern to everyone involved in rugby. It resonates throughout the Laws of the Game and directly affects coaches and players. There are two very good reasons for this preoccupation with safety.

First, rugby is a team game where players repeatedly assemble into set formations. Scrums and line-outs require careful coordination and specific binding of several players to accomplish a collective goal. The combined force of several working together as one is much greater than a single player, and the Laws of the Game reflect this. Coaches are responsible for explaining and enforcing the rules of the game.

Second, rugby is a full-contact sport where players must repeatedly tackle each other. A typical international match might have 150 tackles over 80 minutes of play. Being able to make tackles over and over again without injuring oneself is essential to playing the game. As such, defenders must develop proper tackling techniques and ball-carriers have to learn how to engage the tackler in contact and fall correctly. As the coach, it is your job to ensure that your players learn the correct techniques so they can safely play the game.

Keeping your players safe

The most important factor in preventing rugby injuries is coaching. Injuries often occur when new players are thrust into situations that they are not prepared to handle. For example, coaches must avoid placing beginners in the front row of a scrum without first making certain that they're ready for that particular position. A good coach needs to withstand the temptation to allow new players to participate in matches until they are sufficiently trained in all the skills that will be required in a live game.

For North American coaches, special attention should be paid to teaching your players how to safely tackle in rugby. You can be sure that many of your players will arrive with bad habits learned from playing gridiron. These bad habits are very difficult to overcome, which is why rugby coaches should review safe tackling in training on a regular basis.

Former footballers will be keen to mix it up, but are likely to approach the point of contact with their heads in dangerous positions. They will have been taught to use their helmets as a weapon, and to get their heads across the face of the ball-carrier when making contact. This exposes the head, neck, and spine to serious injury. In rugby, the tackler is instructed to place his or her head alongside either hip of the ball-carrier to avoid frontal collision with the head and neck. The shoulder is used as the main point of contact.

Another factor in preventing injuries is conditioning. Rugby is a demanding aerobic and anaerobic activity that requires short bursts of energy over long periods of sustained exertion. Football players are not rugby fit and without getting their one-minute rest breaks after every five seconds of action, they falter quickly under the strain of continuous play. When players get fatigued, the first thing to suffer is mental concentration, which makes them more prone to fall inappropriately or enter contact with poor technique and get injured.

As a coach, it's your responsibility to ensure that all your players are sufficiently experienced at their particular position, have a solid command of how to safely manage contact, and are in good physical condition before they take the pitch.

False assumptions and the truth about injuries in rugby

Parents often shy away from rugby at the thought of subjecting their children to the rigors of "football without pads." To understand the fundamental difference between rugby and football, a crucial distinction must be drawn here — rugby is a contact sport, whereas football is a collision sport.

False security

Something curious happens when a player suits up in the protective armor worn by football players. With a helmet, shoulder pads, hip, leg, knee, and other assorted pads covering nearly every inch of football players' bodies, a false sense of invulnerability results and is only heightened by gridiron coaches encouraging youngsters to throw their bodies around with reckless abandon. This is further reinforced by the football tackling technique, which places a premium on either stopping the ball-carrier cold in his tracks or driving him backwards. All the padding and the emphasis placed on impacting the runner head-on combine to produce football collisions that are extremely forceful, violent, and unpredictable.

In rugby, players don't have a false sense of security brought on by being encased in body armor. Moreover, and especially at the youth level, safety in contact is a central teaching concern. Not having ten-pound crash helmets to hide within, rugby players are **not** taught to "put their head in there and smash the ball-carrier" like in football, but are specifically warned to keep their heads out of harm's way in the tackle situation.

Learning how to tackle

The point of contact for the tackle in rugby is lower than in football, with the knees to thighs as the target, so the ball-carrier's head and shoulders are avoided by the tackler on impact. The goal of the tackle in rugby is also significantly different. In stark contrast to the football objective of not surrendering even an inch lest the offence make a first down, in rugby tacklers are taught to opt instead for the sure tackle, rather than the big collision.

Also, new players are carefully introduced to tackling, starting first on their knees and then progressing to walking, jogging, and finally running, only after they have demonstrated proper technique and are comfortable enough to advance to the next stage.

In football, all 22 players can hit each other at any time and from almost any direction, which encourages players to make huge "blindside hits," where the victim never sees it coming before getting absolutely smashed. In rugby, unless you're carrying the ball, about to receive it, or directly involved in contesting possession, players on the opposing team are prohibited from hitting you. This means that in rugby, you have a much better sense of when and where the contact is coming from.

Knowing when you're at risk usually allows you to brace before impact and then fall in a manner so as to absorb the kinetic energy through the thick muscles of the back, buttocks, legs, or hips (as opposed to bouncing off the turf, as happens when you're taken by surprise). For these reasons, contact in rugby is much more controlled, predictable, and safer than in football.

Tackling a Tough Job

The coach has the onerous task of successfully putting together the most bewildering of jigsaw puzzles. He or she has to mold 15 very different, often diverse, and sometimes uncooperative individuals into one perfectly inter-locking unit.

The coach has to be an adviser, mentor, psychologist, teacher, diplomat, comrade, leader in arms, master of subterfuge, butcher, baker, and candlestick-maker. If you aspire to be a coach, you need to have:

✔ **A superior understanding of the game:** Coaching is best learned from practical experience, because players soon figure you out if you don't know what you're talking about. It also helps if you are a former player, though you don't have to have reached superstar level! Many of the best rugby coaches were mediocre players who during their playing days developed a good grasp of the game, especially the laws, tactics, and strategies required to win matches.

✔ **A genuine love of the game:** You need to love the game and be fascinated by all its subtleties. Like your players, you must constantly be learning, because you'll never find yourself knowing everything about the sport. Rugby is a game that is continually evolving and throwing up quandaries that confound even the most brilliant of rugby minds.

✔ **A democratic approach:** As a coach you need to be firm without being a dictator, and have the ability to get along with and get the best out of a diverse array of characters. Many coaches fall into the trap of taking all the praise after a victory, and blaming everyone but themselves for a loss. Good coaches don't go on about how their team won because the players followed instructions, or lost because they didn't.

Coaching can't be learned entirely from textbooks. Coaching is a mind game, a skill, and an art. You need initiative, creativity, intuition, and a vast amount of personal get-up-and-go. When you encounter 20 different problems at once you'll soon discover whether or not coaching is for you.

The art of communication

One day at training, Welsh coach John Dawes told his players that if the blindside flanker was to break quickly from the scrum, the halfback would shout a code word beginning with the letter "P." If the openside flanker was to break early, the code word would begin with the letter "S." A scrum was set. Suddenly halfback Gareth Edwards screamed: "Psychology!"

Neither flanker moved.

Do it like Dwyer

Bob Dwyer, who coached Australia's national team in the '80s and '90s, described what is required to be a successful coach. According to Dwyer, a winning coach doesn't require the intellect of a nuclear physicist, but experience, common sense, imagination, and a very, very good memory. As far as Dwyer is concerned, if coaching is approached in the right vein, it is "an honorable profession."

If you want to become the coach of a winning team, the simplest approach is the best. Taking Bob Dwyer's criteria one by one, a successful coach has:

- **Experience:** in order to know what to do when under pressure.
- **Common sense:** in order to stay level-headed and calm no matter what the circumstances.
- **Imagination:** in order to come up with innovative moves and tactics.
- **An excellent memory:** in order to remember the weaknesses and strengths of the opposition so that tactics and strategies to exploit and counter them can be devised.

No one criterion is more important than the others. The key is finding the right balance that suits your individual style of coaching.

Deciding If Coaching Is for You

You won't really know if you have the capabilities to be a coach until you try it. You'll know you have the right temperament for the job when you find yourself on a muddy pitch on a Saturday morning teaching a bunch of children, juniors, young men, or young women — and enjoying it.

Deciding whether coaching is for you requires a bit of self-assessment. The first thing to consider is whether or not you enjoy being around other people — this is a vital characteristic of a rugby coach. In addition, you must:

- Relate well and get along with just about everyone

- Know how to communicate with the many people relying on you to provide them with the right information

- Be even-tempered and able to handle the pressures of being in charge of up to 20 children (or adults who act like children)

You should also ask yourself these questions: Do you love rugby? Do you like offering advice and helping other people? Are you prepared to work hard? Do you excel when under pressure? If the answer to all these is "yes," then give coaching a go.

Once you have been involved in a few games, you'll know whether or not coaching suits you — and whether or not you suit coaching. If you can successfully get the message across to teams that are difficult to organize and motivate, you just might have the coaching touch! (See Chapter 19 for information that will help you get into the coaching game and details about the different coaching opportunities that are available.)

You're Not Alone: Support Staff

A coach may sometimes feel like a rock, solitary and endlessly battered by the elements. At the bottom rung you'll find yourself doing all the jobs necessary to make a team run, but as you progress more help is available.

At higher levels a strong network of support staff surrounds the head coach in order to spread the stress and responsibilities more evenly and to help the team reach its full potential. Such support occurs not just in the professional ranks, but at the top amateur clubs that are well organized and well funded.

For those who don't want the full-blown responsibility of being head coach, numerous other jobs are available that could be perfect for you. A support role can be just as important to the running of a rugby team as is that of the head coach.

At the lower levels of the game, support staff are relatively few and no one gets paid. You usually find a head coach and maybe an assistant coach and a volunteer trainer. At the higher echelons of rugby, however, teams from the representative level and up are usually professional in their approach and the support staff can involve a cast of many.

Coaching: Assistant coach

Most teams from club level upwards have at least one assistant to the head coach. At a typical training session, teams eventually break up into two groups: forwards and backs. As one person cannot oversee both, another pair of eyes and hands are needed.

The best teams usually have a three-man coaching structure, comprising a head coach, a forwards coach, and a backs coach. The forwards coach is usually a specialist at scrums, line-outs, rucks, and mauls. The backs coach has particular expertise in backline strategies and moves and understands the requirements of all the positions from 9 to 15 (see Chapter 2 for details about all player positions). The three coaches work closely together and are usually responsible for selecting the team.

Someone who has played forward does not necessarily make a good forwards coach, nor does a former back automatically make the best backs coach. Sometimes an outsider's perspective is refreshing and more thorough because it comes from someone who has had to learn the intricacies of the position from the ground up without benefit of direct playing experience.

Coaching: Defense coach

In recent years, professional teams and international sides have employed coaches who have focused on improving the defensive strategies of the team. Often, these coaches are former *rugby league* players who, because of the tight defensive structure of their game, are able to pass on important tips on tactics that stop opponents. (Rugby League is a rugby derivative played with 13 men and popular only in Australia and northern England.)

Managing the team

Because the coach is primarily focused on the squad's performance on the field, an effective team manager is needed to make sure that everything runs smoothly off the pitch.

The duties of a team manager normally include ensuring that:

- ✔ Training venues have been reserved and are ready for use
- ✔ Players know exactly where they have to be and at what time
- ✔ Transport for the team and support staff is organized
- ✔ The team has the right playing and training equipment such as rugby balls, tackle bags, and kicking tees

In addition, team managers need to have all the information that's relevant to their team on match day, including directions to the pitch, kickoff times, where the team will change, and who the match officials are.

The team manager has to attend to the needs of the coach and the players, which means becoming mother, father, nurse, and everyone's best friend. The role also encompasses that of psychotherapist, as the team manager's shoulder is the one players usually cry on when they have been dropped from the team or feel as though they have failed.

The team manager's job is probably the most demanding one within the organization, as it requires an abundance of common sense, a tough hide, a willingness to work, and the ability to solve problems logically. While the job can be a thankless one, many consider it to be very rewarding.

Training the team

At lower levels, a team probably won't have a trainer. At representative level, however, teams often have their own fitness gurus.

The trainer puts the players through their drills during training and makes certain that when they are off the field, they are involved in appropriate weight, exercise, and nutritional programs.

Massaging the players: The physiotherapist

For professional organizations, the physiotherapist works closely with the team doctor and trainer to ensure that injured players receive the right course of treatment. A rugby team's physiotherapist specializes in sports science, injury management and treatment, and is an important member of the support staff.

When a player is injured on the field, the physiotherapist runs out onto the pitch with the doctor to treat him or her. Between them, they quickly assess the seriousness of the injury and whether or not the player should come off the field.

The physiotherapist may also pre-tape players on match day and at training sessions. This involves using bandages, braces, and tape to prevent injuries occurring or previous ones from recurring.

Calling the team doctor

At the professional level, the team doctor is a paid position, while at club level, the doctor is usually a volunteer. In addition to working with the physiotherapist to assess injuries sustained during a match, the team doctor helps players recover from those injuries. The team doctor diagnoses injuries on the field and tracks the progress of the injured players while they recover. The coach relies on the team doctor to advise when an injured player has recovered and is available for selection.

In accordance with the blood bin rule, the team doctor is usually found doing quick stitch-up work on injured players during matches so that they can get back into the game as quickly as possible.

Chapter 19

Coaching Certification and Advancement

In This Chapter

▶ Getting certified to coach

▶ Advanced overseas options

▶ Finding the right level for you

*O*nce you make the fateful decision to become a rugby coach, a whole new world of agony and ecstasy awaits. Before you don the clipboard and start barking orders at your new charges, you need to get properly certified as a coach. Rugby Canada and USA Rugby have similar, but slightly different, accreditation programs to assist both new and experienced coaches.

In this chapter, we describe the coaching certification process, discuss international resources to continue your training, and focus on issues presented by the various levels of the game.

Coach Training in Canada

Rugby Canada has a well-established and successful coach education program that's been in existence for more than 30 years. The National Coaching Certification Program (NCCP) consists of a partnership between Rugby Canada, the Coaching Association of Canada, and the Government of Canada, through over 60 provincial and territorial National Sport Federations. The NCCP offers four coaching courses based on the different levels of the game.

For those interested in coaching neighborhood kids, the Community Coach course provides a basic introduction to the principles of play for non-contact rugby, and is designed for new coaches and parents of youths under 12.

The Introductory Coach program is for high school, university, and club-level coaches. This is where full contact is introduced and the concepts of tactical and technical improvements are brought into focus. This course is for coaches who will be responsible for novice to intermediate-level players.

The next step is the Developmental Coaching course where positional play and specialized technical and tactical skills are emphasized. This level is designed to help develop representative team and top club coaches.

The top tier is called the High Performance Coaching course and was created to serve Super League coaches and provide coaching talent for the Canadian national teams. At this stage, positional play, tactical awareness, and technical skills for the national team level are featured. Go to www.rugbycanada.ca for more information and to register for the next coaching course in your neighborhood.

Coaching Accreditation in the U.S.

USA Rugby's coaching accreditation program has certified more than 3,500 coaches since it was launched in 1995. There are three tiers of coaching courses offered: Levels I, II, and III. The program is delivered through a series of clinics that are organized across the country each year. The courses must be taken sequentially from Level I through Level III. The cost to pre-register for the three courses is $160 for Level I, $170 for Level II, and $175 for Level III.

The Level I clinic offers a combination of practical and theoretical material that covers the basic principles of play. When you arrive, you'll receive a *Level I Coaches Manual* focusing on the basics of the game, a *Coaches Workbook* that is used in conjunction with classroom discussion and video analysis, and a *Book of Readings*, addressing a wide variety of relevant topics. The course is held over two days and includes approximately 14 hours of classroom and on-field instruction, culminating in a written examination. Provided you pass the test, you get a certificate that says you're a qualified USA Rugby Level I coach.

After you complete one season of coaching in the field as a Level I graduate, you can sign up for the Level II course. The Level II curriculum expands on the practical skills and theory work of Level I.

Level III is totally theoretical and classroom work is supplemented by extensive video analysis. See www.usarugby.org for more information on dates or to register for the next course in your area.

The International Rugby Academy

The International Rugby Academy (IRANZ) is based in Wellington, New Zealand, and offers a variety of coaching courses. IRANZ was founded by former All Black number 8 Murray Mexted, former All Black coach Laurie Mains, and legendary All Black hooker, Sean Fitzpatrick. The list of course instructors is chock-full of former stars and rugby luminaries unmatched anywhere in the world.

For club-side coaches, the Practical Coaching Course is an outstanding way to discover how the leading coaches in the oval world are preparing their teams. With an all-star staff of former All Blacks, Wallabies, and esteemed experts from other sports, the Practical Coaching Course is well worth the time and money required to attend the program. (We know this first-hand, as we were the first Americans ever to be certified by IRANZ!)

For coaches who aspire to a professional career in coaching, the Elite Coaches Course is the gold standard among coaching academies around the world. This three week course is held in conjunction with IRANZ's Elite Players course at the Adidas Institute of Sport in Palmerston North, so the coaches can work with some of the world's leading talent in a practical setting. With a host of coaching greats on staff and led by Laurie Mains, the Elite Coaches course is the place to go for those seeking the best training available. See www.internationalrugbyacademy.com for more information on dates and custom courses.

Figure 19-1: Coaching at the IRANZ.

Coaching Hatchlings to Eagles

Before the professional era in rugby began in the mid-1990s, almost all coaches from mini rugby to national teams were volunteers or lightly compensated individuals who served because they loved the game. In those days, nearly every coach began his or her progression up the coaching ladder by working with kids. By the time a superior coach had reached the top level, he or she had years of experience in dealing with all age groups and situations, cementing a knowledge of the sport in the process.

Sadly, this is no longer the case in many parts of the world, and coaching has become a big-money occupation. The desire for wins and publicity at the highest levels has attracted recently retired international stars to take the reins of professional clubs without the benefit of ever having coached before, while seasoned veterans of the coaching game look for work.

One place where that is not true is in North America. There are only a very few coaches who make a living running rugby teams, meaning the rest of the multitudes are still in it because they have a passion for the game. Because rugby is a sport played mostly by collegians and adults in the United States and Canada though, there are relatively few coaches who have experience coaching at all levels and appreciate the distinct demands of each rung on the rugby ladder.

Figure 19-2: Youth coaching.

Nurturing the youth

An area of phenomenal growth in North American rugby is the exploding number of children who are being exposed to the game. Unfortunately, there are more kids wanting to play than there are qualified coaches to handle them. Coaching youth players (aged 5 to 15) takes a tremendous amount of patience and a good rapport with nervous parents.

The key element to coaching youngsters of all ages is to always emphasize the fun aspects of the sport. When introducing the game, a coach should never put pressure to win on their juvenile charges. Rather, explaining the inherent value of competition for its own sake is the primary message to be delivered. Instead of striving for victories, the players should be encouraged to enjoy themselves while obtaining the skills necessary to play the game at higher levels.

Having an oval ball in high school

The secondary school setting is rapidly becoming an important entry point for young rugby enthusiasts. This means that the high school coach has to focus on bringing newcomers up to speed more quickly than the youth coach, but without neglecting to instill a healthy respect for the sport itself in a competitive environment. Tackling, passing, and ball-handling drills should be supplemented with lectures on sportsmanship and the overall ethos of the game.

Getting the basics right at this stage is still far more important than wins and losses. No competitive person likes to lose, but learning how to do so is every bit as important for teenagers as is winning with good grace. It always has to be highlighted that rugby is not a sport that tolerates trash-talking, showboating, or disrespectful behavior of any kind to opponents, officials, spectators, or teammates.

The most beneficial concept that high schoolers can take away from rugby is the value of teamwork. By its very nature, rugby is a game that requires trust, communication, cohesion, and shared desire to achieve results. Learning how to work with others and how to be selfless while putting the team first is an invaluable lesson for future success in academics, business, and life in general.

Corralling collegians

The collegiate arena is by far the most difficult milieu in which to coach because of the intensity of the participants involved. Most collegians are new to the sport and many are attracted not just by the game but by the social atmosphere that surrounds it on many campuses. Rugby at this level is often seen as an outlet for athletes who are no longer playing other organized sports, or as a chance to vent pent-up aggression. Channeling this energy in a positive direction is the duty of all college coaches.

As the game grows in North America, more and more collegiate programs are moving away from the traditional free-wheeling, hard-partying set-up to a more structured and better-funded model. Coaches at places where this is the case have a distinct advantage over their colleagues at institutions where the sport is less organized.

Beyond simple instruction in technique and discipline, a critical component of coaching collegians is to impart the necessary information about the game's history, traditions, and worldwide camaraderie. Seeing themselves as part of a bigger picture when they take up the game breeds attention to issues like fairness and situation-specific sociability. A coach shouldn't try to temper the boisterousness and natural experimentation of their burgeoning adults but rather, help them to examine what sorts of behavior are appropriate in the rugby context on and off the pitch.

Catering to the clubs

The requirements for successful club coaches differ depending upon the division in which their teams play.

At lower levels, the coach must be a total club person, dealing with all the elements that affect the entire group. Recruiting players, fundraising, and various other managerial tasks can be a large part of this coach's job description. The ability to teach the basics is also necessary because new players are the lifeblood of the future. Striking a balance at training between preparing a team to win and developing new talent from scratch is the toughest challenge for a coach at this level. Winning in the present is important, but continuously building and solidifying the entire club, including families and supporters, is the key to any coach's long-term success.

At the upper levels, the coach functions more like their professional counter-parts, concerned mainly with strategic decision-making, training programs, and the upcoming weekend's opponent. A coach in this situation is usually a veteran of the sport who has taken on the challenge of guiding a squad of rugby-enthused individuals with a strong desire to perform and win. Coaches at this level can focus directly on the players because they usually have a support staff to take care of the day-to-day running of the club.

BROWNIE SAYS

Godfree's last season

When I initially started playing rugby at Occidental College, Michael Godfree was my first coach. Godfree had numerous ties to the college and was a long-serving volunteer, selflessly donating his time to mentor the somewhat wayward individuals that made up the Oxy Blackshirts team. The veterans on the team at the time informed me that after more than a decade of coaching, 1987 was to be Godfree's last year at the helm because of business and family commitments. Yet, when the next season rolled around, there he was, running practice and distributing sage advice.

It wasn't until at least a dozen years later when I became the coach of the women's rugby team at Occidental that I fully realized the amount of time and effort that Godfree had put into coaching us all those years. I also came to understand that if he hadn't done so, the club would certainly have ceased to exist — it wasn't as if there was a long line of eager applicants for the job. When I started coaching, the options were basically me or no one and I'm sure that's the case at many institutions all across North America. If USA Rugby wants to sustain and capitalize on the recent growth in collegiate rugby, one of their top priorities has to be the recruitment and training of suitable individuals to coach teams throughout the United States.

As for Godfree, 17 seasons later he's still coaching the Blackshirts. But I've heard it's his last year!

Chapter 20

Managing the Game — The Referee

*T*he most important person at any rugby match is the referee — without the services of this crucial official the game could not be played. Despite being the whipping boys for the media at the international level and the victim of ill-informed derision from sideline hecklers on local pitches, referees are almost always unbiased adjudicators and conscientious guardians of the sport they love.

In this chapter we'll look at what it takes to be a referee, what the responsibilities are for those of us who decide to join this honorable society, how to begin refereeing, and how to climb your way up the appointment ladder in North America.

The Responsibility of the Whistle

According to the Laws of the Game the referee is the sole judge of fact and law during a rugby match. To properly discharge that awesome portfolio of absolute authority, a referee must be able to fulfill the requirements in five areas of responsibility:

- Knowledge
- Consistency
- Communication
- Temperament
- Fitness

Knowledge

Referees must know the Laws of the Game. Now that doesn't mean that they have to memorize the entire law book before ever taking up the whistle, but something more than a passing familiarity with the dictates of the law-makers is essential when starting out. Knowledge of the most frequently enforced laws and all the potential choices when things go wrong promotes trust in the referee amongst the players being controlled.

A referee should strive to know more than any player who is subject to his or her decisions for the simple reason that it bolsters confidence in calling the game. Knowledge is indeed power. If referees are uncertain about the law, it will make them hesitant in blowing the whistle (and there is nothing worse than an indecisive referee). The process of becoming a referee, which we get to later in this chapter, provides for constant learning and evaluation. All good referees take quiet pride in their knowledge of the law and don't feel the need to lord it over their less informed rugby brethren.

Consistency

Although it would be ideal if every referee called a match in exactly the same way, inevitably different styles and slightly varying interpretations develop around the world. At the international level, the International Rugby Board (IRB) strives to minimize these deviations as much as possible by careful assessment of all test-match whistle-blowers. At the other end of the spectrum, local referees have less supervision and training and are thus more likely to vary in their performance from week to week. The goal for any individual referee is to work towards personal consistency.

By consistency we mean calling the game in the same fashion from start to finish. A penalty for not releasing the ball in the tackle has to be the same for both teams in all situations, whether it is in the first or 80th minute. Nothing is more frustrating for players than to perform an action at one point in the game and have it be legal, then to be called for a penalty for the same action later on in the match. Consistency breeds respect because even if a player disagrees with a call, if it is always called that way he can adapt his game to reflect the referee's interpretation.

Communication

Until very recently, the only sound that came out of a referee during a match was the high-pitched blast of the whistle. An occasional chat with a touch judge or a serious offender was basically the extent of their conversational output. In the modern game, however, the referee is expected to manage the game by being a consummate communicator.

In professional and test rugby almost all referees are wired for sound. Listening in on their chatter for 80 minutes is like hearing a condensed version of what a preschool worker must sound like when talking to young children. The referee will constantly identify phases of play, admonish potential wrongdoers, give warnings, and signify that everything is okay when players follow his commands. For example, a common refrain might be, "Ruck formed, no hands, leave it alone 7, that's fine, play on." By communicating what they see happening and calling this out to the players, fewer infractions are likely to be committed and thus there will be fewer stoppages in play, which is better for the game. Because players are now coached to actively listen to the ref's directives, smart players are avoiding penalties, which keeps the game flowing.

The referee also has the responsibility of being a teacher for less experienced teams at the lower levels. New players are often more aggressive than they are rugby smart and it's always better for a referee to help these players learn than it is for the other team to show them the consequences of their actions in non-verbal ways; this is especially important at the high school and collegiate levels. Players can learn more in one match with a good referee than in a dozen training sessions. No matter how many times a particular concept is taught at practice by a coach, when a referee provides contemporaneous direction during live competition of what players should and shouldn't be doing, understanding is greatly accelerated.

Temperament

Not everyone is cut out for refereeing. A referee must be intelligent, tolerant, calm under pressure, approachable, and have a genuine love for the game. These qualities are needed to maintain a positive relationship with the players without pretending like they're your best friends or, alternatively, treating them like naughty schoolchildren. Belligerence and arrogance are the two qualities that are least becoming on referees and those that have these characteristics in abundance give the rest of their colleagues a bad name.

Referees must always remember that their role is to be fair and impartial, to let the players decide the outcome, and to call the game as they see it without resorting to bias based on reputation or previous misconduct. As a player, it is horrible to see a certain referee turn up a match and think, "This ref hates us." What you want them to feel is, "This ref's fair." By making decisions dispassionately and without personal animosity, a referee builds a reputation for fairness that goes a long way when trying to control 30 agitated rugby players.

The highest compliment that can be paid to any referee is to go unnoticed at the end of a match. The best referees are stewards of the game who don't try to impose themselves or their beliefs on a particular contest.

Fitness

Referees can satisfy all four of the previous criteria, but if they can't keep up with play enough to see what's going on, it won't do them any good. If they're able to run for 80 minutes without tiring, they're more likely to maintain mental sharpness throughout the entire match.

As most refs are former players, they have an initial sense of what it takes to run for an hour and a half with very few chances to rest. What they don't realize, at least until they take charge of their first few matches, is how much extra running a referee does because he is constantly chasing the ball. As a forward or a back there are few moments in a match where you continually chase after the ball, but that's exactly what a referee has to do the whole time.

Becoming a Ref in the States

A simple fact in the United States is that there are more rugby matches every week than there are qualified referees. The result is that rugby as a whole suffers because it is usually the younger players (who are most in need of quality refereeing) who are neglected. Fortunately though, the upside of this chronic shortage is that anyone who thinks they might want to take up the responsibility of the whistle has ample opportunity to give it a go. If you've ever thought that you could do better than the person out there calling the game, our advice is to get started studying your law book and buy yourself a whistle.

Getting started

Before you head out onto the pitch for the first time as a whistle-blower, it helps to have watched a fair bit of rugby on TV and in person so that you can at the very least be familiar with how to position yourself at set pieces and breakdowns. The next step is to volunteer to referee a second side game or a scrimmage for your club or a team in your area (very few offers to referee are ever turned down; we think the last one was in 1982).

Another option is to first attend a refereeing clinic. These are put on by local referees' societies and are a good introduction to the basics of how to manage a match. If you choose the second route, you'll be assigned second side matches so that a more experienced referee can watch and help explain any questions afterwards.

The first designation you will receive is that of Associate Referee until you get some experience and demonstrate a working knowledge of the Laws of the Game. After you are evaluated a few times by higher ranking referees you'll be assigned to the entry-level C panel at the rank of C-3. This begins a process of evaluation and hopefully, progression up the refereeing ladder, from the C, to the B, and all the way up to the A panel.

Moving up

As you gain experience and are assessed you can be moved up from C-3 all the way to C-1. The higher you rise the more likely you are to receive assignments to referee in top matches, usually among the highest divisional teams in your area. If your performance, desire, and fitness warrant the move, you'll eventually be elevated to the B panel.

The progression through the B panel is much more rigorous than the C panel. You'll be required to travel and referee outside of your home area and you have to receive above-grade evaluations from a National Evaluator. All throughout the march from Associate to B-1 there are multiple clinics and Levels 1, 2, and 3 certification courses on offer for those who aspire to higher honors.

Reaching the top

If you have the skills, knowledge, on- and off-field demeanor, and you're in good enough physical shape, you will receive appointments to referee national level games and show your stuff to the top decision-makers. If they like what they see, you may be moved up to the National, or A Panel, and then be eligible to receive test match appointments.

Very few referees ever gain this distinction and the ones that do seem born to do it. It's crucial to remember, though, that refereeing at any level is a rewarding experience and provides immeasurable service to the game.

Picking Up the Whistle Up North

Taking up the honorable profession in Canada is similar to doing so in the United States with the main differences being terminology and organizational structure. All ten provincial unions are responsible for developing their own referees but every effort is made to provide consistency in evaluation.

Referees in Canada are designated as "Introductory" until they receive their first evaluation, when they are moved up to C-3. This follows the same international structure that is also employed by the Americans, all the way up to the A, or Canada Panel. Advancement is by individual assessment and referees also have the opportunity to enhance their skills at Level 1, 2, and 3 clinics conducted at varying intervals across the country.

One area where Rugby Canada differs from their southern neighbors is in an aggressive push to recruit new referees. Referees have tended to come from the ranks of retired players who take up the whistle to stay involved in the game once their playing days are over. Referee's societies throughout Canada are now encouraging virtually any young player who shows the slightest inclination towards refereeing, to consider making a career switch at an earlier age and potentially make it to international level with a whistle in their mouth instead of in their ear.

GUTHRIE SAYS

Who's the ref?

On a classic junket to the Rugby World Cup 1999 semifinals with Brown, I ran into Welsh international referee Derek Bevan in the media accreditation area before the first semifinal. We had interviewed him in 1998 in Wales as part of our build-up to the 1999 tournament and I was impressed by his graciousness and wanted to let him know that we really appreciated his taking the time to work with us. He recognized me and after exchanging pleasantries, oblivious to the fact that he was in charge of the impending match, I asked him which team he was picking to win the first semi?

In typical Welsh fashion, without so much as uttering a word, he smiled almost imperceptibly, and just then the IRB referee liaison thrust himself between us and directly declared, "Of course, ahem," clearing his throat, and continued, "it would be inappropriate for the match referee to make any comment whatsoever on the outcome of the match." Having realized my gaffe, I immediately retreated from the engagement nodding apologetically, knowing that further exchange of words would only cause greater harm and embarrassment.

Flash forward to one week later at the World Cup Final in Cardiff. I was walking through the stands before the game and noticed Mr. Bevan in the stands holding court, telling a rather animated story to a fellow ref. Just then, Derek looked right at me, pointed and said, "and that's the guy!" Both refs laughed heartily, as I forced an embarrassed smile and waved back, acknowledging my identification as the subject of the story. Ever since then, I've made it a point to check all the referee assignments, which is a good idea if you want to avoid the joke being on you!

Part V
Following the Game: The Informed Fan

The 5th Wave   By Rich Tennant

POLAR LEAGUE RUGBY FANS ARE PARTICULARLY APPRECIATIVE OF A GOOD JUMPER IN A LINEOUT.

In this part...

Now that you know the basics and where you fit into the rugby food chain, you probably want to know where you can get more rugby information, what media outlets can improve your knowledge of the game, and how to get the most enjoyment out of watching it being played.

In this part we explain the tremendous impact that television has had on the development of the game in North America and suggest which channels to watch to catch all the action from around the world. We rate the shows and commentators and explore some of the jargon unique to the game.

Then it's off to the match itself, where you'll learn how to find a contest to watch and how to find your place in the crowd. We finish with a survey of all the best sources of rugby information in magazines, books and Web sites.

Chapter 21

Get Your Game — Rugby on TV

....

In This Chapter

▶ TV's impact on the growth of the game

▶ Following rugby on TV

▶ Surveying the channels and offerings

....

*B*y instantaneously beaming images from London to Los Angeles and all around the globe, television has made the world a much smaller place. It is indisputable that the introduction and regular delivery of rugby on television over the past few years has done more to help the game grow than all other factors combined.

Although you have to know where and when to watch, rugby is now available on at least three TV networks across North America. Once you get the programming lineups all sorted out, you'll know which channels to watch for matches, educational features, and news updates.

In this chapter, we'll survey rugby on television in North America so you can mark your calendar, set your VCR, and never miss your weekly dose of the game they play in heaven.

The History of Rugby on TV in North America

In the dark ages prior to 1995, rugby was a very closely held secret in North America. Unless you played the game in college, or lived in one of the few pockets of rugby activity around the country, chances are you wouldn't have the slightest clue about the game. If you had heard of rugby at all, it was most likely in a negative context, having to do with college kids gone wild, or as an indecipherable foreign game. In effect, rugby didn't really exist because it almost never appeared in mainstream print media and it wasn't regularly covered on television. Of course, there were a few rugby snippets on ABC's *Wide World of Sports* in the early 1970s, and ESPN provided limited coverage

GUTHRIE SAYS

Rugby's long march to your living room

In my travels around the oval planet, rugby-passionate people often comment on how cool it is that I get paid money to produce rugby on TV at Fox Sports World. There's simply no denying the fact that I have a dream job. And while I usually respond with something humble like, "Well, someone has to do it," what I really think is, "They have no bloody idea what a nightmare it's been to get to where we are today."

When this whole mess started in 1994, I was a lawyer minding my own business, making good money, and playing rugby. To his credit, my boss at the firm suggested that I somehow involve rugby and the law to spice up my caseload. After volunteering my services to the Southern California Rugby Union as general counsel, I decided to investigate what it would take to get rugby on television. Being naive enough not to know better, and without any prior television experience, I began a tortuous march to put rugby on TV.

With the crucial backing of Bo Kelly, Bob Watkins, Ed Hagerty, and Dennis Storer, we formed a company and acquired the U.S. rights for the 1995 Five Nations from the BBC. Armed with a product, we secured distribution on the International Channel and launched our venture with England versus Wales on February 18, 1995. Unwittingly and overnight, I became the Executive Producer of a one-man operation, cursed with the responsibilities of selling advertising, acquiring rights, expanding distribution, making a weekly program, and keeping the whole project moving forward. Life as I knew it would never be the same.

If I wasn't working on production, I was pitching to sponsors or networks in a never-ending sequence of daily challenges. Was the satellite feed all set? Did I have the cashier's check for the studio time? Was the talent confirmed? Was the show written? Were all the promises to sponsors being honored? I wore so many different hats my head was getting blisters from constantly changing them. There was barely even time to *play* rugby, in the 20-hours-a-day battle to get everything done to keep rugby on the air every week. After a three-and-a-half-year unpaid struggle to create a niche for the game on TV (and learning to hate Top Ramen along the way since I never got paid), in 1998 Fox Sports World took pity on me and assumed control over the financing and ownership of the show. Since then, they've actually been paying me to do all things I did for love in the early days. I have to confess, though, that I'd still do it for free, and I give a little chuckle each time I get a check for doing something that provides me with so much personal pleasure — the satisfaction of knowing that new fans are being converted to the game I love with every telecast!

of the 1987 Rugby World Cup and the Hong Kong Sevens, but other than those isolated instances, if you wanted to watch rugby on TV the lack of access left you crying in your beer.

If you wanted to watch a live match, your only option was to go to an English pub that carried closed-circuit viewing of the Five Nations. Other than those ten matches per year, there was simply no way to watch rugby from the comfort of your own living room. Rugby enthusiasts were forced to have their overseas friends make recordings, ship them to North America, and then get them converted from PAL (European format) to NTSC (North American format). In total, it might cost you $75 (U.S.) just to watch a match that was two weeks old by the time it arrived.

That all changed in February 1995 with the launch of *Championship Rugby*, North America's first and only weekly rugby program, which delivered the best rugby from around the world. In 1998, *Championship Rugby* became part of the Fox Sports family of properties and continued as the voice of rugby for more than 500 two-hour programs until the final episode in December 2003, when it was replaced by *The Rugby Club*.

Since becoming televised in North America, rugby has grown by leaps and bounds. This is because the game itself is compelling entertainment. North Americans have a natural inclination to enjoy and appreciate many of the basic elements of the sport. Running with the ball, making big hits, and scoring tries are actions easily translated by North Americans raised on football. They love the physical contact and appreciate the fitness of today's players. Television has been the vehicle, but the reality is that the game has sold itself to North Americans. USA Rugby's membership has nearly tripled from 21,000 to 59,000 registered players since rugby has been shown on TV. The inescapable reason for this unprecedented expansion is the availability of rugby on television. As more and more people are exposed to the game, new fans are created, old passions are reawakened, and increasing numbers of parents sign their children up for youth rugby.

Fox Sports World

Fox Sports World is the home for rugby on television in the United States. Since the channel's launch in 1998, Fox Sports World has been the primary source for rugby on TV in the States. Fox Sports World is available in approximately 20 million U.S. households via digital cable or direct broadcast satellite (both DirecTV and DISH Network distribute Fox Sports World).

In addition to rugby union, Fox Sports World also televises Aussie Rules Football, National Rugby League, and daily news covering international sports with the Fox Sports World Report. For soccer enthusiasts, FSW delivers coverage of virtually all the leading soccer competitions including the English Premier League, German Bundesliga, Brazilian League, Argentinean League, UEFA Cup, FA Cup, United Soccer League, French Soccer, Dutch Soccer, Major League Soccer, and the United States Soccer League.

Rugby properties on Fox Sports World

Fox Sports World telecasts more than 75 first-class rugby games each year. The competitions covered include the Super 12, all the tours to Australia, New Zealand, and South Africa, the Tri-Nations Series, the South African Currie Cup, and the Air New Zealand National Provincial Championship (see Chapter 14 for a description of each of the above competitions). Most matches are delivered live via *The Rugby Club* studio show, or straight from the site to your screen at home (see www.foxsportsworld.com for listings).

The Rugby Club

The Rugby Club, Fox Sports World's weekly studio show, raises interest in the sport by functioning as North America's delivery vehicle for the game. *The Rugby Club* consists of five segments, including a pre-game look at the match, the first half of action, halftime highlights and features, the second half of the game, and a post-game loaded with local content, all presented from an authentic rugby clubhouse. The show provides the audience with insightful commentary and the match of the week, and highlights the all-important social aspect of the game. *The Rugby Club* embodies the unique camaraderie that is central to rugby, while promoting sportsmanship, inclusiveness, and friendship.

Figure 21-1:
The Rugby Club's Max, Ray, Brownie, and Viz.

Figure 21-2:
The Rugby
Club boys at
the bar.

Each week, U.S. and Canadian teams appear on *The Rugby Club* as the featured Club of the Week. The guest club's history and current profile are discussed in order to give the North American audience a first-hand glimpse of what a rugby club is all about (if your club would like to be considered for an invitation to appear on the show, send an e-mail to rugby@foxsportsworld.com).

Learning the game — *The Rugby Club's* Rugby For Dummies segment

Every week at halftime on *The Rugby Club*, we present our educational feature entitled "Rugby For Dummies," formerly known as "Laws of the Game." The segment uses match footage together with expert comments from our presenting team to explain the laws, or rules, of the game. The concepts behind the laws are addressed in simple terms, with the goal of making the game easier to understand for beginners, novices, intermediate, and advanced players alike.

Once new fans get a sense of the rules, their enjoyment of the game increases exponentially, as they no longer get frustrated thinking, "Why the heck did the referee stop play again?" Knowledge helps convert fans who would otherwise be confused and have neither the time nor patience to figure out the game on their own.

Getting acquainted with the talent

The Rugby Club is presented by Max Bretos, Brian Vizard, Ray Viers, and everyone's favorite barman, Matt Brown. "Mad Max" Bretos claims to have played rugby for Florida State University and Santa Monica RFC, but without a single frame of video in the library, this seems a dubious claim at best. Mad Max's enthusiasm for the game is infectious and, provided he reads the prompter and stays focused, we're entirely comfortable with all his remarks. He's a workhorse for Fox Sports World, calling heaps of soccer games, but we try not to hold that against him.

Brian "Vizman" Vizard is a former USA Eagles Captain who amassed 22 caps back in the days before television (it was only the 1980s really) and since we actually do have video clips of the Vizman playing for the Eagles (sporting a really cool 1970s-style moustache, lamb-chop sideburns, and a mullet), we're satisfied that he actually did play rugby somewhere in the not-too-distant past. Brian's quiet confidence comes from having been a team leader as a player and he's translated that self-assuredness into his role on the show. A fixture on rugby television from the very beginning, the Vizman has educated more North Americans about rugby than anyone else.

Our irrepressible Aussie, Ray Viers, provides his antipodean perspective gained from playing, coaching, and refereeing rugby in Australia and the United States for over 30 years. A longtime fixture with the Huntington Beach Unicorns, Ray's one of the more familiar and friendly faces on the Southern California rugby scene. Not shy to let his voluminous opinions fly, we'd like Ray a lot more if he could keep his remarks down to manageable sound bites instead of his interminable monologues.

As rugby barmen do, Matt "Brownie" Brown provides background and insight on news and rugby events from around the globe. A distinguished prop of undetermined age and varying rotundity, his extensive rugby CV includes stints with the Oxy Olde Boys, Missoula All-Maggots, and Rigas Miesnieks, to name but a few. Brownie's chock-full of opinions on every rugby subject imaginable and is not afraid to speak his mind, come what may. He profiles the Club of the Week and everyone has to be nice to him since he pours all the drinks and controls the Guinness tap.

Catching the Fox Sports World Rugby Report

On Wednesday nights, the *Fox Sports World Report* contains a ten-minute weekly insert entitled the "Fox Sports World Rugby Report." In the "Rugby Report," Brownie offers his unique "rugby-centric" view of the universe. The segment consists of highlights and observations from the previous weekend's action, news items, previews, and predictions of the upcoming week's matches, plus plenty of Brownie's opinions on anything and everything oval.

Getting Fox Sports World in the U.S.

To get Fox Sports World, call your cable provider and ask them if they offer the channel as part of their digital cable platform. If they don't, or if you're ready to switch over to satellite anyway, contact either DirecTV or DISH Network and sign up for their service. Make sure you mention that you want the package that includes Fox Sports "World," as there are about 30 other regional and national "Fox Sports" channels and you have to have World to get your rugby. World can be found on channel 613 on DirecTV and channel 149 on DISH Network.

Rugby on Television in Canada

Like in the U.S., rugby on television in Canada is a relatively new product. Beginning with the 1999 Rugby World Cup, Canadian rugby fans have been able to watch rugby on regional sports networks on a weekly basis. More recently, with the launch of Fox Sports World Canada, there are now two networks north of the border regularly delivering rugby.

Rogers Sportsnet

Rogers Sportsnet consists of four regional cable sports networks that reach approximately 7 million Canadian households from Halifax to Vancouver. For the past four years, Rogers Sportsnet has distributed Championship Rugby and now telecast *The Rugby Club* via their network of regional sports channels. The program times vary from region to region, but generally speaking, rugby airs on Sunday mornings at 10 a.m. local time.

Sportnet's distribution of *The Rugby Club* provides Canadian viewers with the best game each weekend throughout the year and includes all the competitions that *The Rugby Club* covers. Rogers Sportsnet is available via basic cable service in most areas and on direct broadcast satellite in the more remote areas. To order Rogers Sportsnet, contact your local cable company or satellite provider (see www.sportsnet.ca for listings).

Fox Sports World Canada

Fox Sports World Canada also carries rugby programming in Canada to approximately 500,000 households. Fox Sports World Canada offers coverage of the Super 12, tours to Australia, New Zealand, and South Africa, the South African Currie Cup and the Air New Zealand National Provincial Championship.

Rugby's demographics

Rugby has an extensive presence (759 teams!) on leading college campuses across the country. For example, 42 of the Top 50 U.S. National Universities (as rated by U.S. News and World Report) have a rugby program. And while rugby's audience is still very small by mainstream standards, the quality of the rugby viewer's profile is compelling. Rugby fans are young, affluent, and very well educated. According to an online survey conducted by Fox Sports World in October 2002, 45 percent of the 16,915 respondents reported annual household earnings in excess of $70,000 (U.S.), 85 percent were less than 45 years old, 90 percent had attended college, and 27 percent went on to post-graduate studies.

With the game rising to new heights on the pitch, the steady growth of the game at institutions of higher learning, and more sports fans getting turned onto the game every week, rugby's prospects for long-term success in North America are very bright indeed.

Fox Sports World Canada is available only via digital cable. To order, contact your local cable or satellite provider (see `www.foxsportsworld.msn.com` for more information and scheduling).

Speaking the Language

Rugby has its own unique language. All the major rugby-playing nations of the world have developed their own lexicon of rugby terminology that is used by fans and the media alike (without a domestic rugby vocabulary of our own, we revel in this cornucopia of linguistic diversity). Because 99 percent of televised rugby originates outside North America, before you can understand and fully enjoy foreign play-by-play, you need a short course in the lingo that's used to describe the game and its traditions.

Rugby's TV jargon glossary

The particular dialect of rugby speak depends on the country of origin and the commentators who are calling the game. And while this is by no means intended to be exhaustive in its scope, here's a sampling of a few rugby terms and phrases you might hear and what they really mean in plain English:

- **"They're going to keep it in tight":** The team in question is going to play a conservative game plan and try to keep the ball in the forwards to maintain possession.

✔ **"It's getting a bit niggly out there":** Some of the players are beginning to lose their discipline and are punching, stamping, or otherwise communicating their unhappiness with each other.

✔ **"He's having trouble finding touch":** The player kicking the ball is having difficulty with his accuracy and the ball is not going out of bounds where he wants it to.

✔ **"He launches a huge Garryowen":** The kicker has punted a high ball in the middle of field for his chasers to pursue and hopefully re-gather.

✔ **"Monstered in the tackle":** The ball-carrier is flattened by the tackler and loses control of how the ball is presented for the next wave of attack.

✔ **"They're really working hard in the engine room":** A team's locks are putting in a mighty effort.

✔ **"That's a bit one-eyed":** Someone is only able to see things from a single perspective.

Marvelous Mextedisms

Former All Black number 8 Murray Mexted is a well-respected commentator for Sky Television in New Zealand who has a penchant for spontaneously delivering some of the most interesting lines you'll ever hear. Here's a sampling of things that Murray has actually said on television:

✔ "You don't like to see hookers going down on players like that."

✔ "He's looking for some meaningful penetration into the backline."

✔ "Spencer's running across field calling out, 'Come inside me, come inside me.'"

✔ "I can tell you it's a magnificent sensation when the gap opens up like that and you just burst right through."

✔ "I don't like this new law, because your first instinct when you see a man on the ground is to go down on him."

✔ "Darryl Gibson has been quite magnificent coming inside Andrew Mehrtens, and I'm looking forward to seeing more of the same today."

✔ "There's nothing that a tight forward likes more than a loosie right up his backside."

✔ "Everybody knows that I have been pumping Martin Leslie for a couple of seasons now."

Thanks Murray — enough said.

Figure 21-3:
Murray
Mexted.

The best of the commentators

Having had the distinct pleasure of watching and then rewatching every single rugby match that's been on television over the past nine years, we naturally have our own list of the best rugby commentators:

- ✔ **Grant Nisbett (Sky, New Zealand):** Nisbo is the world's best play-by-play man. He's cool and impartial under pressure, is technically sound in laws knowledge, and communicates a genuine love for the game. A real class act and consummate professional behind the mike.

- ✔ **Miles Harrison (British Sky Broadcasting):** Miles is the best of Northern Hemisphere, but tends toward hyperbole at times. Best when paired with Stuart Barnes.

- ✔ **Greg Clark (Fox, Australia):** Clarkie is smooth as silk at calling all the action and has a solid command of the finer points of the game. He's the best of the Aussies by a wide margin.

- ✔ **Murray Mexted (Sky, New Zealand):** Enough said already about Mex. But seriously, besides the flowery language, Murray's technical knowledge is outstanding and he actually uses the replays to explain what just happened.

- ✔ **Tony Johnson (Sky, New Zealand):** He communicates the excitement of the match without being partial and is extremely well prepared. He gets the hard names right and possesses a wealth of knowledge about the game.

- ✔ **Gordon Bray (Channel 7, Australia):** Bray may be overly dramatic at times, but he makes a point of explaining the laws during his call.

- ✔ **Stu Wilson (Sky, New Zealand):** One of the most outspoken and opinionated color men on TV, he gets it right more often than not.

- ✔ **Phil Kearns (Fox, Australia):** Phil is not afraid to speak his mind and has plenty of opinions to share. He's a no-nonsense type who relishes the battle up front but tends to be a bit one-eyed if the Wallabies or Waratahs are involved.

Chapter 22

Spectating and Staying in Touch with Rugby News

....

In This Chapter

▶ Doing the right thing by your fellow spectators

▶ Making dazzling comments on the game

▶ Making the most of magazines

▶ Surfing the best rugby Web sites

▶ Globe-trotting with your national side

....

Spectating at a rugby match can range from standing on the sideline, cheering on your local club side, to sitting way up at the back of a stadium, rooting your national side to victory. Regardless of the setting, rugby crowds are some of the best behaved and most pleasant in all of sport.

In this chapter, we give you advice on how to get the most from your visit to a rugby match and become the model rugby spectator. For those of you who really want to get into the spirit of things, we offer some tongue-in-cheek tips on how to impress those around you with your incredible rugby knowledge. We also provide a vast array of resources to bring you up to speed with rugby happenings in the U.S., Canada, and around the world.

Finding a Match to Watch

Congratulations — you're about to take the plunge and actually attend a rugby match. Rugby is one of the most user-friendly sports, generally attracting an intelligent, passionate crowd who believe that watching rugby at any level is a wonderful treat.

If you are interested in attending a club match but don't know if there's a team in your area, a little online searching can fill the void. For the United States, go to www.usarugby.org and click on membership in the left hand column, select Find a Club, and the rest depends on where you live. In Canada, go to www.rugbycanada.ca and click on links in the left-hand column. The list on that page includes provincial union, sub-union, and individual club Web sites.

Another option is to use any of the major search engines to find a local club. Type "local rugby unions in _____," filling in the blank with your state, province, or geographic region. That will result in a long list of choices that will at least give you a starting point to track down a club. Most union sites will have links to their clubs, or alternatively, contact details for a responsible party who can supply further information. Most club sites will provide roughly the same details specific to that team.

To find out when and where international and representative matches will be played in Canada and the U.S., check out the above-mentioned Web sites for dates, venues, and how to purchase tickets.

Blending In with the Crowd

Whether you are going to watch a full-blown test match or a local Division II encounter, the spectator areas at rugby games are safe and suitable places for a family outing. Even at 80,000-seat stadiums in rugby hotbeds the atmosphere in the crowd is still relatively restrained and positive.

In this section, we give you guidance on how to behave so as not to upset other spectators. We also give advice on the right kind of clothes to wear to maximize your comfort.

Following rugby etiquette

Rugby definitely has an unwritten code of conduct for its fans. Remember, players, supporters, and everyone involved with the game are rightly proud of the fact that rugby retains its civilized nature even in the age of professionalism. So that you'll know what's acceptable and what's not at a rugby match, we've put together a few words of wisdom that may save you from embarrassment:

✔ **Don't be afraid to ask questions:** If you're a novice fan, feel free to query your neighbor about things you don't understand that are happening in the match. Most rugby fans love nothing better than to help out newcomers with the intricacies of the game because it allows them to show off their superior level of expertise. If you feel like making comments of your own, you should at least sound well informed. You don't need to spout Shakespeare; initially your immortal lines could include phrases like, "Excellent tackle" and "Great take in the line-out." The section on how to sound like an expert later in this chapter can also give you some ideas for comments that sound more deep and meaningful.

- **Criticize, but don't denigrate, the referee:** It's okay to take issue with the referee's decisions — but it's not acceptable to make him or her the target of verbal abuse. Demonstrating regard for the referee shows that you are a spectator who understands the traditions that make rugby the noble game it is. In other sports, referees are called all sorts of horrible names, but in rugby, the referee is a figure of respect, which is why the players always address the person in charge as "sir" or "ma'am."

- **Show respect for the opposition:** The good rugby fan applauds the opposition when they do something impressive. Friendly, civilized behavior makes the occasion more enjoyable — even if your team is losing.

- **Maintain decorum:** When an opposition player is about to take a shot at goal, be silent. Don't imitate the idiots who try to distract the goal kicker. Such antics are frowned upon because most rugby spectators believe that rugby is an intellectual pursuit to be treated as a thinker's game, not as an opportunity for hooligans to misbehave.

- **Check the allegiances of those around you very carefully:** If you are among fans of the same team, you can get away with a lot more than if you are among supporters of the other team. If you find yourself surrounded by people supporting the opposition, be more circumspect in your comments.

- **Buy someone a beer (where available):** If you go off to buy a beer, ask the person next to you if he or she wants one. This will instantly make you a friend. Having friends around you at a rugby match gives you a nice feeling of solidarity and gives you the opportunity to exchange views on the game.

Dressing for the occasion

A good choice at any rugby match is rugby-related gear like jerseys or hats, either purchased from online retailers or obtained from your local club. This allows you to declare your rooting proclivities without saying a word. Some fans believe that the height of fashion is to deck themselves out in clothes that scream out their rugby allegiances (see Figure 22-1).

Figure 22-1:
Showing
their true
colors,
rugby fans
cheer their
team on.

The best clothes to wear to a rugby match combine a bit of fashion with a lot of function. You need to be wearing something that can protect you from whatever type of weather a rugby afternoon or evening can bring. Rugby in many parts of the United States and Canada is a spring and fall sport so you often have to confront chilly or wet weather. Dressing appropriately for the weather conditions usually means more clothes rather than fewer. Don't forget that, as a spectator, it is easier to take layers of clothes off if you get too warm than try and get warm when you haven't got anything else to put on. If in doubt about the weather, at the very least take a waterproof jacket.

Spectating Across North America

The best place to watch a game is near the halfway line because a spot here gives you a good view of the whole field. For test matches, the seats at the halfway line are the most expensive. Another good place that affords a fine view of the action is near the 22-meter lines.

At the club level you can generally follow the ball up and down the sidelines (taking care to stay back far enough to let the touch judge have unfettered access), so you are always in position to see what's going on in every situation.

Going to watch a test match

A *test match* is when the top representative teams of two national unions meet in a game sanctioned by the International Rugby Board (IRB). This is the elite level of competition; playing for your country is the highest honor a rugby player can achieve. Various teams around the world may have adopted nicknames like the All Blacks and the Wallabies, but make no mistake, when they meet it's New Zealand versus Australia, direct country-to-country combat.

Going to see a test match in North America is difficult because of the limited number of games available on an annual basis. For the last five years Canada has averaged four home tests and the United States just over three internationals per year. The advent of the Churchill Cup and the Super Cup (see chapter 13 for details on these tournaments) should eventually raise these paltry numbers and give more fans a chance to see their national teams in action.

A test match, or *full international*, is marked by the playing of both national anthems prior to kickoff and the presence of a neutral country referee. Every player that sees action in a test is awarded a *cap* for their efforts. Many teams around the world mark the occasion of a player's first appearance for his country by actually giving them a ceremonial cap, as was done in years past.

Test matches can be part of a larger competition like World Cup qualifying, the Pan-American tournament, or as part of a tour by the visiting side. There are also one-off tests where sides meet on an irregular basis as determined by the IRB. This is usually done to bolster the lesser teams by having them play rugby powerhouses from around the globe.

Tests in North America are still generally played in smaller stadiums, but in rugby-mad countries they can be held in mammoth venues. The all-time record for a test was set in Sydney in 2000 when an Australia versus New Zealand Tri Nations clash drew 109,874! Whether a test is attended by that number or several hundred diehards the atmosphere is special because the teams are playing for national pride first and foremost.

The club experience

If the you are geographically challenged and unable to make it to a test in North America, don't fret because there's probably plenty of other rugby being played somewhere near you. The beauty of watching matches at the local level is that there are usually no crowds and you can follow the game in its purest form.

Getting a close-up view of the action at club level

A great way to learn the game and enjoy rugby in its essence is to attend a local club game. In most divisions it's free, but at the semiprofessional level of Super League in the States and Canada a reasonable entrance fee is usually charged. Standing close to the action, you get a better appreciation of the intensity and physicality of the game. This is the ideal way to learn the referee's signals, discover what the different players actually do, what is required for each position, and how players react to different tactics. Overall, being close to the sideline helps you get a good feel for the game.

Enjoying the camaraderie of local clubs

At a club match everyone is there because they love rugby or someone playing it. This is where you find the really passionate rugby supporters, who follow their club through thick and thin. Clubs rely on good community spirit and volunteers for their very existence. Quite apart from the outcome of the game, a successful match day means everyone has enjoyed themselves in a welcoming environment.

The atmosphere at club games is generally amiable, and you quickly feel at home. Faster than you can say "kick for touch," someone is usually selling raffle tickets to help make money for the club. Pitch in and buy a ticket or two, because in your own small way you may be helping to develop a club champion, who could eventually end up representing the United States or Canada on the world stage.

Spectators are almost always welcome at the post-match function where the two teams and their supporters get together to share a beer or three and talk about the game. This is when you can sense the genuine bonds that develop in this sport.

Sounding like a rugby expert

You really only need a few phrases to sound like a rugby genius. After the first scrum, turn to your neighbor and say, "That tight-head will have to watch himself, because he's pushing in at an illegal angle." We guarantee you that the person next to you will turn, look at you as if you're a sage old hand, and nod his or her head. You'll get this reaction even if what you say is not happening, because no one can really tell if the tight-head prop is pushing into the scrum at the wrong angle — it is such a fine line of judgment. (We discuss scrums in detail in Chapter 8.)

Another crucial phrase to remember is, "They're offside." No matter which team you are following, or whether the opposition is offside or not, every person in the crowd believes the opposition is offside, and just loves telling the referee about it. If you say "they're offside" at various well-timed moments of the game, you are sure to get knowing nods from those around you. (See Chapter 6 for an explanation of the Offside Law.)

All kidding aside, if you're in doubt about the kind of reception your comments may attract, just applaud when everyone else applauds and you'll be safe.

Touring Overseas

Touring to far-distant places is a great rugby tradition. Due to the strong international flavor of the game, any club, no matter what level, is usually able to find plenty of overseas clubs willing to offer them a match. So, if someone in your club is up to the task, a fascinating itinerary can be organized, enabling players to discover the delights of playing and watching the game in some of the most unexpected rugby pockets of the world.

A tour can be organized around a major event like the Rugby World Cup or a British and Irish Lions tour, or undertaken for no reason other than that everyone wants to get out of the country and play some rugby. When and where you go is a decision for individual clubs, but certain elements are common to successful touring.

Cost is number one because unless at least 20 players can go, it makes for a lonely and body-battering tour. Itinerary is also crucial. Trying to squeeze too much into a couple of weeks of travel is more taxing than relaxing. Finding the right clubs to play is another necessary component. This can be achieved by being honest about your club's capabilities and skill level. It's no fun to be beaten by huge margins in every tour match because you are playing teams way above your level.

For players and fans, rugby tours are the ultimate way of letting their hair down and getting to know each other. Living with your teammates and fellow club members for a couple of weeks in the close quarters of buses and hotel rooms is an ideal way to build spirit and cohesiveness. Of course, one maxim that always has to be followed is that *what goes on tour, stays on tour,* meaning that particularly funny, embarrassing, or debauched moments are for consumption only by the tourists themselves and not casual listeners back home.

Learning More About the Game

Once you watch some rugby either at club or test level, or anywhere in between, you'll probably want to find out more about this fascinating sport. While there is still very little coverage available in most North American newspapers and on broadcast television, there are a multitude of other resources that can help you to fill in your knowledge gaps about the game played with the oval ball.

North American magazines

The best way to get a feel for rugby in North America is to pick up the two magazines that cover the sport in their respective countries. These are both all-purpose magazines designed to keep fans informed on events and all facets of the game within their nation.

Don't hesitate to read these rugby magazines — there is something for everyone. The more you read, the more fluent you will become in the special language of rugby. (For other magazines from around the world see Appendix C at the back of this book.)

National Rugby Post

If you want to know what's going on in Canadian rugby, the *National Rugby Post* is a must-read. Canada's rugby magazine is published in Edmonton on a bi-monthly basis. It covers all aspects of the game in Canada, including international competition and provincial news. Inside every issue you'll find player profiles, match reports and schedules, Super League news and provincial standings, commentary and opinion, plus feature articles on a wide variety of rugby topics and events.

Amidst the informative and entertaining writing are advertisements for everything from rugby gear to far-flung tournaments. To find out how to obtain a copy go to `www.rugbypost.com` for more information.

Rugby magazine

Rugby magazine, now in its 30th year, provides complete coverage of U.S. and international rugby, numerous departments geared to improving the level of U.S. play, and a National Directory/Yearbook. During a 12-month cycle, *Rugby* posts detailed reports on each of the 21 U.S. National Championships, plus the results of all matches played by the eight U.S. National Teams. *Rugby* also covers the local and territorial union championships, plus many of the 250 independent tournaments that take place in the U.S. each year.

A signature feature is the inclusion of "transferable information" pieces: in-depth interviews with members of the U.S. community who have found innovative ways to fund fields and clubhouses, conduct successful youth programs, make inroads with school administrators, and more. *Rugby* also profiles members of the rugby community who distinguish themselves in various ways outside of the game. Included among the departments to be found in each issue are: profiles of male and female players, referee and coach profiles, referee's corner, coach's corner, masters rugby, nutrition, and domestic and international calendars. *Rugby*'s International Round-Up provides a digest of all significant matches and developments around the world.

BROWNIE SAYS

Rugby books

Rugby books generally fall into three categories: autobiographical or biographical, instructional, or events-related non-fiction. Rather than providing an endless list of titles, I'll give you my favorite title from each of these classifications.

Autobiography: *Boots 'n All* by Andy Haden

This remains my personal favorite because it was the first book I read about rugby after starting to play. Haden is a legendary All Black lock with a wild streak and a healthy appetite for challenging the established order. It was published in 1983 so it's hard to find and is a bit dated, but still a pleasure to read.

Instructional: *Thinking Rugby* by Josh Kronfeld, Ken Hodge, and Alex McKenzie

Rugby is a thinking game and this book takes that idea to another level. This was the first book to examine in a clinical way the steps necessary to becoming a better rugby player through Psychological Skills Training. Co-author Ken Hodge is also a fellow All-Maggot! (See chapter 16 for a description of Maggotfest.)

Non-fiction: *The Rugby War* by Peter FitzSimons

This book tells the inside story of the battle for the soul of rugby when it first went professional in 1995. The author is a former Wallaby who knows all the key players in the saga and presents it in a very readable fashion. The book was updated and re-released in a new edition in 2003.

Finally, each year *Rugby* produces a 168-page National Directory, which provides updated information on the over 2,000 U.S. clubs and comprehensive records of all U.S. National Championships and players. For more information visit www.rugbymag.com.

Rugby news in cyberspace

Rugby is blessed with some excellent Web sites, so it isn't hard for the addict to get his or her daily fix of information, the latest news, or in-depth detail on any aspect of the game. Most of the leading sites also have excellent archive sections, where you can easily access background information on a wide variety of rugby-relevant subjects. Some Web sites focus on the game in a particular country while others present broader coverage reflecting rugby's status as a global game.

As rugby television producers and journalists we rely on several of these Web sites to stay up-to-date on everything that's going on in the competitions.

Fox Sports World

Fox Sports World's Web site (www.foxsportsworld.msn.com) has a rugby page that can be found on the top border of the home page. Click onto rugby and you'll find up-to-date news articles and Brown's weekly rugby column, where he previews the upcoming matches and offers his rugby-centric view of the universe.

Planet Rugby

Planet Rugby (www.planet-rugby.com) is the world's leading rugby Web site. We use this site every single day. Based in the United Kingdom, it gives in-depth coverage on what is going on in the northern hemisphere and around the world. Planet Rugby also has a string of international correspondents who report on what is going on in their part of the world.

This site offers a good balance of news, analysis, opinions, and background. If you want to check up on a player and find out his age and number of test appearances, Planet Rugby provides the information. This site is also useful to the enthusiast who wants to know how a team performed in previous years; match reports on all test matches are kept on the database.

Scrum

Scrum (www.scrum.com) is another UK-based Web site. It covers the international game but is particularly strong in the areas of Six Nations, Heineken Cup, and Zurich Premiership information. Scrum also features Rugby Today, which presents a sampling of rugby articles from newspapers and Web sites around the globe, all in one easily accessible place.

Rugby Heaven

Rugby Heaven (www.rugbyheaven.com.au) is the leading Australian rugby Web site. The site relies on the resources of the *Sydney Morning Herald*, the *Daily Telegraph* in London, *Australian Associated Press*, and various other news agencies, enabling Rugby Heaven to provide the latest news from around the globe.

This site boasts numerous interesting sections, such as World Cup, Six Nations, Tri Nations, Super 12, Provincial, and Off the Field. Rugby Heaven also has on-line competitions, chat rooms, polls, and many interactive services. At the start of the 2003 season, Rugby Heaven underwent a revamp, giving it a cleaner, more authoritative look, ensuring that the latest tables, stories, and articles can be found easily. This site is a good spot to start to find out what is going on in the game.

Stuff

Stuff (www.stuff.co.nz) is a useful Web site if you're looking for information about rugby in New Zealand. By going to the sports section of this all-Kiwi site you can find out what's going on all over New Zealand in regards to rugby. Articles from newspapers throughout New Zealand appear alongside original commentary from various luminaries.

SuperSport Zone

If you want to follow the game in South Africa, SuperSport Zone (www.superrugby.co.za) is the recommended site. It provides plenty of news and commentary on the Currie Cup, Vodacom Cup, and all other domestic issues in the republic. The site also follows the Springboks religiously.

IRB and union sites

A good starting point to find out about the game of rugby is the Web site for the worldwide governing body of the sport, the International Rugby Board (www.irb.com). This site gives information on every national union in the world, and features sections on all IRB sponsored competitions, as well as a complete version of the Laws of the Game, and other relevant material. You can also find useful tidbits on refereeing, coaching, and training, or you can look at the current world rankings.

Many individual unions have Web sites that comprehensively cover the game in their country. You can find these either on the IRB site or by typing the name of the country, followed by the word "rugby," into any search engine. The best of the bunch is put up by New Zealand.

The New Zealand Rugby Union Web site

As one would expect from the official site of the organization in charge of the country's unofficial religion, the New Zealand Rugby Union (NZRU) site (www.nzrugby.co.nz), cleverly caters to the passionate rugby fan. In a section called "Fanzone," supporters can express their love towards the teams and players that they root for.

The site also offers the latest breaking news, details of upcoming games and results, and extensive information about the New Zealand team. You'll find information about the union's leading players and what is happening at all levels of New Zealand rugby.

The United States and Canadian Rugby Union sites

USA Rugby's official site (www.usarugby.org) contains a wealth of information on the USA National Teams, plus the various annual National Championships, news, and membership data.

Rugby Canada's site (www.rugbycanada.ca) offers a full array of information on the game from youth development programs to the Super League and everything Canadian in between.

Part VI
The Part of Tens

The 5th Wave   By Rich Tennant

© RICHTENNANT

PAINTING THE DEAD BALL LINE
ON A RUGBY FIELD

In this part...

Every *For Dummies* book includes a Part of Tens, chapters that each contain ten or so interesting pieces of information.

In this part, we offer our list of the ten best North American rugby players as a ploy to get the debate flowing. Next, we list and explain our ten best moments, with five from around the world and five from the USA and Canadian experience. We conclude with a look at some of the more peculiar facts about rugby, a game that is played by some of the world's most colorful people and where anything can, and often does happen on the day.

Chapter 23

The Ten Greatest North American Players

● ●

In This Chapter

The Men:

▶ Gareth Rees

▶ Dan Lyle

▶ Al Charron

▶ Dave Hodges

▶ Brian Vizard

▶ Winston Stanley

The Women:

▶ Jen Crawford

▶ Diane Schnapp

▶ Gillian Florence

▶ Jane Mitchell

● ●

*I*n this chapter we profile the ten greatest players ever to pull on a United States or Canadian national team jersey. These are the very best to have ever graced our North American fields with their rugby genius.

Compiling a list of the ten best Canadian and American rugby players of all time was no easy task considering how many outstanding men and women have played the game in North America. In making our selections we considered not only their individual accomplishments, but more importantly, how their particular talents helped their teams to succeed. As with any top ten list, there are some very qualified candidates that didn't make the cut. To recognize their accomplishments, we've added an honorable mention section.

Gareth Rees

Gareth Rees is the highest profile North American rugby player of all time. He made his debut against the United States in 1986. In an international career that spanned 13 years he earned 55 caps for Canada. He was the only player to appear in each of the first four World Cups from 1987 to 1999. Rees retired following the 1999 Rugby World Cup as Canada's all-time leading scorer, amassing a career total of 487 points. He played for several leading professional clubs in Europe including Castres (France), Wasps and Harlequins (England), and Newport (Wales).

With outstanding vision and an excellent tactical and goal-kicking boot, Rees stands head and shoulders above all other North American flyhalves. In May 2002, he became the Chief Executive Officer of Rugby Canada and reinstated national team coach David Clark before stepping down on the eve of the 2003 Rugby World Cup.

Figure 23-1:
Gareth Rees

Dan Lyle

Dan Lyle is the best rugby player ever to put on an Eagle jersey. He was a talented tight-end who played college football at the Virginia Military Institute. Like so many Americans who switch from football to rugby, Lyle was introduced to the sport in his 20s, yet still managed to assimilate the finer points of the game using intelligence and hard work. He debuted for the USA Eagles in 1994 against Ireland, then went on to play professionally in England for Bath and Leicester. He became one of Europe's finer players, setting up the only try in Bath's 1997 European Cup triumph. Dan earned 45 caps (24 as captain) before retiring following the 2003 Rugby World Cup, on the heels of a towering performance where he earned our praise as the outstanding number 8 of the tournament.

Figure 23-2:
Dan Lyle
soars for a
line-out.

At 6'5" and 250 pounds, Lyle's solidly built frame was impressive, but his greatest assets were his intelligence and tremendous athleticism. A number 8 with power, speed, and good distribution skills, Lyle was also an imposing defender. Perhaps his greatest skill was claiming restarts and line-outs, where he was one of the world's best players at contesting possession in the air.

Al Charron

Al Charron is an ironman who appeared 72 times for Canada since his debut against Argentina in 1990. A tall and rangy back-row forward, Charron played flanker, number 8, or lock with equal skill. He was invited to play with the Barbarians RFC five times and was named to a World XV in 1999. Following Rees' lead, Charron's participation in the 2003 Rugby World Cup earned him the distinction of having appeared in four World Cups. He captained Canada 22 times during his career and was a fixture for many years on the Canadian Sevens Team.

Dave Hodges

Only the second American to earn 50 caps, USA Eagles Captain Dave Hodges is just the kind of player you want leading your team into battle. At 6'4" and 235 pounds, Hodges is a fierce defender who leads by example, putting his body on the line every time he takes the field. He's a versatile forward possessing a full complement of back-row and locking skills. Since 1997, he's played professionally in Wales for Llanelli and Bridgend and was named Llanelli's 2001–2002 Player of the Year.

A 1989 All-American linebacker at Occidental College, Hodges played professional football in Europe for the Hamburg Blue Devils in 1993–94, before dedicating himself full-time to rugby. Like Lyle, Dave's intelligence and tremendous work ethic enabled him to smoothly adjust from football to rugby without missing a beat.

Winston Stanley

Winston Stanley is a fantastic finisher whose speed and rugby IQ seem to improve with age. The balding winger may have lost some hair follicles, but he's managed to maintain his speed over the years at a position where few can. He made his debut for Canada against the United States in 1994 and has earned 63 caps while notching 123 points. He's played professionally in Europe for Blackheath, Worcester, and Leeds, and was a member of the 2001 European-Cup-winning Leicester Tigers. A veteran of the 1997 and 2001 Canadian Sevens World Cup teams, he's just as comfortable and even more dangerous in the abbreviated version of the game.

Brian Vizard

The Vizman debuted for the Eagles against Japan in 1986 and went on to earn 22 caps for the United States, captaining the team eight times. An imposing figure at 6'6" and 230 pounds, Vizard played number 8 in the days before lifting in the line-out, when having a tough line-out enforcer was absolutely critical. Foolhardy would-be tacklers encountered an Edward-Scissorhands-like fury of razor sharp elbows and relentlessly churning knees. He made numerous appearances for the Eagles Sevens side in Hong Kong and elsewhere around the world. Viz played the majority of his club rugby for the Old Mission Beach Athletic Club leading them to six USA Rugby National Club Championships along the way. From what we can gather from tall tales, artifacts, and fossil remains, Viz was the kind of player that everyone wanted on their team, but dreaded playing against — a big, strong, determined, aggressive, and angry man who wanted to win more than anyone else on the pitch.

Diane Schnapp

North America's most gifted and technically sound ball-fetcher, Diane Schnapp heads the list of game winners that never seem to get their names in the headlines. At 5'6" and 150 pounds, she's solidly built and low to the ground, making her a monster when the ball is on the turf. She excels at reading the game and is usually the first to arrive at the breakdown. Once there, she has the strength and courage to go in and win the ball without any regard for her body. She's a firefighter in Oakland, California, and a member of the Berkeley All-Blues juggernaut. Schnapp would be the first player chosen if we were selecting a women's side.

Figure 23-3:
Diane
Schnapp.

Jen Crawford

Jen Crawford is the finest female player that North America has ever produced. The U.S.'s all-time leading try scorer, Crawford captained the Eagles to the final of the 1998 Women's World Cup while earning a record 20th cap. Still a force in the club game, she's led the Berkeley All-Blues to six consecutive USA Rugby National Women's Club Championships.

She has an instinctive feel for the game and a deadly ability to set up defenders and either sell the dummy or blow straight through them. She's a devastating finisher when the goal line is in sight and has led representative sides to national titles in 15s and 7s.

Gillian Florence

A powerful and aggressive flanker who's amassed 26 caps representing her country, Florence earned the game MVP in her test debut at the 1994 World Cup. A devastating tackler and hard runner with the ball in hand, she was a key performer on the fourth-place Canadian team at the 1998 Women's Rugby World Cup. Gillian was selected to the 2003 All World Team.

Jane Mitchell

The U.S.-based half of the famous Anglo-American rugby-playing Mitchell twins, Jane's rugby IQ is simply off the charts. Although we have no idea how old she really is, somehow, like a fine Northern California red wine, she just keeps getting better with age. With the most enticing dummy imaginable, Jane has littered fields across the world with wayward defenders grasping air in her slipstream. She's a master game controller from the pivot and equally devastating from the midfield. Another mainstay of the Berkeley All-Blues, Mitchell is a champion who exudes confidence and inspires her teammates.

Honorable Mentions

Whenever you construct a list like the preceding one, you're forced to leave off some worthy candidates. To properly acknowledge their achievements, we've come up with a list of notables who deserve recognition.

On the Canadian men's ledger, the following players are worthy of an honorable mention:

- **Dan Baugh:** Although hampered by injuries, the 30-times capped and very athletic Baugh plays for Cardiff in Wales.

- **Mike James:** A force in the Canadian line-out since 1994, Mike has earned 50 caps and played for Stade Français in Paris.

- **Dave Lougheed:** This rangy and deceptively fast winger is a veteran of three World Cups and is still one of Canada's best finishers.

- **Bob Ross:** The world's longest serving international debuted in 1989 against Ireland, earned 54 caps, and is Canada's second all-time leading scorer.

- **Rod Snow:** A versatile prop, Snow is a rock of consistency with 50 caps and was named to a World XV in 1999.

The Canadian women who deserve to be singled out include:

- **Shari Sparling:** A long-serving captain and reliable fullback, Sparling holds the most caps at her position among Canadian women.

- **Dawn Keim:** A free-spirited London Wasps back-rower, Dawn was the MVP of the 1999 Can Am match.

- **Josee Lacasse:** The most-capped Canadian woman retired after the 2002 Women's Rugby World Cup having earned 29 caps at prop.

Outstanding male players from the Eagles that deserve mention include:

- **Vaea Anitoni:** A speedy wing, Anitoni is the Eagles' all-time leading try scorer in 46 tests.

- **Tom Billups:** The Eagles' fittest hooker and one of the first Americans to play professionally in Europe (Harlequins), Tom was a no-nonsense player who's brought that same intensity to his current position as coach of the U.S. Men's National Team.

- **Luke Gross:** At 6'10", Gross was a monster in the line-out and the most-capped American with 62 appearances for the Eagles.

- **Fred Paoli:** Perhaps the U.S.'s best all-time prop, Paoli was a no-nonsense captain and natural team leader who earned 20 caps.

- **Dennis Jablonski:** A standout fullback in defense and attack (and the first in a long line of Eagles from Occidental College), Jabbo was also the first American ever named to a World XV representative team.

For the U.S. women, this trio stands out:

- **Kathy Flores:** A slightly undersized number 8, Flores was an integral part of the 1991 and 1994 Eagles World Cup champion and runner-up teams. Kathy now coaches the USA Rugby Women's National Team and was named the IRB's Female Personality of the Year in 2003.

- **Candi Orsini:** This gifted and ageless center combined speed, agility, and power to wreak havoc from the midfield. Another veteran of the U.S.'s 1991, 1994, and 1998 Rugby Women's World Cup squads, Candi now serves as an assistant coach with the national team.

- **Phaedra Knight:** The only American woman named to the 2003 World XV, the athletic prop combines size, power, and quickness, plus good technique up front. Her contribution is huge in attack and on defense.

Chapter 24

The Ten Best Rugby Moments

*R*ugby fans are particularly passionate about the history of their game and love nothing more than to discuss fantastic moments from the past over a cold beverage. Good-natured debate about the greatest game, best try, and most awesome team is a staple activity in clubhouses around the globe.

In this chapter, we provide our picks of the five greatest moments in the history of the game from around the oval planet and then put forth our selections for the top five moments in the game for North American teams.

Top Five Around the World

In the more than 125 years since the first test match was played between England and Scotland in 1871, rugby has delivered hundreds of great games marked by dramatic finishes and featuring monumental team and individual performances. The process of paring this mountain of history into just five games demonstrated to us yet again why rugby is such an amazing sport. Here's our list of the five best games of all time.

The greatest test ever

On July 15, 2000, Australia hosted New Zealand at Olympic Stadium in Sydney in what we believe was the single best test ever played. The setting befit the occasion, as a world-record rugby crowd of 109,874 filled the stadium to watch the defending World Champion Wallabies face the New Zealand All Blacks with the Bledisloe Cup on the line in the opening match of the Tri Nations. The match started with a flurry as Tana Umaga scored an intercept try off an ill-advised pass by Chris Latham. From the ensuing kickoff, the Kiwis controlled the ball and Jonah Lomu got into the action, by putting Pita Alatini in the clear after a break down the touchline. Fullback Christian Cullen was next on the scoresheet stunning the Aussie crowd with a burst through the Wallaby defense for the third try. Then, after an Andrew Mehrtens penalty, with just nine minutes gone, the scoreline read Australia 0, New Zealand 24. With 70 minutes left to be played, it was shaping up to be the worst beating that the All Blacks had ever inflicted on the Wallabies.

Wallaby Captain John Eales summoned his troops and told them to keep their cool and stay focused on the game plan — the key thing was not to panic. From the next restart, Stephen Larkham broke the line and put Stirling Mortlock into the clear with a perfectly weighted pass. The huge crowd let out a collective sigh of relief as they all wondered . . . "Can the boys come all the way back?" Over the next 25 minutes the World Champions did exactly that to level the scores at 24–all at the half.

The Aussies took the lead 27–24 with a penalty in the 58th minute, but the All Blacks answered with a try by Justin Marshall to reclaim the lead 29–27. After the conversion and a Mehrtens penalty the Kiwis led 34–27. Stirling Mortlock then added a penalty, and the lead was down to 34–30 with only a few minutes remaining. In the 78th minute, Wallaby hooker Jeremy Paul drove over the tryline in the corner and raised his arms in triumph, as the all-time record crowd went absolutely nuts, celebrating yet another amazing comeback by their beloved boys who had moved ahead of their biggest rivals 35–34.

All that remained was to run out the clock. Trailing by one point, the All Blacks had to score on their last possession. After several phases of slowly advancing the ball, reserve scrumhalf Byron Kelleher moved the ball wide to Taine Randell, who drew two defenders and passed over the top to Jonah Lomu. The big man rumbled around the corner, beating Larkham's last-ditch tackle attempt to score the match winning try!

We've seen the match at least 15 times and it still gives us chills to watch the finish. If you ever want to explain to someone who's unfamiliar with rugby what the game's all about, and you're lucky enough to have it on tape, show them this match — they'll be a believer in no time.

The 2003 World Cup final

The 2003 Rugby World Cup final pitted host Australia against the pre-tournament favorites, England. The home nation against the former colony, the best of the north against the best of the southern hemisphere, this match had a storyline that was longer than the queues waiting to catch a train after the match at Homebush station. The stadium was half full of English and half full of Aussie supporters, as white and gold jerseys dominated the jam-packed venue. The match started well for the home side when Lote Tuqiri hauled in a cross field bomb by Stephen Larkham and the Wallabies took a five-point lead.

England kept their composure as Jonny Wilkinson converted three shots at goal to put England in front 9–5. Then just before halftime, Wilko put Jason Robinson into the clear down the right sideline and England went into the changing rooms with a well-deserved 14–5 halftime lead.

The second half settled into a contest of wills: The Wallabies scratched their way back into the match with two penalty goals, but England still led 14–11 as fulltime approached. On the Wallabies' final possession in injury time, a penalty gave Elton Flatley his chance to level the scores and force extra time. With ice water coursing through his veins and the rugby world holding its breath, he calmly slotted the goal and the fulltime whistle was blown, leaving the world's two best teams even at 14–all.

In extra time, the teams continued the pattern. England took the lead on a penalty, and then Australia leveled the scores with 30 seconds left in the second of the two ten-minute periods. With just seconds remaining and the commentators speculating about a third ten-minute sudden death period, England's scrumhalf Matt Dawson somehow broke through the Wallaby defense and got close enough to the line for Jonny Wilkinson to line up a final drop goal attempt. Everyone in the stadium knew what was coming: Jonny stroked the drop and history was made when the ball sailed through the uprights and England became the first northern hemisphere nation to ever win the World Cup. All hail Sir Clive Woodward and England!

Barbarians versus New Zealand 1973

Before July 15, 2000, when the subject of greatest games came up, the 1973 contest between the Barbarians RFC and the New Zealand All Blacks topped the list. The game matched a Barbarians team chock-full of Welsh legends, including the incomparable Gareth Edwards, JPR Williams, Phil Bennett, and John Dawes, plus Irish icons Willie John McBride, Mike Gibson, and Fergus Slattery, and other notables from Scotland and England. The All Blacks featured the uncompromising Ian Kirkpatrick, Alex Wyllie, Sid Going, and Brian Williams who had just shut out England 9–0 and now faced the star-studded Barbarians to finish up their tour.

After the opening kickoff, the teams traded deep kicks, jockeying for field position until the All Blacks' Brian Williams launched a high kick deep behind the Welsh 22-meter line. Instead of taking the sensible option and kicking for the safety of touch, Phil Bennett counterattacked, beginning an 80-meter movement that would be forever etched in the memories of rugby fans around the world.

Bennett picked up the ball around his own 10-meter line, and made three successive side-steps to elude Alister Scown, J.A. Hurst, and Ian Kirkpatrick. Bennett then passed on to JPR Williams, who nearly had his head ripped off, but still managed to offload to John Pullin. Pullin transferred the ball to John Dawes who sold a dummy, covered more ground, and passed inside to Tom

David as he crossed the halfway line. David made a one-handed pass inside to Derek Quinnell, who moved the ball on with another one-handed pass inside. Just then, Gareth Edwards blasted from nowhere to join the line at precisely the right angle and pace to round the corner, evaded Joe Karam's covering tackle, and covered the final 20 meters to dive headfirst into the left-hand corner of the River Tafft end to score what is now known as "The Try." The capacity Cardiff Arms Park crowd erupted into a delirious state of rapture and the Barbarians went on to defeat the mighty All Blacks 23–11.

If you ever get lucky enough to hear Gareth Edwards describe "The Try" in person, you'll see his eyes light up as he relives every step of the movement from 30 years ago like it was yesterday, despite the fact that it's the 25,000th time he's told the story. Some things really do improve with age.

The British and Irish Lions versus Australia 2001

The 2001 British and Irish Lions Tour of Australia featured the then defending World Champion Wallabies against a formidable assembly of the best stars from England, Ireland, Wales, and Scotland. The first two matches of the three test tour went according to plan with the Lions winning the first and the Wallabies taking the second, setting up a winner-takes-all decider in the third and final test. The Lions had never been beaten in a test series on Australian soil, but the 2001 Wallabies were proven champions, with perhaps their best Captain ever, the unflappable John Eales.

Going into the final 12 minutes with the score tied at 23, Matt Burke slotted two penalties to put the home side in front 29–23. The Lions roared back with time running out and had several charges at the Wallaby line, but somehow, they came up just meters short. The series victory was the icing on the cake in the storied careers of both skipper John Eales and coach Rod MacQueen — truly the zenith of Australian rugby.

1995 World Cup final

The 1995 Rugby World Cup was staged in South Africa and marked the return of the mighty Springboks to the international order after years of isolation because of their government's apartheid policies. The tournament started with a bang for the hosts, when they beat the defending Champion Wallabies in the opening match. The Boks eventually faced a heavily favored New Zealand side in the final.

The 1995 World Cup final was not the most exhilarating exhibition of try scoring rugby ever played — neither team was able to touch down over the more than 100 minutes of play. However, the contest's dramatic ending made up for this: with time running out in the second extra-time period, Springbok flyhalf Joel Stransky drop-kicked a monster goal that sailed high through the uprights, to set the 62,000 spectators into a frenzy of delight.

South Africa had indeed returned to claim the top spot on the world stage and when Nelson Mandela joined Francois Pienaar on the podium for the trophy presentation and pumped his fists in the air to celebrate the Boks victory, sport had transcended politics; the Rainbow Nation rejoiced in harmony as one.

Top Five North American Moments

While the United States and Canadian Men's National Teams have yet to win the Rugby World Cup, that doesn't mean North American rugby teams have failed to impress around the world. In fact, if you look back in time, both the American and Canadian men's and women's teams have had their fair share of moments over the years.

Women's Rugby World Cup final 1991

The first Women's Rugby World Cup was staged in Cardiff, Wales, in 1991, as the United States, France, the former Soviet Union, Wales, Japan, Sweden, Canada, the Netherlands, Italy, and New Zealand battled it out for the inaugural unofficial women's world championship. The United States beat the Netherlands and the former Soviet Union to qualify for the semifinals, where they faced the New Zealand Black Ferns. The Eagles defeated the New Zealanders and qualified to meet England in the final. The Eagles soared over the Arms Park and defeated England 19–6, much to the delight of the Welsh crowd and the U.S. supporters. Women's rugby had finally arrived as a real sport, and the Eagles were perched on top of the world.

Canada versus France 1994

In June 1994 Canada played host to France in a test match played in Nepean. The highly rated French brought over their first team, which included the likes of Philippe Sella, Emile N'Tamack, Philippe Saint-Andre, Abdelatif Benazzi, and Laurent Cabannes. The upstart Canadians were quietly confident after having defeated Wales at the Arms Park the previous November (see later).

Even though the French scored the only try of the match, flyhalf Gareth Rees carried the Canucks on his back with six penalty goals, and the locals came out the winners, 18–16 to take their biggest scalp of all time.

U.S. Olympians versus France (1920 and 1924)

In 1920 in Antwerp, and again four years later in 1924 in Paris, the United States defeated France in the Olympic gold medal rugby match. The U.S. team was composed primarily of players from Stanford University and the University of California at Berkeley. In 1924 the Americans beat Romania to advance to face France in the gold medal game.

The match was the first gold medal contest of the Games and a partisan French crowd expected their countrymen to dispose of the Americans with ease. To the shock of the 50,000-plus in attendance at Stade Colomiers, the United States defense totally frustrated the Tricolors attack and when it was all over, the upstart Americans were victorious 17–3, to take the gold. Since rugby was dropped following the 1924 Games, the United States are technically the two-time defending Olympic gold medal champions.

Wales versus Canada 1993

On November 10, 1993, the Canadian team posted their first-ever win over an International Rugby Board (IRB) founding nation, when they defeated Wales at the venerable Cardiff Arms Park. The final score was Wales 24–26 Canada, but what made the victory even sweeter was the fact that Canada scored two tries and managed to keep the Welsh from scoring a try, with all of the Dragons' points coming from the boot of Neil Jenkins. Canadian Captain Ian Stewart and future skipper Al Charron both scored five-pointers, while Gareth Rees was perfect with his kicks, converting both tries and slotting four penalties of his own.

Canada versus Scotland 2002

The most recent high point for the Canadian men's team occurred at Vancouver's Thunderbird Stadium when they hosted Scotland on June 15, 2002. The Scots were ranked seventh in the world and had just smashed the 13th-ranked Canadians the week before in Markham, Ontario, 33–8.

With 13 minutes remaining, the hosts were trailing by seven points with the score at 23–16. Prop Jon Thiel blasted over the line to score under the posts and Jared Barker kicked the easy conversion, the game was even at 23-all. Over the final 12 minutes, both sides had chances to score, but each time a defensive gem or offensive miscue kept the scores locked. Then with just seconds remaining in injury time, referee David McHugh awarded Canada a penalty goal shot to win the game. Jared Barker then calmly slotted the goal and when fulltime was blown, Canada had beaten Scotland for the first time, 26–23!

Chapter 25

Ten Peculiar Facts About Rugby

"To play rugby union, you need three things: a good pass, a good tackle and a good excuse." Though we wish we were the ones to coin that phrase, we have to hand the credit to that ubiquitous person, Anonymous.

This chapter is a good excuse for us to tell you about some of the strange, odd, even bizarre things that happen in the world of rugby. If you are a collector of rugby trivia, you are in for a treat.

Rugby Attracts Some Surprising People

Rugby players come in many political stripes. Just take a look at the names of some of the famous (and in at least one case, infamous) men who once wore rugby jerseys before rugby jerseys became fashion statements:

✔ **Che Guevara:** Best known as a failed exporter of revolution and as a guerrilla leader, Ernesto "Che" Guevara was also a passionate rugby player. Che was a medical student at the University of Buenos Aires in Argentina when he developed a love of the game. An enthusiastic halfback, Guevara played several seasons of club rugby before being distracted by a belief that he had to change the world.

✔ **Idi Amin:** Before becoming the president of Uganda and an infamous despot, the all-imposing Idi Amin was not only a keen heavyweight boxer, he was a better-than-average rugby forward, playing the occasional representative match. Amin was educated in Britain. They didn't know it at the time, but when the British Lions squad touring Africa in 1955 prepared to take on East Africa, they almost played the man who became one of the most despised dictators of the 20th century. He didn't take the field against the British Lions, rather, he remained on the reserves bench. In 1964, the British Dominion Office described Amin as "...a splendid type and a good rugby player...he is virtually bone from the neck up and needs things explained in words of one letter."

✔ **Bill Clinton:** Yes, it's true. Bill Clinton actually played the 15-man game. His rugby career was fleeting, but he was a keen participant. After completing college in 1968, Clinton won a Rhodes Scholarship, which allowed him to study at Oxford University in England. Clinton, a big believer in doing what the locals do, was soon lured into trying his luck on the Oxford rugby fields. He didn't make much of an impression, but he did run around in several low-grade games.

✔ **George Bush Jr:** The presidential successor to Bill Clinton went one better than the sax-playing leader. In 1968, George Dubya, allegedly a wild man at college, played in the Yale First XV. *Sports Illustrated* even has pictures to prove it!

Unlikely Lads Can Make It to the Top

As a clear reminder that in rugby you should never give up, we offer the stories of three players who came out of nowhere to achieve great things:

✔ **Which cocky player?** After the main England trial for the test team against the first Springboks tour in 1906, it seemed a certainty that Liverpool and Lancashire representative Noel Slocock, a forward, would be selected. Slocock was a formidable lineout jumper, something desperately required against the touring South Africans. Although the national selectors put Slocock's name on the test list, an administrative bungle led to the name of Arnold Alcock appearing on the list instead. Alcock was a little-known medical student who had played in a hospital cup team. Somehow, Alcock played for England and managed to help his country to a 3–all draw.

✔ **Whose autograph?** One man who did all he could to get noticed was England international winger Carston Catcheside. After his first international game, Catcheside made certain that the people who mattered knew who he was. He wrote his name all over the bald head of one of the selectors!

✔ **Deserves a Merrick increase?** One player who wasn't expected to get there, but did anyway, was Australian test scrumhalf Steve Merrick, who emerged from the small New South Wales country town of Singleton to play in the two-Test series against New Zealand in 1995. When rugby turned professional later that same year, the salaries that could be earned turned the heads of a number of Australian players. Merrick was different: He didn't want to be a well-paid, high-profile sportsman. He simply didn't want to move from peaceful Singleton to be part of the Sydney rat-race — so he turned his back on lucrative player contracts and the chance of holding both the New South Wales and Australian scrumhalf positions.

Siblings Like to Battle It Out Together

Rugby seems to run in the blood of some families. Brothers frequently wind up playing side by side — usually on the same team. The following list names some of the firsts in sibling players:

- The first brothers to appear together in a rugby international were John and Francis Luscombe, who played for England in 1871.

- The first instance of three brothers in a test match occurred in 1875 when Scotland's N. J, A. B. and J. F. Finlay played in a scoreless draw against England.

- The first time that brothers appeared on both test teams was in 1885 when George and Richard Maitland played for Scotland and Bob and Arthur Gould appeared for Wales.

- Stewart and Jim Boyce became the first twins to play in a test when they played for Australia against New Zealand in 1964.

- Gordon Brown of Scotland was the first brother to replace a brother when he replaced his injured brother Peter in a match against Wales in 1970.

- When Jane and Emma Mitchell lined-up opposite of each other in Bermuda in 2002, the twins earned the distinction of playing against each other for different countries. Emma played for England and Jane for the U.S.

Players Injure Themselves in Bizarre Ways

Much as we would like you to believe otherwise, it is a sad fact of life that, yes, players do sometimes get injured while playing rugby. Some of the better-known accidents are better known because of the utter embarrassment of the players concerned.

- **Blinded by the sun:** In 1969, French flanker Jean-Pierre Salut could not contain his excitement as he prepared to face Scotland at the great Parisian stadium, Stade Colombes. To calm himself down, he decided to be the last player to run onto the field. To get to the ground from the dressing rooms, the players had to run down a very long corridor and negotiate several flights of stairs before emerging into the sunlight. Everything was going really well — until Salut tripped on the final step and broke his ankle.

✔ **Manouvering around the media:** Northern Transvaal center Pieter Nel missed the 1990 Currie Cup final when he injured his ankle running onto the Loftus Versfeld pitch in Pretoria. Nel tried to get around a photographer with a side-step then slipped on some dung left behind by a bull (which happened to be the local mascot!).

✔ **Kneecapped in midair:** In 1997, after struggling with a string of injuries, Scottish halfback Andy Nicol was delighted he had returned to full fitness and was able to lead his country on its tour of South Africa. He was happily sleeping away on the flight to Johannesburg when an errant drink cart smashed into his knee. Nicol was sidelined for several weeks.

Rugby Players Hate to Cancel Games

Some rugby players are so passionate about the sport that nothing (and we mean nothing) will get in the way of a match.

✔ **Portsmouth Victoria versus Southampton Trojans:** Numerous matches have been interrupted by stray dogs running onto the pitch, but only one dog has ever been used to score a try. In an 1890s game between Portsmouth Victoria and Southampton Trojans, a ball kicked into the Trojans in-goal area rebounded off a dog. One of the Portsmouth players gathered the ball and claimed a try. Although the Trojans protested, the try stood. The Rugby Football Union ruled that the decision was correct, because dogs were not classified as spectators. If the ball had bounced off a spectator, it would not have been allowed.

✔ **Williams versus Randall:** In 1909, two Welsh families decided to play each other in a sevens game, with £100 in prize money to the winners. Seven brothers of the Williams clan from Pembrokeshire met seven from the Randall clan of Llanelli on neutral ground at Carmarthen. Several thousand spectators crowded the ground to watch the match degenerate into a wrestling bout. While the match hardly resembled a rugby game, the Williams boys still won the money.

✔ **East Midlands versus Barbarians:** Former England halfback Adrian Stoop refereed the 1921 East Midlands versus Barbarians match. Somehow he managed to blow the final whistle 14 minutes early. After complaints and protests, the players and referee had to get out of their baths and finish the match.

✔ **All Blacks versus Tahiti 15:** When international teams play, the after-match function is usually held, well, *after* the match. Not so when the All Blacks decided to play a friendly game against a Tahitian 15. The Tahitians decided to have their function *before* kick-off. They offered the New Zealanders a sumptuous feast including copious amounts of wine and champagne. The tactic backfired when the Tahitian team decided to join in and have a few drinks, too. They ran onto the field somewhat worse for wear and suffering from extremely blurred vision. The All Blacks won by more than 70 points.

Rugby Is Played in Extreme Weather and in Strange Locations

Since the game was developed in England in the 19th century (see Chapter 1 for more details), rugby has turned up in some rather unexpected places. Equally unexpected are the settings of some rugby playing fields and the extraordinary range of climate and weather in which the game is played.

✔ **Antarctica:** Rugby is truly a global game that's played on all 7 continents! In 2001, the United States and New Zealand research teams faced-off on a snow covered pitch over ancient sea ice in Antarctica. The Kiwis from the Scott Base defeated the Yanks from McMurdo Sound station 9–3.

✔ **Bahrain:** Some countries, such as Bahrain, play rugby on the desert sand, often in the highest temperatures imaginable.

✔ **England:** Teams touring England have often discovered the delights of playing in the fog. The 1978 Australian Schoolboys team, playing the England under-19s at Twickenham, could not see more than a meter in front of them. The fog was so thick the spectators couldn't see a thing — so they were allowed to stand on the sidelines and near the dead ball lines in the hope that they might be able to follow the game.

✔ **Indonesia:** One of the main rugby grounds in Indonesia is found deep in a jungle, while another is almost at the summit of a mountain, near a tea plantation.

✔ **Jordan:** Few grounds can beat the Amman Rugby Club, whose players play on the floor of the Dead Sea. The pitch, whose surface is soft sand, lies 385 meters below sea level.

✔ **Russia:** Some of the coldest rugby venues are in Russia. In 1978, Krasnoyarsk played Polyechnika Alma when the temperature was minus 23 degrees Celsius. No one even contemplated calling the game off — the team from Krasnoyarsk had travelled 2,000 kilometers in order to play. To overcome the chill, the players wore stocking masks, gloves, and several pairs of tracksuits.

✔ **Western Samoa:** Rugby legend has it that when Western Samoa began playing tests, their home ground had a large coconut tree growing on the halfway line. Sounds unbelievable, but then again, Samoans have always prided themselves on their relaxed style.

Players Score in Unorthodox Ways

The aim of rugby is to score more points than the opposition. No surprises there. However, over the years, some rather unorthodox methods of scoring have been observed on the field. (You can read about the regular scoring system in Chapter 2.)

✔ **The unlikeliest try:** During a game in Builth Wells in Wales about a century ago, the visiting fullback kicked the ball into some tree branches that were overhanging the pitch. Surprise, surprise — the ball got stuck. While officials went off to find another ball and the players had a rest on the pitch, the ball suddenly fell from the tree. A quick-thinking player grabbed the ball and scored under the posts. The opposition naturally complained but the referee awarded the try because, under local rules, the ball had not gone out of play.

✔ **The fastest try in test history:** This is an honour claimed by Scotland's New Zealand import, John Leslie. Leslie scored with only nine seconds gone on the clock in the test against Wales at Murrayfield in 1999.

✔ **The only jointly awarded test try:** Welsh players Howie Jones and Harry Peacock shared credit for scoring in a test match against Ireland in 1930. The referee was unable to work out which player grounded the ball, so the only joint try in an international game was awarded.

✔ **The accidental try:** In the late 1950s, George Nepia, probably recognized as New Zealand's greatest fullback, was well into retirement but continued to play in social matches. In one of these games, the ball hit him perfectly in the chest. Noticing a gap straight in front of him, he sprinted for the line and grounded the ball right under the posts. Only one problem — he was the referee.

Sometimes Officials Make Unofficial Calls

A *send-off* occurs when a player commits a serious violation and is ordered by the referee to leave the field for the rest of the game. Sometimes even the officials are not safe from the wrath of other officials. For example, at a Plymouth club game in England in 1967, the referee ordered his own touch judge sent off after he was involved in a melée with players and spectators.

Even the most serious rules can be taken too seriously. For example, the strangest send-off wasn't actually meant to be a send-off. In 1988, former Irish test front-rower Gerry McLoughlin was playing for Welsh club-side Gilfach Goch when he was involved in a brawl. According to Irish and Welsh lore, when referee Roy Rees had sorted the fight out, he looked at McLoughlin and told him, as a general warning, "Push off and let's get on with the game."

When a scrum was set about 15 minutes later, Rees discovered that the local club was missing their tight-head prop — Big Gerry. McLoughlin had misinterpreted what Rees had said and thought "push off" meant that he had been sent from the field. By the time Gerry was told of his error, he was in his street clothes. Gilfach Goch had to make do with 14 men for the rest of the game. Somehow Gilfach won.

Rugby Blunders Into Multicultural Minefields

When a player is sent off, he or she usually has to appear before a judiciary committee, which is a rather formal occasion. Unfortunately, formal occasions have a habit of being undermined by human folly, especially in cross-cultural exchanges, and sometimes result in embarrassment all around.

One of the more entertaining judiciary committee incidents occurred while Malcolm McPhee was chairman of the Sydney Rugby Union Judiciary Committee. As Neil Marks wrote in his book *Tales from the Locker Room* (Ironbark Press), McPhee and his committee had to interview two players, both recruited from overseas, who had been cited by referees. One was a large Samoan second-rower from the Drummoyne club in Sydney, and the other an even larger Fijian second-rower from the Sydney club of Hornsby.

The Hornsby player was the first to arrive, wearing a Fijian lap-lap and sandals. Accompanying him was his wife, a very large woman dressed identically to her husband. The player introduced himself as Charlie Levula from Hornsby.

"How do you do, Charlie," the chairman replied, politely shaking the big forward's hand. McPhee then noticed Levula's wife standing in the background. Thrusting out his hand, he said, "And you must be from Drummoyne!"

Rugby may need to introduce a new law — for sending judiciary officials to the sin bin when they make social blunders.

If It's Going to Happen, It'll Happen on Tour

Strange as it may seem, some of the most memorable things that happen on a rugby tour do not occur on the pitch. Touring teams often like to play with the minds of local journalists. When the Fijian team toured Britain in 1970, a young scribe asked one of their huge forwards how they celebrated after matches. "The winners eat the losers," was the reply. The scribe thought he was serious and included it in his report.

✔ **Nobody meets the Queen:** The highlight of several Wallaby tours to the United Kingdom has been the chance to meet Queen Elizabeth at Buckingham Palace. Not surprisingly, these meetings have had their hiccups. In 1984, Australian team manager "Chilla" Wilson forgot the name of winger Ross Hanley as he was about to introduce him to the Queen. Similarly, in 1988, Wallaby manager Andy Conway struggled to maintain his composure when ACT center Paul Cornish met the Queen — the Queen turned to Conway and asked, ever so nicely, "Doesn't this player have a name?"

✔ **A right royal salute:** During the 1984 visit, another royal incident occurred when Queensland back-rower Chris Roche decided to perch himself on an antique hall table. Within a few seconds, the table, unused to heavy weights like Roche, crashed to the floor. As Roche looked for somewhere to hide, Prince Philip turned around and casually said, "Don't worry. There are plenty more of them in the storeroom."

✔ **War stops play:** Unfortunately, not everything that happens on tour is amusing — tragedy strikes everywhere. During their 1939 tour, the Wallabies arrived in the United Kingdom just before World War II was declared. The tour was immediately abandoned. After spending several days filling sandbags to protect their hotel in Torquay, the players returned home without a game being played. But they still endured a hazardous trip, with their boat forced to zigzag to throw off submarine attacks.

Appendix A

U.S. and Canada Tests

United States Test Record

Date	Match	Score	Location
31 Oct 2003	United States versus France	14–41	Wollongong, Australia
27 Oct 2003	United States versus Japan	39–26	Gosford, Australia
20 Oct 2003	United States versus Scotland	15–39	Brisbane, Australia
15 Oct 2003	United States versus Fiji	18–19	Brisbane, Australia
30 Aug 2003	United States versus Uruguay	31–17	Buenos Aires, Argentina
27 Aug 2003	United States versus Canada	35–20	Buenos Aires, Argentina
23 Aug 2003	United States versus Argentina	8–42	Buenos Aires, Argentina
28 Jun 2003	United States versus England XV	6–43	Vancouver, Canada
21 Jun 2003	United States versus England XV	10–36	Vancouver, Canada
18 Jun 2003	United States versus Canada	16–11	Vancouver, Canada
17 May 2003	United States versus Japan	69–27	San Francisco, U.S.
27 Apr 2003	United States versus Spain	58–13	Fort Lauderdale, U.S.
12 Apr 2003	United States versus Spain	63–13	Madrid, Spain
31 Aug 2002	United States versus Uruguay	9–10	Montevideo, Uruguay
24 Aug 2002	United States versus Chile	13–21	Santiago, Chile
15 Aug 2002	United States versus Uruguay	28–24	San Francisco, U.S.
10 Aug 2002	United States versus Chile	35–22	Salt Lake City, U.S.
13 Jul 2002	United States versus Canada	13–36	Chicago, U.S.
29 Jun 2002	United States versus Canada	9–26	Markham, Canada
22 Jun 2002	United States versus Scotland	23–65	San Francisco, U.S.
01 Dec 2001	United States versus South Africa	20–43	Houston, U.S.

Date	Match	Score	Location
16 Jun 2001	United States versus England	19–48	San Francisco, U.S.
26 May 2001	United States versus Uruguay	31–28	Markham, Canada
23 May 2001	United States versus Argentina	16–44	Hamilton, Canada
19 May 2001	United States versus Canada	10–19	Kingston, Canada
18 Nov 2000	United States versus Wales	11–42	Cardiff, Wales
04 Nov 2000	United States versus Scotland	6–53	Edinburgh, Scotland
15 Jul 2000	United States versus Samoa	12–19	San Francisco, U.S.
07 Jul 2000	United States versus Tonga	6–29	Nuku A'lofa, Tonga
30 Jun 2000	United States versus Fiji	21–37	Apia, Samoa
10 Jun 2000	United States versus Ireland	3–83	Manchester, U.S.
03 Jun 2000	United States versus Canada	34–25	Manchester, U.S.
27 May 2000	United States versus Japan	36–21	Osaka, Japan
14 Oct 1999	United States versus Australia	19–55	Limerick, Ireland
09 Oct 1999	United States versus Romania	25–27	Dublin, Ireland
02 Oct 1999	United States versus Ireland	8–53	Dublin, Ireland
21 Aug 1999	United States versus England	8–106	London, England
26 Jun 1999	United States versus Samoa	20–27	Apia, Samoa
19 Jun 1999	United States versus Canada	18–17	Toronto, Canada
12 Jun 1999	United States versus Japan	31–47	Honolulu, U.S.
22 May 1999	United States versus Fiji	25–14	San Francisco, U.S.
15 May 1999	United States versus Tonga	30–10	San Francisco, U.S.
22 Aug 1998	United States versus Uruguay	21–16	Buenos Aires, Argentina
18 Aug 1998	United States versus Canada	14–31	Buenos Aires, Argentina
15 Aug 1998	United States versus Argentina	24–52	Buenos Aires, Argentina
25 Jul 1998	United States versus Fiji	9–18	Suva, Fiji
20 Jun 1998	United States versus Hong Kong	17–27	San Francisco, U.S.
13 Jun 1998	United States versus Japan	21–25	San Francisco, U.S.
06 Jun 1998	United States versus Canada	3–37	Burlington, U.S.

Date	Match	Score	Location
23 May 1998	United States versus Canada	15–17	Vancouver, Canada
16 May 1998	United States versus Hong Kong	25–43	Hong Kong
10 May 1998	United States versus Japan	38–27	Tokyo, Japan
12 Apr 1998	United States versus Spain	49–3	El Puerto de Santa Maria, Spain
08 Apr 1998	United States versus Portugal	61–5	Lisbon, Portugal
12 Jul 1997	United States versus Wales	23–28	San Francisco, U.S.
05 Jul 1997	United States versus Wales	20–30	Wilmington, U.S.
28 Jun 1997	United States versus Canada	11–22	San Francisco, U.S.
14 Jun 1997	United States versus Hong Kong	17–14	San Francisco, U.S.
07 Jun 1997	United States versus Japan	51–29	San Francisco, U.S.
25 May 1997	United States versus Japan	20–12	Osaka, Japan
17 May 1997	United States versus Hong Kong	9–46	Hong Kong
10 May 1997	United States versus Canada	12–53	Vancouver, Canada
11 Jan 1997	United States versus Wales	14–34	Cardiff, Wales
21 Sep 1996	United States versus Uruguay	27–13	Markham, Canada
18 Sep 1996	United States versus Canada	18–23	Hamilton, Canada
14 Sep 1996	United States versus Argentina	26–29	Nepean, Canada
06 Jul 1996	United States versus Japan	74–5	San Francisco, U.S.
29 Jun 1996	United States versus Hong Kong	42–23	San Francisco, U.S.
16 Jun 1996	United States versus Japan	18–24	Tokyo, Japan
08 Jun 1996	United States versus Hong Kong	19–22	Hong Kong
18 May 1996	United States versus Canada	20–24	Vancouver, Canada
11 May 1996	United States versus Canada	19–12	San Francisco, U.S.
06 Jan 1996	United States versus Ireland	18–25	Atlanta, U.S.
09 Sep 1995	United States versus Canada	15–14	Markham, Canada
05 Nov 1994	United States versus Ireland	15–26	Dublin, Ireland
20 Jun 1994	United States versus Argentina	11–16	Buenos Aires, Argentina

Date	Match	Score	Location
28 May 1994	United States versus Argentina	22–28	Long Beach, U.S.
21 May 1994	United States versus Canada	10–15	Long Beach, U.S.
12 Mar 1994	United States versus Bermuda	60–3	Devonshire, Bermuda
02 Oct 1993	United States versus Australia XV (non-cap)	22–26	Riverside, U.S.
19 Jun 1993	United States versus Canada	9–20	Winnipeg, Canada
13 Jun 1992	United States versus Canada	9–32	Denver, U.S.
18 Apr 1992	United States versus Hong Kong	23–16	San Francisco, U.S.
11 Oct 1991	United States versus England	9–37	London, U.S.
08 Oct 1991	United States versus New Zealand	6–46	Gloucester, England
05 Oct 1991	United States versus Italy	9–30	Otley, England
20 Jul 1991	United States versus France	3–10	Colorado Springs, U.S.
13 Jul 1991	United States versus France	9–41	Denver, U.S.
08 Jun 1991	United States versus Canada	15–34	Calgary, Canada
18 May 1991	United States versus Scotland XV (non-cap)	12–41	Hartford, U.S.
04 May 1991	United States versus Japan	27–15	Chicago, U.S.
27 Apr 1991	United States versus Japan	20–9	Blaine, U.S.
23 Sep 1990	United States versus Japan	25–15	Tokyo, Japan
08 Jul 1990	United States versus Australia	9–67	Brisbane, Australia
09 Jun 1990	United States versus Canada	14–12	Seattle, U.S.
07 Apr 1990	United States versus Argentina	6–13	Santa Barbara, U.S.
08 Nov 1989	United States versus Argentina	6–23	Buenos Aires, Argentina
05 Nov 1989	United States versus Uruguay	60–6	Montevideo, Uruguay
23 Sep 1989	United States versus Canada	3–21	Toronto, Canada
09 Sep 1989	United States versus Ireland XV (non-cap)	7–32	New York, U.S.
25 Sep 1988	United States versus Soviet Union	16–31	Moscow, Russia
17 Sep 1988	United States versus Romania	17–7	Moscow, Russia
11 Jun 1988	United States versus Canada	28–16	Saranac Lake, U.S.

Date	Match	Score	Location
14 Nov 1987	United States versus Canada	12–20	Victoria, Canada
07 Nov 1987	United States versus Wales	0–46	Cardiff, Wales
03 Jun 1987	United States versus England	6–34	Sydney, Australia
31 May 1987	United States versus Australia	12–47	Brisbane, Australia
24 May 1987	United States versus Japan	21–18	Brisbane, Australia
10 May 1987	United States versus Canada	9–33	Vancouver, Canada
03 May 1987	United States versus Tunisia	47–13	Pebble Beach, U.S.
08 Nov 1986	United States versus Canada	16–27	Tucson, U.S.
31 May 1986	United States versus Japan	9–9	Torrance, U.S.
16 Nov 1985	United States versus Canada	10–21	Vancouver, Canada
21 Apr 1985	United States versus Japan	16–15	Tokyo, Japan
09 Jun 1984	United States versus Canada	21–13	Chicago, U.S.
09 Jul 1983	United States versus Australia	3–49	Sydney, Australia
11 Jun 1983	United States versus Canada	9–15	Burnaby, Canada
19 Jun 1982	United States versus England XV (non-cap)	0–59	Hartford, U.S.
12 Jun 1982	United States versus Canada	3–3	Albany, U.S.
25 Sep 1981	United States versus South Africa	7–38	Glenville, U.S.
06 Jun 1981	United States versus Canada	3–6	Calgary, U.S.
08 Oct 1980	United States versus New Zealand XV (non-cap)	6–53	San Diego, U.S.
08 Jun 1980	United States versus Canada	0–16	Saranac Lake, U.S.
10 May 1980	United States versus Wales XV (non-cap)	18–24	Long Beach, U.S.
09 Jun 1979	United States versus Canada	12–19	Toronto, Canada
28 May 1978	United States versus Canada	12–7	Baltimore, U.S.
15 Oct 1977	United States versus England XV (non-cap)	11–37	London, England
21 May 1977	United States versus Canada	6–17	Burnaby, Canada
12 Jun 1976	United States versus France	14–33	Chicago, U.S.

Date	Match	Score	Location
31 Jan 1976	United States versus Australia	12–24	Los Angeles, U.S.
18 May 1924	United States versus France	17–3	Paris, France
10 May 1924	United States versus Romania	37–0	Paris, France
10 Oct 1920	United States versus France	5–14	Paris, France
05 Sep 1920	United States versus France XV (non-cap)	8–0	Anvers, Belgium
01 Jul 1919	United States versus Romania	21–0	Paris, France
15 Nov 1913	United States versus New Zealand	3–51	Berkeley, U.S.
16 Nov 1912	United States versus Australia	8–12	Berkeley, U.S.

Canada Test Record

Date	Match	Score	Location
29 Oct 2003	Canada versus Tonga	24–7	Wollongong, Australia
21 Oct 2003	Canada versus Italy	14–19	Canberra, Australia
17 Oct 2003	Canada versus New Zealand	6–68	Melbourne, Australia
12 Oct 2003	Canada versus Wales	10–41	Melbourne, Australia
30 Aug 2003	Canada versus Argentina	22–62	Buenos Aires, Argentina
27 Aug 2003	Canada versus United States	20–35	Buenos Aires, Argentina
23 Aug 2003	Canada versus Uruguay	21–11	Buenos Aires, Argentina
02 Aug 2003	Canada versus New Zealand Maori	9–30	Toronto, Canada
26 Jul 2003	Canada versus New Zealand Maori	27–65	Calgary, Canada
18 Jun 2003	Canada versus United States	11–16	Vancouver, Canada
14 Jun 2003	Canada versus England XV (non-cap)	7–43	Vancouver, Canada
23 Nov 2002	Canada versus France	3–35	Paris, France
16 Nov 2002	Canada versus Wales	21–32	Cardiff, Wales
31 Aug 2002	Canada versus Chile	29–11	Santiago, Chile

Date	Match	Score	Location
24 Aug 2002	Canada versus Uruguay	23–25	Montevideo, Uruguay
17 Aug 2002	Canada versus Chile	27–6	Calgary, Canada
10 Aug 2002	Canada versus Uruguay	51–16	Edmonton, Canada
13 Jul 2002	Canada versus United States	36–13	Chicago, Canada
29 Jun 2002	Canada versus United States	26–9	Markham, Canada
15 Jun 2002	Canada versus Scotland	26–23	Vancouver, Canada
08 Jul 2001	Canada versus Japan	7–39	Tokyo, Japan
03 Jul 2001	Canada versus Fiji	23–52	Tokyo, Japan
09 Jun 2001	Canada versus England	20–59	Burnaby, Canada
02 Jun 2001	Canada versus England	10–22	Markham, Canada
26 May 2001	Canada versus Argentina	6–20	Markham, Canada
23 May 2001	Canada versus Uruguay	14–8	Hamilton, Canada
19 May 2001	Canada versus United States	19–10	Kingston, Canada
11 Nov 2000	Canada versus Italy	22–17	Rovigo, Italy
15 Jul 2000	Canada versus Japan	62–18	Markham, Canada
07 Jul 2000	Canada versus Fiji	11–42	Apia, Samoa
01 Jul 2000	Canada versus Samoa	22–41	Apia, Samoa
17 Jun 2000	Canada versus Ireland	27–27	Markham, Canada
10 Jun 2000	Canada versus South Africa	18–51	East London, South Africa
03 Jun 2000	Canada versus United States	25–34	Manchester, U.S.
20 May 2000	Canada versus Tonga	29–11	Vancouver, Canada
14 Oct 1999	Canada versus Namibia	72–11	Toulouse, France
09 Oct 1999	Canada versus Fiji	22–38	Bordeaux, France
02 Oct 1999	Canada versus France	20–33	Beziers, France
28 Aug 1999	Canada versus England	11–36	London, England
21 Aug 1999	Canada versus Wales	19–33	Cardiff, Wales
03 Jul 1999	Canada versus Tonga	10–18	Nuku A'lofa, Tonga
19 Jun 1999	Canada versus United States	17–18	Toronto, Canada

Date	Match	Score	Location
29 May 1999	Canada versus Samoa	13–17	Vancouver, Canada
15 May 1999	Canada versus Fiji	29–40	Vancouver, Canada
01 May 1999	Canada versus Japan	21–23	Tokyo, Japan
22 Aug 1998	Canada versus Argentina	28–54	Buenos Aires, Argentina
18 Aug 1998	Canada versus United States	31–14	Buenos Aires, Argentina
15 Aug 1998	Canada versus Uruguay	38–15	Buenos Aires, Argentina
21 Jun 1998	Canada versus Japan	34–25	Vancouver, Canada
13 Jun 1998	Canada versus Hong Kong	38–12	Shawnigan Lake, Canada
06 Jun 1998	Canada versus United States	37–3	Burlington, U.S.
23 May 1998	Canada versus United States	17–15	Vancouver, Canada
09 May 1998	Canada versus Hong Kong	17–23	Hong Kong
03 May 1998	Canada versus Japan	30–22	Tokyo, Japan
30 Nov 1997	Canada versus Ireland	11–33	Dublin, Ireland
19 Jul 1997	Canada versus Wales	25–28	Markham, Canada
28 Jun 1997	Canada versus United States	22–11	San Francisco, U.S.
14 Jun 1997	Canada versus Japan	42–18	Vancouver, Canada
07 Jun 1997	Canada versus Hong Kong	17–16	Vancouver, Canada
24 May 1997	Canada versus Hong Kong	35–27	Hong Kong
18 May 1997	Canada versus Japan	31–32	Tokyo, Japan
10 May 1997	Canada versus United States	53–12	Vancouver, Canada
21 Sep 1996	Canada versus Argentina	21–41	Markham, Canada
18 Sep 1996	Canada versus United States	23–18	Hamilton, Canada
14 Sep 1996	Canada versus Uruguay	24–18	Nepean, Canada
13 Jul 1996	Canada versus Japan	51–30	Vancouver, Canada
06 Jul 1996	Canada versus Hong Kong	57–9	Vancouver, Canada
29 Jun 1996	Canada versus Australia	9–74	Brisbane, Australia
09 Jun 1996	Canada versus Japan	45–18	Tokyo, Japan
01 Jun 1996	Canada versus Hong Kong	18–12	Hong Kong
18 May 1996	Canada versus United States	24–20	Vancouver, Canada

Date	Match	Score	Location
11 May 1996	Canada versus United States	12–19	San Francisco, U.S.
09 Sep 1995	Canada versus United States	14–15	Markham, Canada
03 Jun 1995	Canada versus South Africa	0–20	Pt Elizabeth, South Africa
31 May 1995	Canada versus Australia	11–27	Pt Elizabeth, South Africa
26 May 1995	Canada versus Romania	34–3	Pt Elizabeth, South Africa
22 Apr 1995	Canada versus New Zealand	7–73	Auckland, New Zealand
08 Apr 1995	Canada versus Fiji	22–10	Nadi, Fiji
10 Mar 1995	Canada versus Argentina	26–29	Buenos Aires, Argentina
07 Mar 1995	Canada versus Uruguay	28–9	Montevideo, Uruguay
21 Jan 1995	Canada versus Scotland	6–22	Edinburgh, Scotland
17 Dec 1994	Canada versus France	9–28	Besancon, France
10 Dec 1994	Canada versus England	19–60	London, England
11 Jun 1994	Canada versus Wales	15–33	Markham, Canada
04 Jun 1994	Canada versus France	18–16	Nepean, Canada
21 May 1994	Canada versus United States	15–10	Long Beach, U.S.
10 Nov 1993	Canada versus Wales	26–24	Cardiff, Wales
09 Oct 1993	Canada versus Australia	16–43	Calgary, Canada
19 Jun 1993	Canada versus United States	20–9	Winnipeg, Canada
05 Jun 1993	Canada versus England XV (non-cap)	14–19	Nepean, Canada
29 May 1993	Canada versus England XV (non-cap)	15–12	Burnaby, Canada
17 Oct 1992	Canada versus England	13–26	London, England
13 Jun 1992	Canada versus United States	32–9	Denver, U.S.
20 Oct 1991	Canada versus New Zealand	13–29	Lille, France
13 Oct 1991	Canada versus France	13–19	Agen, France
09 Oct 1991	Canada versus Romania	19–11	Toulouse, France
05 Oct 1991	Canada versus Fiji	13–3	Bayonne, France
08 Jun 1991	Canada versus United States	34–15	Calgary, Canada

Date	Match	Score	Location
25 May 1991	Canada versus Scotland XV (non-cap)	24–19	Saint John, Canada
11 May 1991	Canada versus Japan	49–26	Vancouver, Canada
16 Jun 1990	Canada versus Argentina	19–15	Buenos Aires, Argentina
09 Jun 1990	Canada versus United States	12–14	Seattle, U.S.
30 Mar 1990	Canada versus Argentina	15–6	Burnaby, Canada
23 Sep 1989	Canada versus United States	21–3	Toronto, Canada
02 Sep 1989	Canada versus Ireland XV (non-cap)	21–24	Victoria, Canada
11 Jun 1988	Canada versus United States	16–28	Saranac Lake, U.S.
14 Nov 1987	Canada versus United States	20–12	Victoria, Canada
03 Jun 1987	Canada versus Wales	9–40	Invercargill, New Zealand
30 May 1987	Canada versus Ireland	19–46	Dunedin, New Zealand
24 May 1987	Canada versus Tonga	37–4	Napier, New Zealand
10 May 1987	Canada versus United States	33–9	Vancouver, Canada
08 Nov 1986	Canada versus United States	27–16	Tucson, U.S.
07 Jun 1986	Canada versus Japan	21–26	Burnaby, Canada
16 Nov 1985	Canada versus United States	21–10	Vancouver, Canada
23 Jun 1985	Canada versus Australia	15–43	Brisbane, Australia
15 Jun 1985	Canada versus Australia	3–59	Sydney, Australia
09 Jun 1984	Canada versus United States	13–21	Chicago, U.S.
15 Oct 1983	Canada versus England XV (non-cap)	0–27	London, England
01 Jul 1983	Canada versus Italy	9–37	Toronto, Canada
25 Jun 1983	Canada versus Italy	19–13	Burnaby, Canada
11 Jun 1983	Canada versus United States	15–9	Burnaby, Canada
12 Jun 1982	Canada versus United States	3–3	Albany, U.S.
29 May 1982	Canada versus England XV (non-cap)	6–43	Burnaby, Canada
18 Apr 1982	Canada versus Japan	6–16	Tokyo, Japan

Date	Match	Score	Location
11 Apr 1982	Canada versus Japan	18–24	Osaka, Japan
03 Oct 1981	Canada versus Argentina	0–35	Buenos Aires, Argentina
06 Jun 1981	Canada versus United States	6–3	Calgary, Canada
11 Oct 1980	Canada versus New Zealand XV (non-cap)	10–43	Burnaby, Canada
08 Jun 1980	Canada versus United States	16–0	Saranac Lake, U.S.
24 May 1980	Canada versus Wales XV (non-cap)	7–24	Burnaby, Canada
29 Sep 1979	Canada versus France XV (non-cap)	15–34	Paris, France
09 Jun 1979	Canada versus United States	19–12	Toronto, Canada
30 Sep 1978	Canada versus France XV (non-cap)	9–24	Calgary, Canada
28 May 1978	Canada versus United States	7–12	Baltimore, U.S.
11 Jun 1977	Canada versus England Under 23	9–29	Toronto, Canada
04 Jun 1977	Canada versus England Under-23	13–26	Ottawa, Canada
21 May 1977	Canada versus United States	17–6	Burnaby, Canada
12 Jun 1976	Canada versus Barbarians	4–29	Toronto, Canada
25 Oct 1974	Canada versus Tonga	14–40	Vancouver, Canada
09 Jun 1973	Canada versus Wales XV (non-cap)	20–58	Toronto, Canada
02 Oct 1971	Canada versus Wales XV (non-cap)	10–56	Cardiff, Wales
28 Nov 1970	Canada versus Fiji	17–35	Burnaby, Canada
30 Sep 1967	Canada versus England XV (non-cap)	0–29	Vancouver, Canada
17 Sep 1966	Canada versus British Lions XV (non-cap)	8–19	Toronto, Canada
01 Dec 1962	Canada versus Wales Under-23	0–8	Cardiff, Wales
17 Nov 1962	Canada versus Barbarians	3–3	Gosforth, England
11 Feb 1932	Canada versus Japan	5–38	Tokyo, Japan
31 Jan 1932	Canada versus Japan	8–9	Osaka, Japan

Appendix B

Glossary

● ●

age grade rugby: The term for all rugby from ages six to eighteen.

ACT Brumbies: Australian Super 12 team based in Canberra in the Australian Capital Territory. In 2001 they became the only non-Kiwi team to win the Super 12 title.

advantage: Occurs when a referee allows play to continue even though there has been an infringement. The referee gives the non-offending team the chance to do something positive with the ball. If the team is unable to do so, the referee goes back to the site of the original infraction and restarts play with the appropriate method. The goal of advantage is to minimize stoppages and keep play flowing.

ankle tap: When a defender attempts to stop a ball-carrier by tapping him on the ankle from behind in an attempt to bring him down. This is a last-ditch, desperation tackle.

back row: The third line of the scrum, comprising a number eight and two flankers. These three are known as back-rowers.

back three: The fullback and the two wingers.

backs: Numbers 9–15, generally faster players.

ball-carrier: The player carrying the ball.

binding: Firmly grasping another player's body from the shoulder to the hips with the whole arm from hand to shoulder.

Bledisloe Cup: Trophy played for by Australia and New Zealand, usually in an annual series. Named after the former Governor General of New Zealand, Lord Bledisloe.

blindside: The area between the ball and the closest sideline.

blindside flanker: The flanker who binds onto the scrum on the blindside, usually wears number 6, except in South Africa.

blood bin: If a player is bleeding, he must leave the field of play until the wound is covered or dressed. While he is being treated, he is said to be in the blood bin but it's not an actual place.

Blues: Auckland-based Super 12 team, encompassing the Auckland, North Harbour, and Northland Unions. Three-time champions with titles in 1996, 1997, and 2003. One of five New Zealand franchises in the competition.

bomb: A high kick generally aimed at the opposition fullback in the hope that under pressure he'll drop it and lose possession.

box kick: A high kick aimed to land in front of the opposition winger, usually taken by the scrumhalf.

breakaway: Another name for flankers who wear numbers 6 and 7. They bind on the side of the scrum and breakaway when the scrum is over. Their primary jobs are to win the ball at rucks and mauls and to make tackles.

breakdown: When play transitions from one phase to another, usually because of a tackle and the resultant struggle for possession.

Bulls: South African Super 12 team based in Pretoria. Formerly called the Blue Bulls.

Calcutta Cup: A trophy crafted from melted Indian silver rupees played for annually by England and Scotland as part of the Six Nations.

caps: A term used to denote the number of times an individual has played for his national team in a test match. When someone is said to have 22 caps for the United States, it means that he has played in 22 tests for the Eagles.

Carisbrook Stadium: Located in Dunedin, New Zealand. The home of the Highlanders, Otago, and the scene of numerous All Blacks triumphs. Also known as the House of Pain and frequented by Otago University students who are known as Scarfies.

Cats: Johannesburg-based South African Super 12 team. Made up mostly of players from the two provincial teams named the Lions and the Cheetahs.

Celtic Cup: A newly created cup competition for the Celtic League sides which is played in the early part of their season.

Celtic League: An Irish, Scottish, and Welsh competition meant to rival the Zurich Premiership. There are 12 teams that play in a home and away format.

centers: The players wearing number 12 (inside center) and number 13 (outside center). They are the heart and soul of a team's attack. Also called the midfielders.

channel: The path a ball takes when coming back through the scrum between the legs of the forwards.

charge down: The blocking of a kick by an opposing player.

Chiefs: New Zealand Super 12 team based in Hamilton in the Waikato region. Also includes the Bay of Plenty, Counties-Manukau, King Country, and Thames Valley unions.

chip kick: A short kick, usually directed over the top of the opposition's defensive line, hopefully to be regathered by the kicker or a teammate.

clearing kick: A kick aimed to go over the touchline as a way of relieving pressure and gaining territory.

Colts rugby: The under-19 age group level before adult rugby.

conversion: After a try is scored, the attacking team is given a kick at goal from a spot in line with where the try was touched down. If good, it's worth two points, making a converted try good for seven total.

counterattack: An attacking move in response to an opposition attack when the ball has changed possession.

crossbar: The bar joining the two uprights of the goalposts. For a conversion or penalty goal to be successful it has to go over the crossbar.

cross kick: A kick across the field aimed towards the attacking team's openside winger, who plans to run through the defense and re-gather the ball.

Crusaders: Christchurch-based Super 12 team that is made up mostly of Canterbury players but also includes the provincial unions of Nelson Bays, Marlborough, Buller, West Coast, Mid Canterbury, and South Canterbury. The franchise won three straight championships from 1998–2000, then earned a fourth crown with a perfect season in 2002.

Currie Cup: The name of the competition and the trophy awarded to the winner of South Africa's premier provincial competition. Originally given by Sir Donald Currie, a Scotsman who donated it as a cricket trophy.

cut-out pass: A pass that deliberately misses one or more players and goes to the next player in the attacking line.

dead: Means that the ball is out of play. This occurs when the ball has gone outside the playing area and remained there, or when the referee has blown the whistle to indicate a stoppage, or when a conversion kick is being taken.

dead-ball line: The furthest lines at the back of the in-goal areas at both ends of the field.

decoy: A player who pretends that he is about to receive the ball in an attempt to deceive the opposition's defensive line.

defense: Used by one team to stop another when it is attacking.

dive pass: Passing the ball while diving towards the person for whom the pass is intended.

drawing the man: Making an opponent commit to tackling you just before you pass to a teammate.

drift defense: A defensive system which has the defending players drift sideways across the field.

driving maul: A maul where the opposition is driven back through sheer force and coordination.

driving tackle: The tackler pushes the ball-carrier backwards.

drop goal: When a player kicks the ball over the opposition's crossbar during general play. The ball must hit the ground before being kicked. It is worth three points.

drop kick: A type of kick where the ball hits the ground first, used for a drop goal or to restart play after a score or at the beginning of a half.

drop out: A drop kick used to restart play from a team's 22-meter line.

Eden Park: Stadium in Auckland, New Zealand. Home of the Blues, Auckland, and site of the 1987 World Cup final. More All Blacks tests have been played there than any other venue.

Ellis Park: Stadium in Johannesburg, South Africa and scene of many Springbok victories since 1928. Home of the Cats, the Gauteng Lions, and site of the 1995 World Cup Final.

Ellis, William Webb: The alleged creator of rugby. In 1823 Ellis, a student at the Rugby School, reportedly picked up a ball and ran with it during a soccer game, thus inspiring a new form of football called rugby. No evidence actually supports the account, similar to Abner Doubleday supposedly founding baseball in Cooperstown.

European Cup: A 24-team tournament featuring club and provincial sides from England, France, Ireland, Italy, Scotland, and Wales. Sponsored for many years by Heineken.

feed: The placing of the ball into the scrum by the scrumhalf.

fend: An attacking player uses an arm to push away a defender. The same as a straight-arm in American or Canadian Football.

field goal: Another name for a drop goal.

five-eighth: Another name for the flyhalf, used in Australia and New Zealand.

five-meter scrum: A scrum that is set five meters from the defending team's tryline.

flick pass: A quick pass to a teammate. The player throwing the ball flicks his wrists to quicken the pace of the ball.

flyhalf: The back who wears jersey number 10. The flyhalf is one of the most important players in the team, often dictating the flow of play.

forward pass: An illegal pass that travels forward when released.

foul play: Play deemed by the referee to be illegal. The offending player is penalized or in serious cases, given a yellow or red card.

free kick: A kick awarded to a team for a minor penalty.

front row: The forwards in the first line of the scrum, the loose-head prop, the hooker, and the tight-head prop. These players are called front-rowers.

fullback: The back who wears the number 15 jersey, who is the last line of defense.

fulltime: The end of the game.

Garryowen: A high kick, also known as an up and under, designed to be chased and taken. Named after the Irish club renowned for using the tactic.

goal: A successful kick between the goalposts.

goal kicker: The designated player in the team who has the task of kicking conversions and penalty goals.

goal line: The line that has to be reached for a team to score a try. For this reason, the goal line is often called the tryline.

Grand Slam: The term used in the Six Nations when one country beats all its opponents during the tournament. (Also applies to touring sides if they beat all the Home Unions.)

grubber kick: A kick that travels along the ground and bounces unpredictably.

halfback: Another term for scrumhalf.

halfback pass: A fast, accurate pass thrown by the halfback.

halves: The term used for the scrumhalf and flyhalf.

halfway line: Marks the middle of the field where the game is started and also restarted after tries or successful penalty goals.

Heineken Cup: Named after its sponsor, this is another name for the European Cup.

Highlanders: Dunedin, New Zealand–based Super 12 team made up of the Otago, North Otago, and Southland provincial unions.

high tackle: A dangerous tackle which hits the opponent above the line of the shoulders. Punished with either a penalty or a yellow or red card depending upon the severity of the tackle.

hit and spin: The ball-carrier commits himself to being tackled and then spins out of the tackle.

Home Nations: England, Ireland, Scotland, Wales.

hooker: The forward in the number 2 jersey who is a central figure. In the front row of the scrum he is supported by the two props and hooks the ball backwards. In the line-out he throws the ball in.

hospital pass: A badly timed pass which puts the person catching the ball in great danger as it arrives just before he is about to be smashed by an opponent.

Hurricanes: Super 12 team based in Wellington, New Zealand. Comprised of the East Coast, Poverty Bay, Hawkes Bay, Wairarapa-Bush, Wellington, Horowhenua-Kapiti, Manawatu, Wanganui, and Taranaki provincial unions.

infringement: Occurs when a team is guilty of breaking a law, prompting the referee to blow the whistle, or play advantage.

injury time: During a match the referee stops the clock whenever play is halted for an injured player. After normal time has finished (40 minutes each half), play continues for the amount of time lost for the injury stoppages.

inside center: The back who wears number 12. Also known as the second five-eighth in Australia and New Zealand.

International Rugby Board: The governing body which controls the world game, runs the World Cup, and determines the Laws of the Game.

judiciary committee: A group of officials (usually three) who determine whether a player should be suspended and for how long after serious incidents on the field of play.

kickoff: Used to start a game. One team kicks the ball from the center of the halfway line to the opposition.

knock-on: A knock-on occurs when a player loses possession of the ball and it goes forward. Or, when a player hits the ball forward with the hand or arm, or when the ball hits the hand or arm and goes forward, and then the ball touches the ground or another player before the original player can catch it.

Lansdowne Road: Ireland's national rugby stadium in Dublin. It's the oldest venue in world rugby and a fantastic place to watch a match.

lifting: A player is helped into the air by his teammates, either to secure a line-out or a restart kick.

line-out: How play is restarted when the ball goes into touch, or out of bounds. The two sets of forwards line up in a row beside each other and the team with the ball throws it in. The throw must go straight down the middle of the tunnel formed by the two rows.

lob pass: A high, looping pass, aimed to go over the heads of the opposition.

locks: The two forwards who wear jerseys number 4 and 5. Usually the tallest players in the team, the locks are charged with providing strength in the scrum and winning the ball in the line-outs. Together they form the second row or the engine room.

loitering: Refers to someone who is standing or jogging in an offside position, preventing the opposing team from playing the ball as they wish.

loop: A player runs around a teammate to whom he has just passed in the hope of receiving the ball back from him.

loose-head prop: The prop on the left hand side of the scrum, closest to his scrumhalf when his team is putting the ball in the scrum.

loosie: A term used for the three members of the backrow: the number eight and the two flankers. So called because they are supposed to be the first to the loose ball.

man-on-man defense: A form of defense where the tackler takes on the man directly opposite him.

mark: A player who catches a kick inside his own 22-meter line while calling "mark" can be awarded a free kick by the referee.

match ball: The high-quality rugby ball used in a match.

maul: A maul occurs when a player carrying the ball is held by one or more opponents, and one or more of the ball-carrier's teammates bind on the ball-carrier. All the players involved are on their feet and moving towards a goal line. Open play has ended.

Millennium Stadium: Retractable roof, Welsh national stadium in Cardiff. Site of the 1999 World Cup final.

Murrayfield: Scottish national rugby stadium located in Edinburgh. Opened in 1925 with a Scotland victory over England.

National Provincial Championship (NPC): New Zealand's domestic competition. Contested by 27 provincial unions in three divisions.

Newlands: Stadium in Cape Town, South Africa. Home to the Stormers and Western Province.

obstruction: Unfairly getting in the way of an opposing player.

offside: A player is offside if he is in front of a teammate who is carrying the ball or in front of a teammate who last played the ball. Offside means that a player is temporarily out of the game. Such players are liable to be penalized if they take part in the game.

Olympic Stadium: Now known as Telstra Stadium, the Sydney venue was the site of the 2003 World Cup final and also holds the world record for a crowd at a test match with 109,874 for an Australia versus New Zealand clash in 2000.

onside: A player is onside if he is behind a teammate who has the ball. An onside player can participate fully in the match.

openside: The area between the ball and the furthest sideline.

openside flanker: The flanker who binds on the openside of the scrum and usually wears number 7.

outside center: The back who wears jersey number 13.

overlap: A team has more players in an attacking line than the opposition.

pack: The term for the entire group of forwards.

pass: A player throws the ball to a teammate.

peel: A forward runs around the front or back of the line-out to take the ball upfield from a catch or tap.

penalty: When the referee rules that a team is guilty of an indiscretion or has contravened the laws of the game he awards a penalty to the non-offending team.

penalty kick: A team chooses to kick at goal after they have been awarded a penalty.

penalty try: When the referee believes a team would have scored if not for the opposition's illegal play, he can award the try anyway.

pick-and-go: A forward charge where the ball is placed on the ground at the tackle and another forward quickly picks it up and continues the attack.

pill: Another name for the ball.

Powergen Cup: The English knockout cup, which dates back to 1972.

props: The two forwards who wear jerseys number 1 (loose-head) and number 3 (tight-head). They support the hooker in the scrums and lift the jumpers in the line-out.

punt kick: The most common form of kick used in a match.

pushover try: A try that happens during a scrum when the pack is able to keep the ball under their feet and push the opposition scrum across the tryline.

quick throw-in: The ball is thrown in before the line-out forms.

red card: The card shown to a player when the referee is sending him off for the rest of the match.

Reds: Australian Super 12 team based in Brisbane, Queensland. They play at historic Ballymore Stadium.

referee: Person appointed to officiate a match by the organizers. Called "Sir" by the players, but also known as the whistle-blower.

reserve bench: The name given to the place where the replacements sit during the match.

restart kick: The kick that restarts play at each half and after points have been scored.

ruck: One or more players from each team, who are on their feet and in contact, close around the ball on the ground. Once a ruck has been formed, players cannot use their hands to get the ball but are allowed to use their feet.

scissors pass: Passing to a teammate who cuts back in the opposite direction in a bid to disorientate the opposition.

screw punt: A form of punt where the ball spirals in the air, which increases the distance it travels.

scrum: Players from each team come together in a formation, where eight forwards bind in against eight opposing forwards, with the aim of winning the ball which is thrown-in between the front rows of the two packs.

scrumhalf: The player wearing jersey number 9 who puts the ball into the scrum and usually distributes it from scrums, rucks, mauls, and line-outs. Also called a halfback.

scrum machine: An apparatus used at training where teams practice their scrummaging skills.

second row: Another name for lock.

sevens: An abbreviated form of rugby where just seven players play on a full field for seven minutes a half.

Sharks: South African Super 12 team based in Durban with most players coming from Natal province. They play their matches at ABSA Stadium, also called the Shark Tank.

shortened line-out: The team throwing the ball in decides to have fewer than seven players in the line-out.

shove: The players in an attacking scrum push in unison.

side: Another name for a team.

sideline: The same as the touchline.

side-on tackle: A tackle used when a ball-carrier is trying to run in-between defenders.

sidestep: A way to evade a tackler by stepping to one side and then quickly to the other.

sin bin: The referee can send players to the sin bin for ten minutes if they are guilty of foul play, a repeated infringement, or a professional foul. The sin bin is usually a seat on the sideline where the player waits for his time to expire so he can re-enter the match.

Six Nations: The oldest annual tournament in international rugby, involving England, Ireland, Wales, Scotland, France, and Italy.

spiral pass: A pass where the player imparts spin on the ball to improve its trajectory.

squad: A group of players who make up a rugby team. A squad usually is made up of 22 team members.

Stade de France: New home of the Tricolors in Paris, where France plays their home fixtures.

Stormers: Super 12 team made up mostly of players from Western Province in South Africa. They play their matches at Newlands Stadium in Cape Town.

Super 12: The annual tournament involving the 12 best provincial teams from South Africa (4), Australia (3), and New Zealand (5).

support: Following the ball-carrier in order to help if he is tackled or needs to pass.

swerve: A form of run where the attacking player attempts to swerve past his opponents.

tackle: A player brings an opponent carrying the ball down to the ground.

tackle area: The general area in which a tackle has been made, usually defined as several meters around where the player has been brought to ground.

Television Match Official (TMO): During most televised matches, the TMO can be asked by the referee to assist on in-goal decisions.

throw-in: The ball is thrown into the line-out.

tight five: The term given to the three front rowers and the two second rowers.

tight-head: The prop on the right-hand side of the scrum who packs in on the opposite side of where his scrumhalf puts the ball in. This player is the anchor of the scrum. "Winning a tight-head" happens when the team that didn't put the ball in is able to win possession.

touch judges: These two officials assist the referee during the course of the game. They patrol either sideline and determine the exact position where line-out throws are taken, check whether teams are offside, watch for foul play and decide whether penalty goals and conversions are successful.

touchline: The two lines situated on either side of the field. A ball is described as going "into touch" when it crosses either of these two lines and goes out of the field of play.

training ball: The type of rugby ball used for training purposes.

Tri Nations: An annual tournament involving Australia, New Zealand, and South Africa which began in 1996.

Triple Crown: The term used in the Six Nations if one of the Home Unions (England, Scotland, Ireland, or Wales) beats all the others during a season.

try: The grounding of the ball by an attacking player in the opposition's in-goal area. It is worth five points.

tryline: The line marked at either end of the field of play that must be crossed to score a try. Also called the goal line.

Twickenham: Home of the Rugby Football Union in London where England plays their home matches.

up and under: A tactical kick that goes high in the air and tests the catching ability of the opposition as defenders run at him. Also called a Garryowen.

Waratahs: Sydney based Australian Super 12 team. They play home matches at Aussie Stadium.

wheel: A scrum turns more than 90 degrees.

wing: The two attacking players that wear jersey numbers 11 and 14, who play closest to the touchline and are usually the fastest on the team.

Wooden Spoon: The term used in many tournaments to designate the last-place team.

yellow card: A card shown to a player by the referee if that player is considered guilty of foul play, a professional foul, or a repeated infringement. This results in a ten-minute suspension in the sin bin.

Zurich Premiership: The English domestic competition with 12 teams who play home and away.

Index

• D •

• O •

• P •

penalty try, 20
pushover try, 122
scoring a try, 19, 69
try line, 17
tunnel, 116, 127
turnover, 127
turnover balls, 174
22-meter drop-out. *See* drop kick
22-meter line, 17
Twickenham, 201
two-man cut-out, 148

• U •

Under-21 Rugby World Cup, 203
Under 19 World Championship, 12
Under 21 World Cup, 12
unfair play, 89
unique ethos, 10
United States. *See* American rugby
United States of America Rugby Football
    Union (USARFU), 223
  see also USA Eagles
United States Rugby Football Union (USA
    Rugby), 13, 14, 197–198
up and under kick, 59, 152, 153
U.S. Olympians *vs.* France, 313
USA Eagles, 155, 197, 198, 212, 223–225
USA National Club Championship,
    233–234
USA Rugby, 223–225, 231, 242
  see also American rugby
USA Rugby National High School
    Championship, 240
USA Rugby Super League, 232–233
USA Rugby Web site, 296
USA Sevens, 212

• V •

velocity of passes, 147
vests, 37
video referee. *See* television match
    official (TMO)
Viers, Ray, 278
Vizard, Brian, 155, 278, 302
volunteer administrators, 11

• W •

Wales, 196, 313
warm up, 180–181
watching rugby. *See* spectating
water intake, 188
Watkins, Bob, 233, 274
Watson, Andre, 85
weather conditions, 170–171, 319–320
Web sites, 293–296
weight-lifting program, 184
Western Samoa, 320
wheeling the scrum, 120–121
Wilkinson, Jonny, 23, 196
William Webb Ellis Cup, 11, 194
Williams family, 318
Wilson, Chilla, 322
Wilson, Stu, 283
wing forward. *See* flankers
wings (jersey numbers 11 and 14), 26, 57–58
women's rugby
  American, 224–225, 242
  Canadian, 219
  growth of, 242
  NCAA, and women's rugby, 239
Women's Rugby World Cup, 12, 202–203, 219
Women's Rugby World Cup (1991), 312
World Cup. *See* Rugby World Cup
World Sevens Series, 211, 226
  see also Sevens World Cup

• Y •

yellow card, 89
Youth Development Officers (YDOs), 241
youth rugby
  American, 240–241
  Canadian, 236–237
  coaching, 260–264
  non-contact, 241
  youth development, 241

• Z •

Zen Theory of Rugby Fitness, 185
The Zone, 187
Zurich Premiership, 215

RUGBY LEAGUE
SUPER 12
TRI NATIONS
NPC
CURRIE CUP
JUNE TOURS

FOX SPORTS WORLD

foxsportsworld.msn.com

>>> America's Global Sports Channel

© 2004 Fox Sports International ™ Twentieth Century Fox